LEGENDARY LOCALS

OF

EAST BOSTON

MASSACHUSETTS

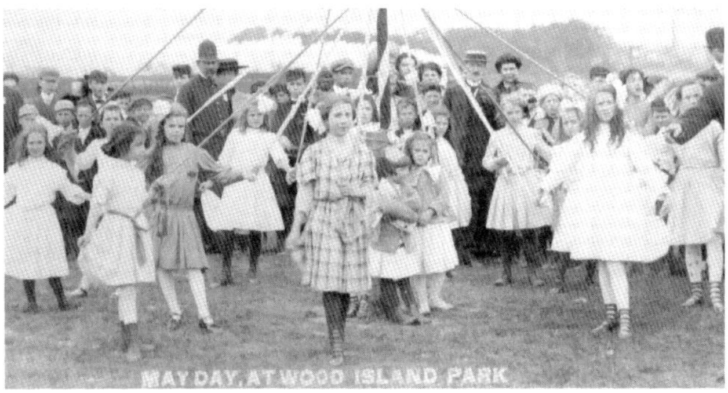

I0805757

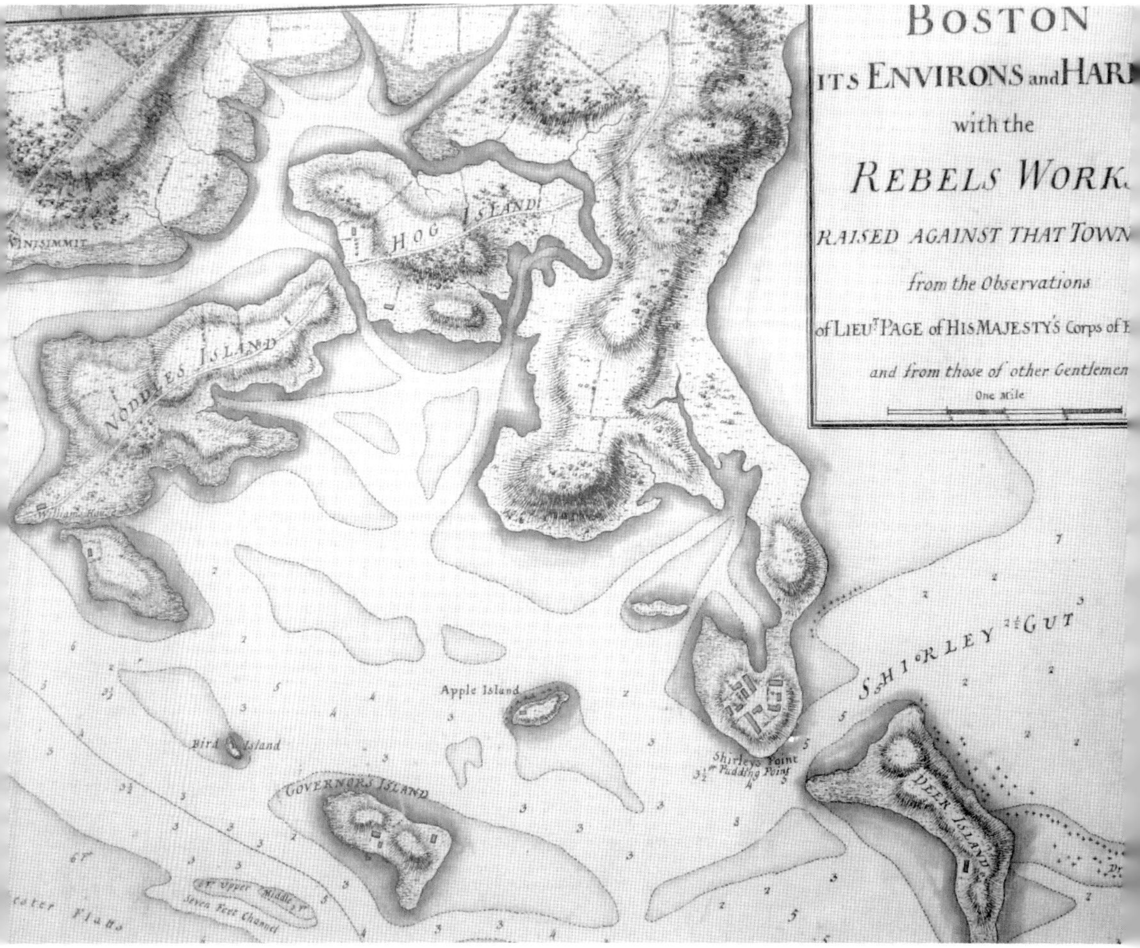

Boston and Its Islands
This is a 1775 map of Boston, showing (in order of size) Noddle's Island, Hog Island, Governor's Island, Apple Island, and Bird Island. North of Noddle's Island, across the river, is Chelsea, then called Winisimmit. Winthrop is on the right. (Author's collection.)

Page 1: **May Day**
A May Day Celebration at Wood Island Park is pictured here in the early 1900s. (Courtesy of Boston Public Library.)

LEGENDARY LOCALS

OF

EAST BOSTON

MASSACHUSETTS

DR. REGINA MARCHI

LEGENDARY LOCALS

Copyright © 2015 by Dr. Regina Marchi
ISBN 978-1-4671-0205-6

Legendary Locals is an imprint of Arcadia Publishing
Charleston, South Carolina

Printed in the United States of America

Library of Congress Control Number: 2014957736

For all general information, please contact Arcadia Publishing:
Telephone 843-853-2070
Fax 843-853-0044
E-mail sales@arcadiapublishing.com
For customer service and orders:
Toll-Free 1-888-313-2665

Visit us on the Internet at www.arcadiapublishing.com

Dedication
This book is dedicated to the people of East Boston and, above all, my parents, Roberta and Richard Marchi, and the rest of my family, who raised me to love East Boston and its history.

On the Front Cover: Clockwise from top left:
Clipper ship builder Donald McKay (courtesy of BPL; see page 26), activist Anna DeFronzo (author's collection; see page 37), *The Sopranos* screenwriter Frank Renzulli (courtesy of Jean Reisman; see page 64), Joseph P. Kennedy (courtesy of JFK Library; see page 32), Red Sox star Tony Conigliaro (courtesy of BPL; see page 93), Santarpio's sign (author's collection; see page 110), activist Evelyn Morash (author's collection; see page 40), Madonna National Shrine (author's collection; see page 54), jazz musician John Neves (courtesy of Isabel Nicks; see page 60)

On the Back Cover: From left to right:
Our Lady of the Assumption Cadets drill team, 1950s (courtesy of Mary Ellen Welch; see page 92), Patrick J. Kennedy and family playing cards at the Kennedy home on Webster Street in 1899 (courtesy of the JFK Library; see page 30)

CONTENTS

ACKNOWLEDGMENTS

Many of the images in this volume appear courtesy of the Boston Public Library (BPL), the John F. Kennedy Presidential Library (JFK), the New England Historic Genealogical Society (NEHGS), the *East Boston Community News* archives at Northeastern University's Snell Library (EBCN), and the Massachusetts Historical Society (MHS). I am extremely grateful to family, friends, and neighbors who generously shared their stories, photographs, and enthusiasm for this book. Many people, including individuals who did not even know me, went out of their way to be helpful. In particular, I wish to thank Roberta, Richard, and Christopher Marchi, Mary Ellen Welch, Debra Cave, Adrian Madaro, John Lynds, Kevin Farrell, Roberto Verthelyi, John White, Evelyn Morash, Michael Laurano, Madeleine Steczynski, Nancy Lee, Barbara McDonough, Edith DeAngelis, Mary Cahalane, Isabel Nicks, Joe Incagnoli Jr., Barbara Bishop, Paul Travaglini, Jacqueline Hopkinson, Leo Lew, Andrew Ruotolo, Thomas Philbin, Bob Nakashian, Laura J. Brown, Jamila Raquib, Sam and Lucille Bolognese, Margaret Kelly of the East Boston Branch Library, Jane Winton and staff in the print department of the Boston Public Library Copley Square, Maryrose Grossman at the JFK Library, David Allen Lambert and Tim Salls at the New England Historic Genealogical Society, Giordana Mecagni and Andrew Begley at Northeastern University's Snell Library, Jasmine Records, and editors Erin Vosgien and Jason Humphrey at Arcadia Publishing.

INTRODUCTION

Viewing East Boston today, it is difficult to imagine that it was once entirely marshlands, drumlins, and forests. Prior to the arrival of British colonists in the 1600s, the Massachuset Indians thrived on the area's abundant fish, fowl, and berries. They moved with the seasons, spending winters hunting on the mainland and setting up summer villages to farm and fish on the harbor islands that would later become East Boston. East Boston was originally a series of five islands located across the channel from Boston proper: Noddle's Island, Hog Island, Governor's Island, Apple Island, and Bird Island (where pirates were hung from the 1600s until the mid-1800s). From the 1830s through the 1960s, these islands were connected by landfill to form a single landmass that can be accessed from mainland Boston only by bridge, boat, or tunnel. East Boston's geographical isolation from the rest of Boston has been a defining characteristic throughout its history, creating a close-knit community where residents have had to work together to solve problems.

The largest of the five islands and the first settled by British colonists, Noddle's Island was named for William Noddle, "a freeman of good character" who sometimes camped there. No records indicate that he had a house or stayed for long. In 1859, the *Boston Herald* wrote, "He seems to have been a Robinson Crusoe without his man Friday, and to have cruised about in his canoe until he found a watery grave." Hog Island eventually became Orient Heights, named in honor of the prosperous China and East India shipping trade that brought great wealth to Boston. Apple, Bird, and Governor's Islands eventually became part of Logan Airport.

In historical writings, Noddle's Island is described as a paradise with seemingly endless quantities of seafood, game, and fowl. The shallow flats around the island teemed with oysters, clams, and lobsters. One could cast a net and easily catch hundreds of fish, and the island's trees brimmed with birds. A diary entry from September 2, 1795, notes that two men went hunting on the island at 1:00 p.m. and shot six dozen birds. After refilling their gunpowder, they resumed hunting and shot three dozen more by 5:00 p.m. The area was a favorite picnic, hunting, fishing, and swimming spot for Colonial Bostonians, who would row over for the day and build campfires to boil caldrons of clam chowder and fry fresh fish.

Noddle's Island became part of Boston in 1636 but was scarcely populated before the 1830s. Its first documented permanent resident was Samuel Maverick, a wealthy trader who moved to the island with his wife, Amias, in 1629, building a home and plantation. The island allowed Maverick, an Episcopalian, to live a sumptuous lifestyle away from the disapproving eyes of Boston's austere Puritans. His hospitality was legendary, as he entertained all guests with lavish foods, alcohol, and tobacco. When the earliest governor of the Massachusetts Bay Colony, John Winthrop, first arrived in Boston, he made a point of docking on Noddle's Island with his entourage before setting foot on mainland Boston. He spent a couple of days enjoying Maverick's hospitality and getting an orientation from him about the political and economic affairs of the colony. Winthrop's associates described Maverick as "the most hospitable man in all the country, giving entertainment to all comers gratis." While the Puritans disliked Maverick and eventually persecuted and jailed him, he was tolerated for years by virtue of his business acumen and the key impact he had on trade in the region. Noddle's Island provided a temporary haven for other dissidents. Although the Puritans came to America for religious freedom, they had no religious tolerance for others. They discriminated against Baptists, Episcopalians, and other non-Puritans, punishing them with fines and incarceration. After being persecuted in Charlestown, Thomas Gould and other nascent Baptists moved to Noddle's Island in 1665, establishing Boston's first Baptist church.

In Colonial times, Noddle's Island was a farming region with orchards, fields, and livestock that supplied Boston with milk, meat, produce, and hay. Horses from the mainland were brought to graze there, sometimes swimming across the channel. At the start of the American Revolution, Noddle's Island had only two estates and some laborers' cottages, but it became a crucial locale in the war as a result of its role as a regional breadbasket. On May 27, 1775, revolutionaries evacuated the island's residents and livestock, setting fire to the homes, fields, orchards, and forests in order to prevent British troops from obtaining food supplies there. When the British saw their main source of provisions in flames from across the harbor, they immediately dispatched 400 troops to attack the "raiders." They also sent a heavily armed schooner, the *Diana*, up the Chelsea Creek to cut off the colonists' retreat. From Noddle's Island and Chelsea, colonists defeated the British troops and destroyed the *Diana*. Adding to British humiliation, the valuable canons and ammunition on the *Diana* were confiscated by the colonists and used against the British. The Battle of Noddle's Island and Chelsea Creek, which occurred a month after the Battle of Lexington and Concord, was the first naval battle of the American Revolution. Although rarely mentioned in history books, this was a major victory that badly shook British confidence and proved that the upstart Colonials could hold their own against the mightiest navy in the world.

After changing ownership several times, Noddle's Island was officially renamed East Boston in 1833 when developer William H. Sumner gained possession of the land. Recruiting 32 investors, he formed the East Boston Company with the goal of turning the sleepy island into a prosperous trading center and vacation resort. The company built wharves, railway tracks, and port facilities to attract shipping and other industries. While the rest of Boston relied on haphazard cow paths for roads, the East Boston Company laid straight wide streets with modern sewers and created detailed architectural plans for housing lots, schools, parks, and businesses. These designs made East Boston the first planned

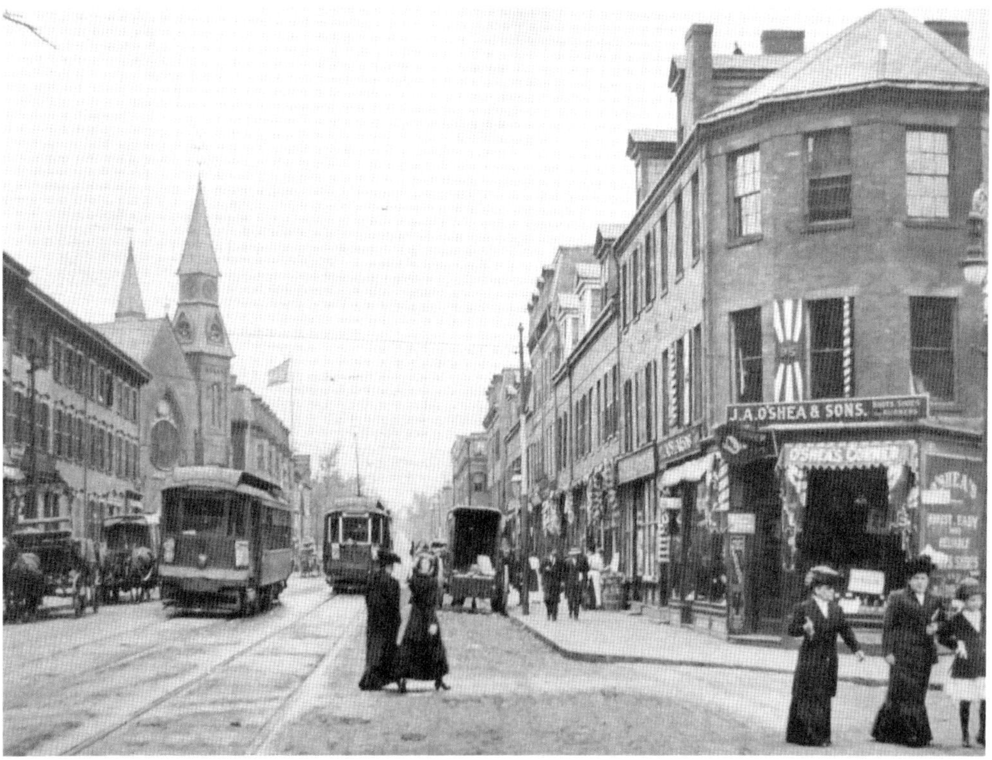

Meridian Street

Pictured here is a shopping scene on Meridian Street between Maverick and Central Squares, about 1908. (Courtesy of BPL.)

neighborhood in Boston and one of the earliest planned communities in the United States, after Washington, DC.

East Boston's docks accommodated large vessels from the age of sailing ships through the era of steamships and ocean liners. The community became a major port, where the world's fastest clipper ships were built in the 1840s and 1850s, carrying tea, porcelain, jade, and other products from the Orient and going to and from California during the Gold Rush. At the time, New England ships had to round the tip of South America to get to California. Donald McKay's clipper ships, built on Border Street, made the journey in record-breaking time, bringing East Boston international fame. In 1857, the first iron steamship in America was built at East Boston's Atlantic Works, leading to the eventual demise of clipper ships. Previously, in 1840, the Cunard Company, known for its wooden and later iron steamships, located its US headquarters in East Boston. These ships carried mail, merchandise, and passengers between Boston and Europe, making East Boston the second-largest immigration port of entry in the United States after Ellis Island.

Thousands of immigrants from around the world passed through customs at the East Boston Immigration Center on Marginal Street. Some settled in East Boston, ascending "the Golden Stairs" between Marginal and Webster Streets in search of new lives. Many found work on the docks or in the factories and transportation-related businesses (railway, ship, and air) that developed in East Boston from the mid-1800s onward. The shipbuilding industry of the 1840s and 1850s attracted Swedish and Norwegian craftsmen renowned for their Norse shipbuilding traditions, Canadians from the maritime provinces of Nova Scotia and New Brunswick, and Portuguese and Cape Verdean sailors. As East Boston's English Protestants began moving to less-congested communities, large numbers of Irish immigrants arrived from the 1840s through 1880s. They established East Boston's first Catholic church, the Most Holy Redeemer, in 1844. Originally barred from skilled occupations because of anti-Catholic discrimination, the Irish formed the bulk of manual labor that built East Boston's piers, extended the railroads, and loaded and unloaded the ships. One of these young longshoremen was Patrick "P.J." Kennedy, grandfather of Pres. John F. Kennedy. P.J. and his son "J.P." Kennedy became prominent businessmen in East Boston, where they first developed the economic and political clout that eventually gave rise to the Kennedy dynasty.

In 1842, about 10 Jewish families established a religious community in East Boston, and in 1844, they purchased land on the corner of Byron and Homer Streets to establish the Ohabei Shalom Cemetery, today the oldest Jewish cemetery in Massachusetts. Soon, more Russian, Polish, and German Jews arrived—tinkers, tailors, shopkeepers, and industrial laborers—making East Boston the largest Jewish community in New England by 1905. Interviewed in 1976, lifelong resident Joseph Shapiro, who was born in 1895, fondly recalled the East Boston of his youth: "Peddlers went out every day from house to house selling fruits and vegetables. Fish you could buy from a wagon; people sold meat from house to house." On Saturdays, when Jews could not light coal fires, "Christian kids would go around making fires for us" as a way to earn a bit of money. There were seven synagogues in East Boston and Hebrew school outings were regularly held at Wood Island Park.

As the Irish and Jews prospered and moved to the streetcar suburbs, the early 20th century saw four decades of Italian immigration in East Boston. Up until 1880, East Boston homes were single-family structures, but by 1930, triple-deckers built to house the neighborhood's growing working-class immigrant population were the norm. Many Italian men worked as stonemasons and plasterers or helped build the underwater subway and auto tunnels. Many Italian women worked as seamstresses and did elaborate beadwork for elite wedding-dress companies such as the House of Bianchi and Priscilla's of Boston. Some Italians came directly from Italy, but many relocated from Boston's North End, drawn to East Boston by its relatively larger homes and yards where they could have vegetable gardens. Consequently, for most of the 1900s, East Boston was a predominantly Italian neighborhood. While still boasting the highest concentration of Italians in Boston today, the community is now ethnically diverse. In the 1980s and 1990s, 1,500 refugee families from Cambodia and more than 3,000 Vietnamese, escaping war and political turmoil, called East Boston home. Starting in the 1980s, immigrants from Colombia, Brazil, Mexico, El Salvador, Guatemala, Peru, and other Latin American countries arrived, many fleeing war and poverty. These new immigrants reinvigorated East Boston's rental market, and many later became homeowners. They also revitalized East Boston's business districts, filling abandoned storefronts with vibrant small businesses. While most of the Southeast Asian immigrants have relocated to other areas, East Boston now has the largest Latino population in Boston. In the 2000s, families from the Middle East joined the community, along with growing numbers of artists, university students, and urban professionals. All of these diverse residents continue to create a dynamic, innovative, and family-oriented community.

East Boston is the site of many important developments that have positively influenced Boston and the nation—a crucial battle in the American Revolution, a shipping industry that produced the fastest sailing ships in the world, the construction of the country's first underwater subway tunnel, the first planned community in Boston, the first public branch library in America, the first free public gymnasium in America, and more. Based on archival research and personal interviews, *Legendary Locals of East Boston* tells the neighborhood's history through profiles of some of the remarkable people who have called East Boston home over the years.

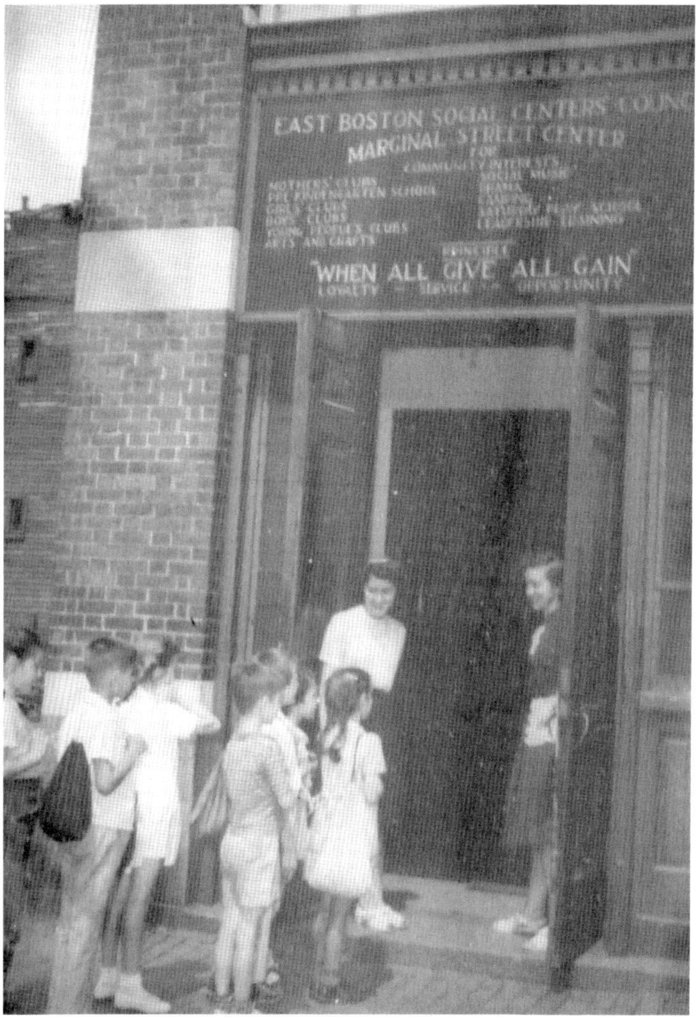

East Boston Social Centers Building
Pictured here is the East Boston Social Centers building on Marginal Street around 1947. (Courtesy of EBSC.)

CHAPTER ONE

East Boston's Early History

In Colonial times, some of the most important individuals in New England, including Gov. John Winthrop, Judge Samuel Sewall, and entrepreneurs Samuel Maverick and Henry Howell Williams, had homes on the islands that became East Boston. Developer and businessman Gen. William H. Sumner acquired Noddle's Island in 1833 and forever transformed it. Renaming it East Boston, he hired surveyors and engineers to level hills, fill marshes, and develop a modern city design. With Colonial structures no longer existing on the island at the time, East Boston became Boston's first planned community, with streets on a grid system, sewers, streetlights, and designated tracts of land for housing, tourism, and industry. Streets were named after the directors of the East Boston Company (Haynes, Sumner, Lamson); European ports (Bremen, Liverpool, Havre), famous poets (Coleridge, Horace, Byron), American birds (Falcon, Eagle, Condor) and American Revolutionary battles (Lexington, Princeton, Trenton). Until 1904, when the country's first underwater subway tunnel opened, the only communication between East Boston and downtown Boston was via boat. In the winter, the harbor would often freeze, making boat travel impossible and cutting off communication with the mainland. A historical diary notes that the ice was sometimes thick enough for "thousands of people to walk across the channel."

East Boston's earliest residents were affluent English Protestants from New England's most prominent families. They were attracted by the prospect of undeveloped land so close to the city center, where they could construct stately homes with large yards and establish new businesses. Most of the men were investors, manufacturers, and other entrepreneurs, but there were also doctors, lawyers, and craftsmen. Most of the women were homemakers and society ladies involved in volunteer groups that helped build East Boston's schools, churches, and libraries. Quite a few women were deaconesses of the neighborhood's first parish—the Maverick Congregational Church—established in 1836. Early community life revolved around this church, and women held important leadership positions in its affiliated associations, performing unpaid work on behalf of the community. Clara Whittemore was president of the East Boston Benevolent Society, Mary Bailey was president of the Home Missionary Society, Helen Gillette was president of the Ladies' Aid Society, and Catharine Ordway was president of the East Boston Maternal Association. In 1836, Eliza Pierce, East Boston's first teacher, began instructing 38 primary school students in a makeshift classroom inside the Malleable Steel Company on Meridian Street. In the mid-to-late-1800s, the island was abuzz with the opening of new shops and industries, ferries and trolleys, several churches, and three schools—the Lyman (1837), the Chapman (1850), and the Adams (1856).

In 1833, Guy and Susan Haynes built the first house on East Boston's new street grid system and became prominent citizens. Guy, a businessman and activist, was the first (unofficial) census data collector in East Boston, keeping meticulous notes of marriages, births, deaths, and executions of pirates, along with people's ages, religions, and ethnicities. Susan started East Boston's first Sabbath school in 1834 to teach children the scriptures. The couple actively volunteered in associations related to schools, churches, helping the poor, beautifying the community, and improving city services. One can gain an idea of how active East Bostonians were in civic life by the following partial list of community associations founded in the mid-1800s and early 1900s: the Friends of the East Boston Library Association, the Old Settlers'

Society, the New Temperance Society, the East Boston Ornamental Tree Association, the East Boston Home Club, the East Boston Milk and Baby Hygiene Association, the Orient Heights Association, the Seafarer's Federation, Associated Charities, Hebrew Charities, and numerous other religious societies and ethnic clubs. Since it was easier to stay on the island than travel across the harbor, residents built elegant and ornate meeting halls for holding social events, lectures, dances, plays, and concerts. Pythian Hall, Lyceum Hall, Maverick Hall, Washington Hall, Grand Army Hall, Knights of Columbus Hall, and two Masonic halls were sites of jubilant socializing and political debate, where nationally prominent speakers such as Frederick Douglass, Julia Ward Howe, and others addressed the crucial political issues of the times. Socializing and political debate are still strong in East Boston today through civic groups such as the Jeffries Point Neighborhood Association, the Eagle Hill Civic Association, the Orient Heights Neighborhood Association, and many other community groups.

Knowing that industry would not come to East Boston without excellent transportation, the East Boston Company developed large wharves and railroad tracks for the efficient transfer of products to areas north of Boston, including wool and cotton bales bound for the mills of Lowell. It also recruited a sugar refinery, an iron and steel company, a mattress factory, a timber company, lumberyards, plaster suppliers, pottery works, fish packers, and commercial shops. When Samuel Cunard established his transatlantic steamship service from Europe to the United States in 1840, William Sumner convinced him to make East Boston the company's only US port. This was a boon to East Boston's economy, and, although the Cunard Company later opened a New York port (because New York's harbor did not freeze as often), the East Boston port remained an important source of development and growth until the 1930s.

Reflecting his dream of creating a fashionable shore resort in East Boston, Sumner led efforts to build the Maverick House Hotel on Maverick Square (where the Health Center now stands) in 1835. Accommodating up to 700 guests, it was one of the most modern luxury hotels of its day. Boston's most distinguished residents attended the grand opening, including congressmen, judges, doctors, lawyers, business tycoons, sea captains, editors, and the president and faculty of Harvard University. Maverick Square became a tourist destination where visitors disembarking from boats and trains could spend restful days and elegant evenings enjoying views of the harbor and city along with modern amenities such as indoor plumbing and the latest in summer comfort, iced drinks. Sumner established two ferries, the *Maverick* and the *East Boston*, to take guests back and forth from Maverick Square to the mainland.

In 1858, another state-of-the-art hotel came to Maverick Square, the Sturtevant House, named for East Boston industrialist Noah Sturtevant. The gala opening was attended by 150 of the wealthiest couples in Massachusetts. Newspapers reported that the hotel was "beautifully painted and frescoed for concerts, lectures and balls" and that "a more magnificent affair never took place in East Boston." Industries and factories continued to develop along East Boston's waterfront, eventually ending the community's status as a shore resort. In response to East Boston's rapid population growth, the Boston Elevated Railroad built the first underwater tunnel in North America (1901–1904) to connect East Boston's trolley lines to the citywide trolley network.

From Colonial times to the Industrial Revolution and the early 20th century, East Bostonians such as Maverick, Sumner, Jeffries, McKay, and the Kennedys influenced the economic and political landscape of Boston and the region. Massachusetts governor John Lewis Bates, of Monmouth Street, pushed to build the first underwater trolley tunnel in America, while another East Boston native, Mayor Frederick Mansfield, led Boston through the Great Depression. Susan Haynes, Judith Winsor Smith, Clara Bates, Armeda Gibbs, and other women were active in volunteer groups that established East Boston schools, churches, social programs, and libraries, to which William Sumner's wife, Mary, donated many valuable books. And, while East Boston's clipper ships became internationally famous, few know that the world's first female clipper ship commander, Mary Ann Patten, came from East Boston. Below are the fascinating stories of these and other residents of East Boston's early history.

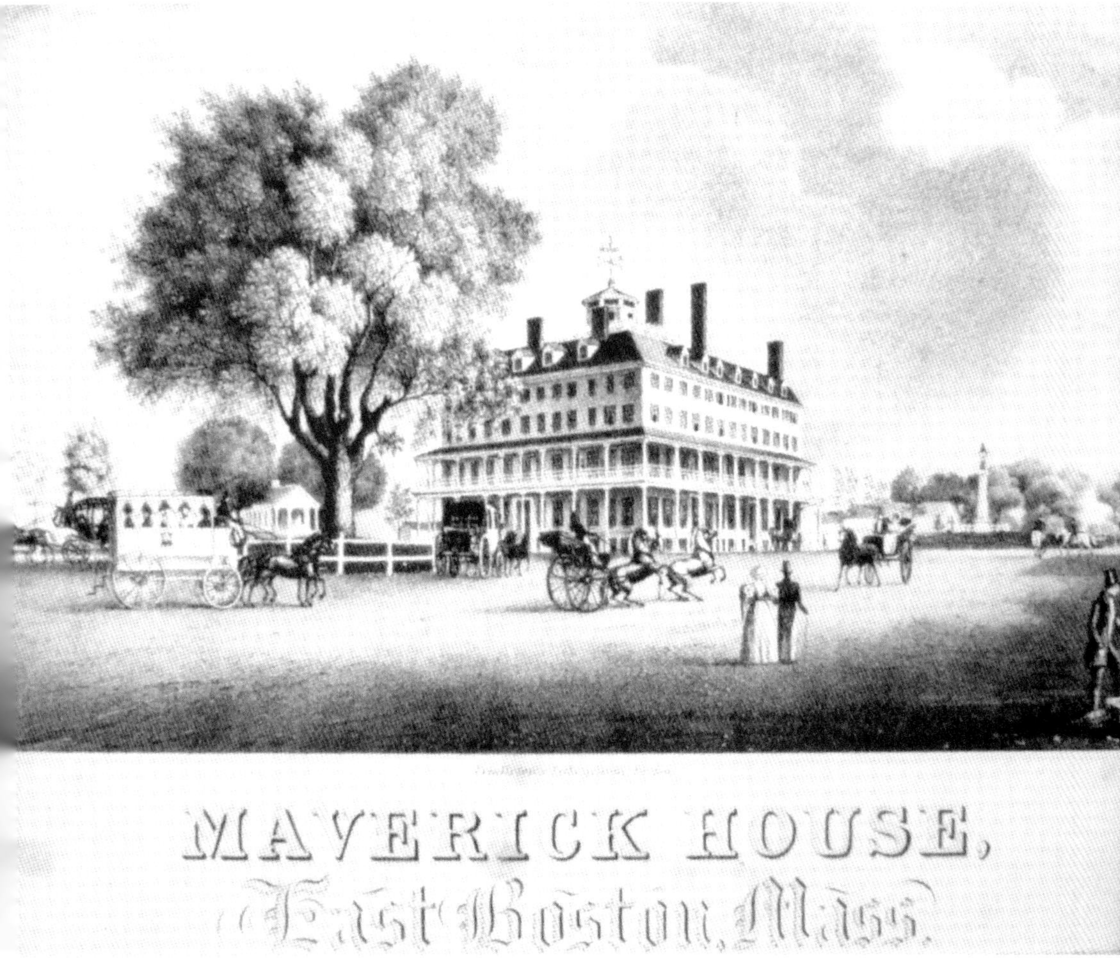

Samuel Maverick (c.1602–c.1670)
A prosperous merchant who was key to the commercial success of Colonial Boston, Samuel Maverick was East Boston's first documented resident. He moved to Noddle's Island with his wife, Amias, in 1629, and their home was the first documented residence ever built there. Maverick was disliked by the Puritans for his Episcopalian religion, loyalty to the British, and lavish lifestyle. Ironically, while he shipped enslaved Africans to Boston in 1638 and is believed to be the first slave owner in New England, he worked "to obtain equal civil and religious rights and privileges for people of every religious belief," denouncing Puritan religious intolerance. The Maverick House Hotel, built in 1885, was named after him, as were Maverick Square and Maverick Street. (Courtesy of BPL.)

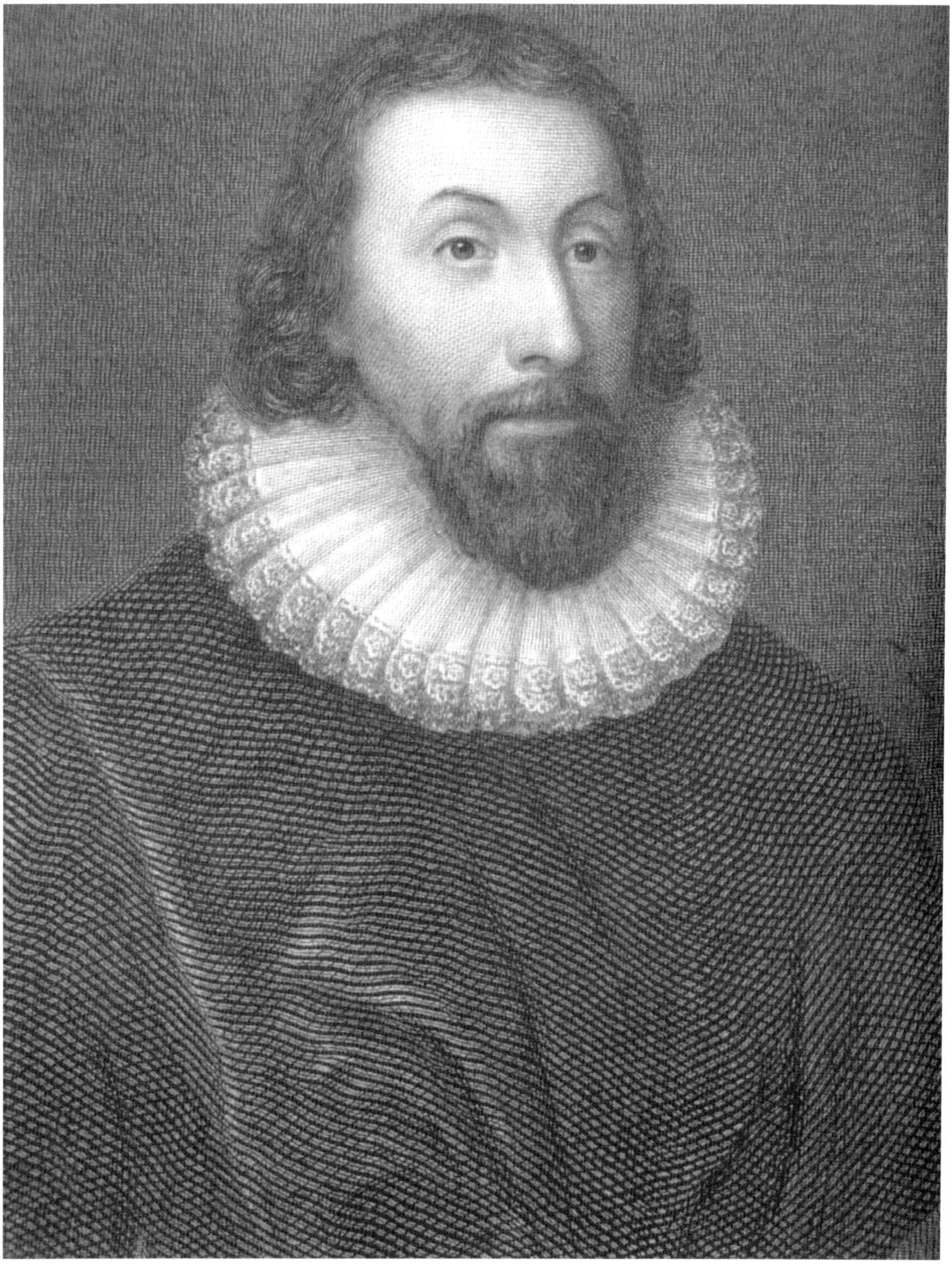

Gov. John Winthrop (1588–1649)
In 1632, Bostonians granted John Winthrop, the first governor of the Massachusetts Bay Colony, an island, naming it Governor's Island. Winthrop and his wife, Margaret, built a country home there and planted the first apple and pear orchards in New England. They spent many peaceful days enjoying the island's sea breezes and panoramic views of Boston. In 1808, the US government bought the island from the Winthrop family and built a military fort. In the 1920s, it became part of Logan Airport. (Courtesy of BPL.)

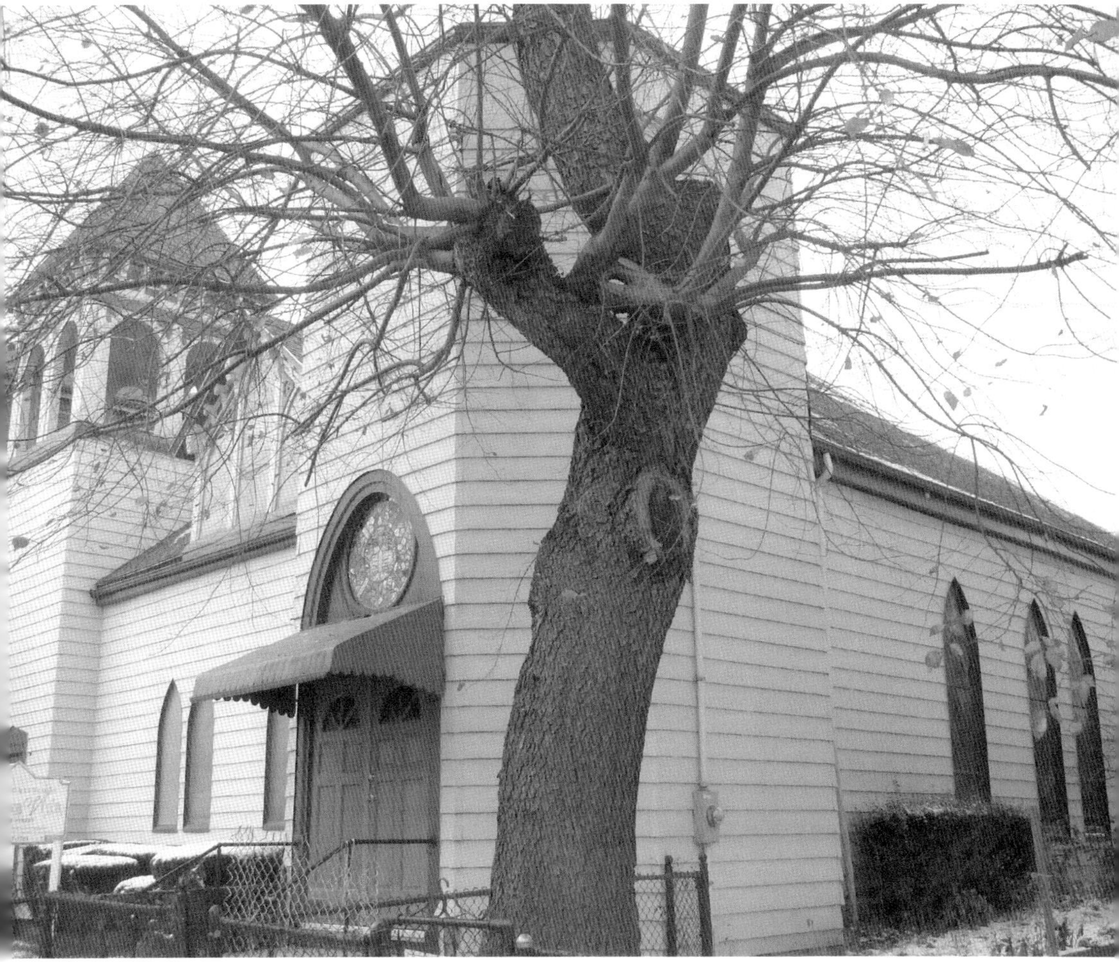

Thomas Gould (c.1619–1674)

The founding father of the first Baptist church in Boston, Thomas Gould was a wheelwright who believed that individuals should be baptized only when old enough to choose their religion. Refusing to have his baby son baptized, he broke away from the Puritans to worship clandestinely with like-minded people in Charlestown. Fearing imprisonment, Gould moved to Noddle's Island in 1665, where he established the city's first Baptist church and became its minister. Excommunicated, disenfranchised, and fined by the Puritans, he was summoned to Boston General Court. When he refused to pay the fines or stop holding Baptist meetings, he was imprisoned, spending significant time in jail and owing unpaid fines upon his death in 1674. He is remembered as a man who fought for the ideals of religious freedom. Pictured here is the White Street Baptist Church, built in 1890. (Author's collection.)

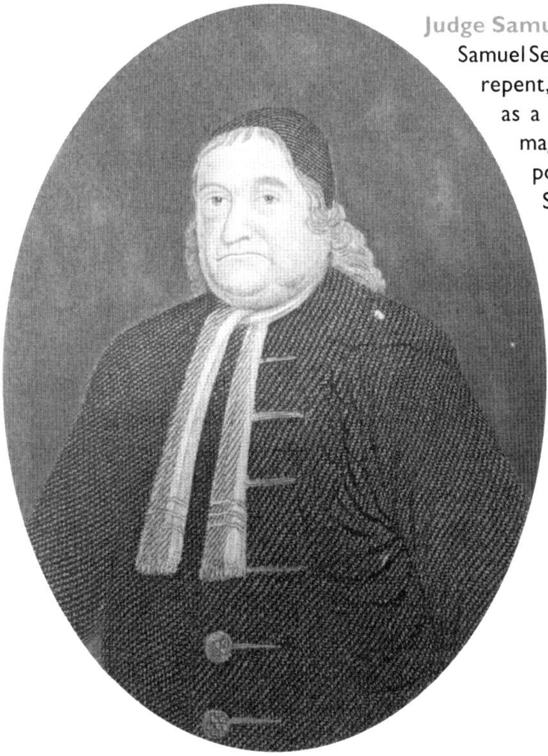

Judge Samuel Sewall (1652–1730)

Samuel Sewall, the only Salem witch trial judge to publicly repent, bought Hog Island (Orient Heights) in 1687 as a rural retreat for his family. As the superior magistrate of the judicature and one of the most powerful men in the state, he presided over the Salem witch trials in the early 1690s, resulting in the conviction and execution of innocent people. In 1697, he wrote an apology that was read aloud in Boston's Old South Meeting House, as he stood with head downcast to demonstrate his penitence. (Courtesy of Michael Laurano.)

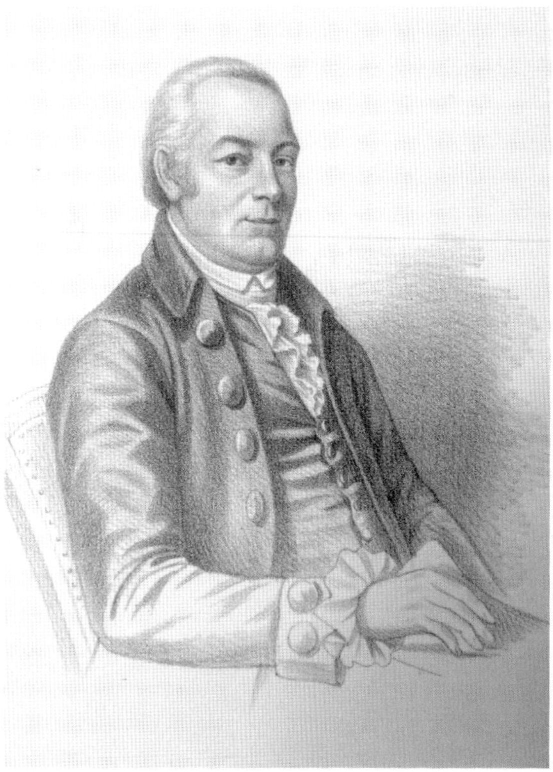

Henry Howell Williams (1726–1802)

Prosperous tenant Henry Howell Williams leased a home, plantation, and orchards on Noddle's Island from 1762 to 1800. He grew rich producing hay and supplying ships leaving Boston with cows, sheep, pigs, geese, turkeys, and ducks, which were loaded from the island's docks. A British loyalist, he furnished the redcoats with provisions and suffered great financial losses in 1775 when revolutionaries burned his property and confiscated his livestock to prevent their being used by the British army. (Courtesy of BPL.)

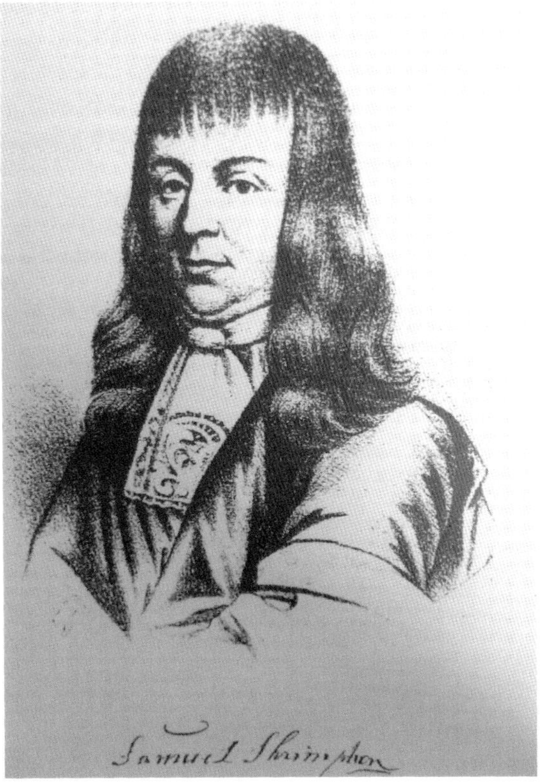

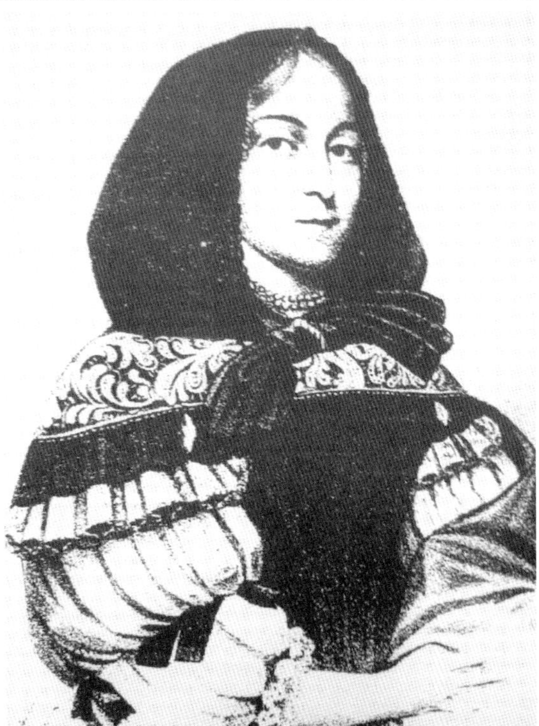

Samuel Shrimpton (1643–1697) and Elizabeth Shrimpton (1645–1673)
Originally a brazier (brass worker), Samuel Shrimpton became one of Boston's wealthiest merchants and landowners. He purchased Noddle's Island in 1670, where he maintained a large estate until his death. His widow, Elizabeth (pictured), bequeathed the island to their granddaughter Elizabeth Shrimpton, who married John Yeamans and died in childbirth. Upon Yeamans's death, the island went to their only child, Shute Shrimpton Yeamans, and was later acquired by one of his heirs, William H. Sumner. (Both, author's collection.)

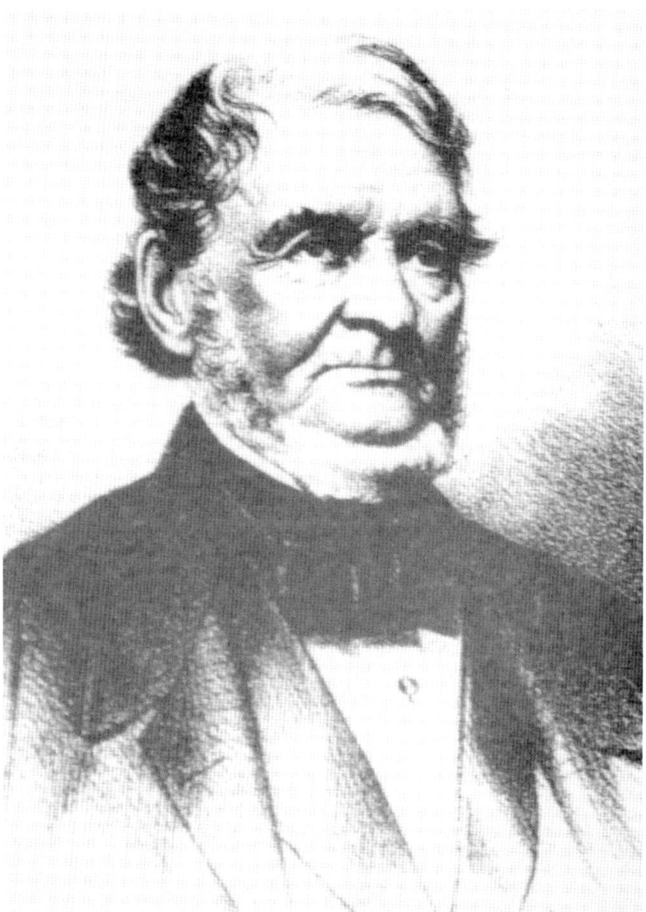

Gen. William H. Sumner (1780–1861)
William H. Sumner acquired Noddle's Island in 1833, renamed it East Boston, and created Boston's first planned community. Founder of the East Boston Company, he was a major social and economic leader of his time, facilitating visionary initiatives that transformed East Boston from a rural refuge to a major port destination. In 1858, he wrote *A History of East Boston*, the most detailed book available on the community's early years. Sumner Street and the Sumner Tunnel are named for him. (Both, courtesy of BPL.)

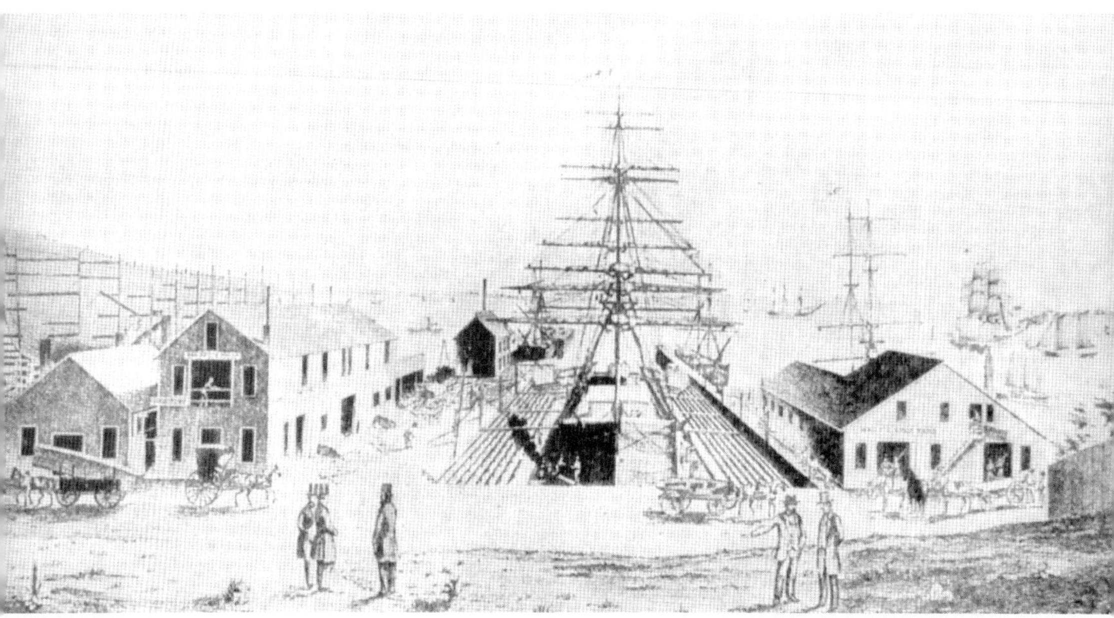

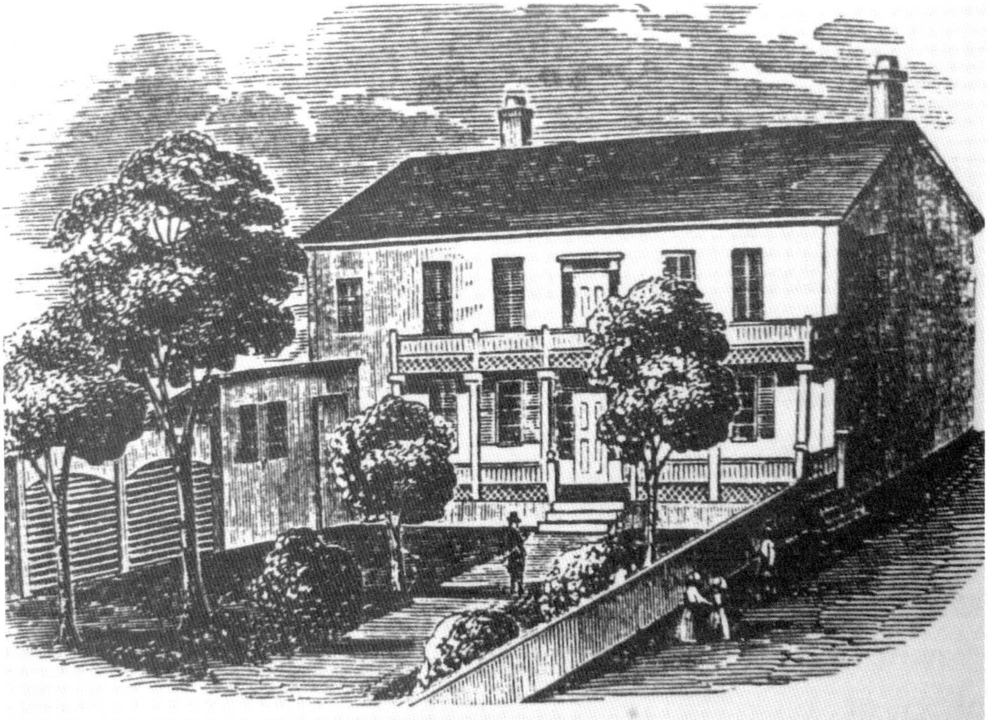

Residence of Guy C. Haynes, First House erected in East Boston, August, 1833.

Guy Haynes (1786–1877) and Susan Haynes (1783–1855)

In 1833, on the corner of Webster and Cottage Streets, Guy and Susan Haynes built the first house in East Boston after the East Boston Company established a grid street plan. One of the community's most prominent citizens, Guy Haynes left a wealth of information about early East Boston in his personal journals. (Courtesy of MHGS.)

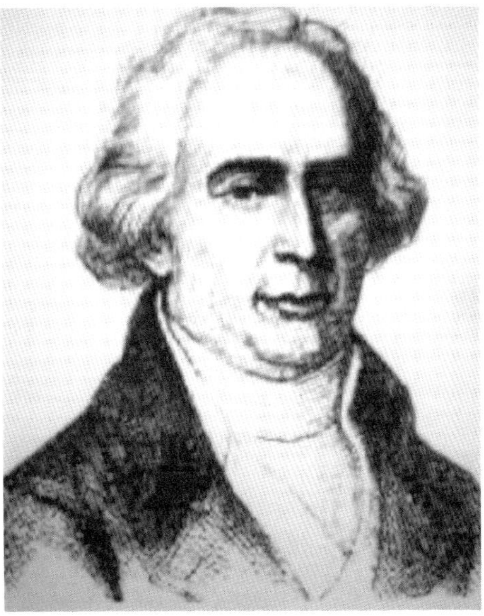

Dr. John Jeffries (1796–1876)

In 1834, Dr. John Jeffries built the second house on East Boston's street grid. He helped establish the state board of health and cofounded the Massachusetts Eye and Ear Infirmary. Jeffries Point and Jeffries Yacht Club are named for him. An avid yachtsman, he spent much time at the club and taught all his sons and daughters to sail. His father, John Jeffries (1744–1819), was a renowned physician and scientist who played a key role in the Boston Massacre trial. As the surgeon who tended one of the men shot in the incident, he was a witness for the defense. He was also Boston's first meteorologist, recording daily weather data from 1774 until 1816. He gained international fame when he made the first balloon trip over London in 1784 to perform a weather study of air at various altitudes. (Courtesy of Jeffries Yacht Club.)

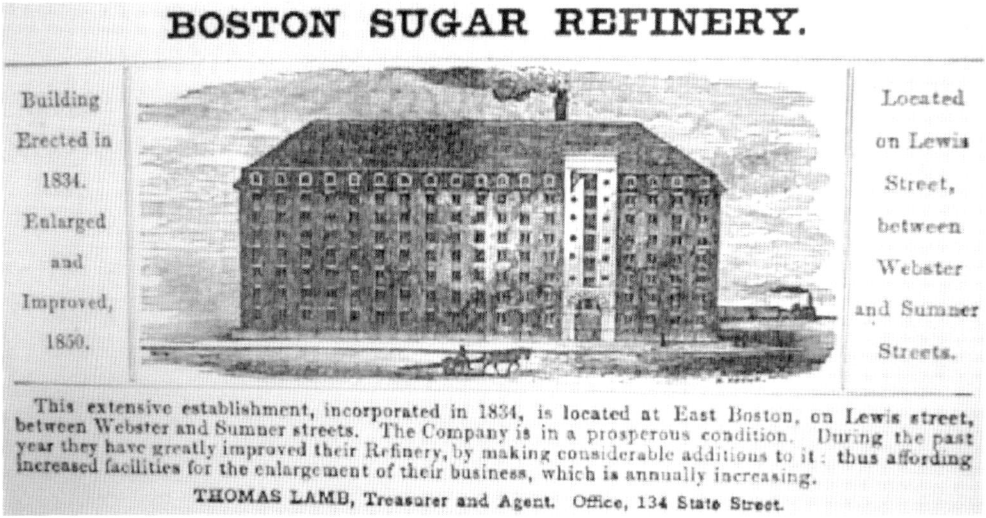

John Brown

In 1834, John Brown opened the region's first sugar refinery in East Boston. He traveled to London, where the industrial revolution was booming, to acquire factory designs and equipment. In an eight-story brick refinery on Lewis Street, he produced sugar for New England and beyond. Competing British sugar interests tried to discredit his mode of refining, but they were unsuccessful. The Boston Sugar Refinery paved the way for future manufacturers to locate in East Boston. (Courtesy of BPL.)

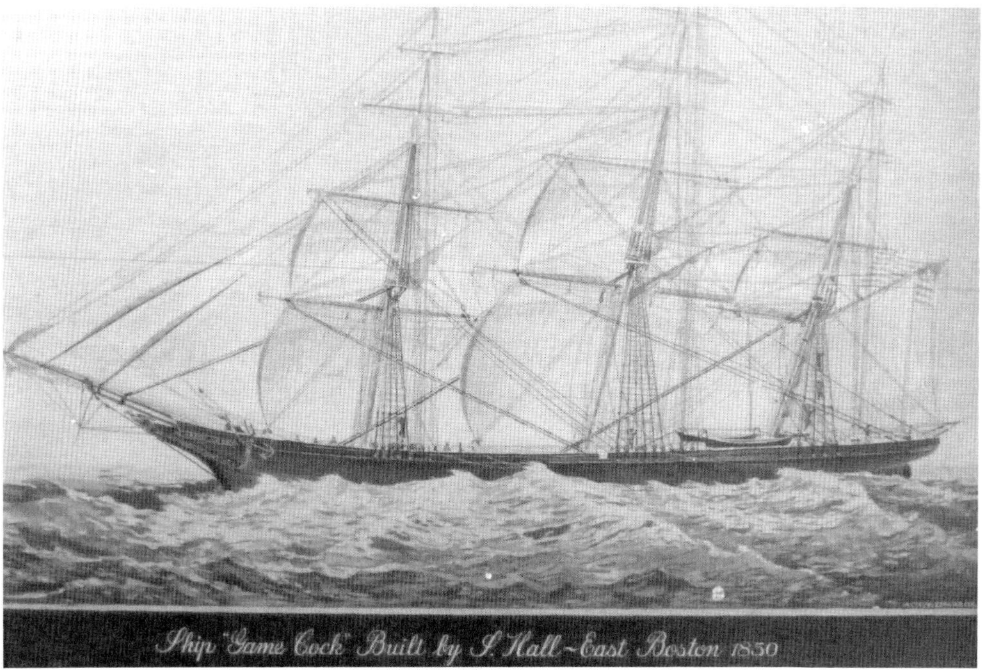

Samuel Hall (1800–1870)

Samuel Hall moved to East Boston in 1839 and opened a shipyard; he built 110 ships over 30 years. He became one of the most famous shipbuilders in the world and the driving force behind the East Boston Drydock Company, the East Boston Ferry Company, and the Maverick National Bank. (Courtesy of Mary Ellen Welch.)

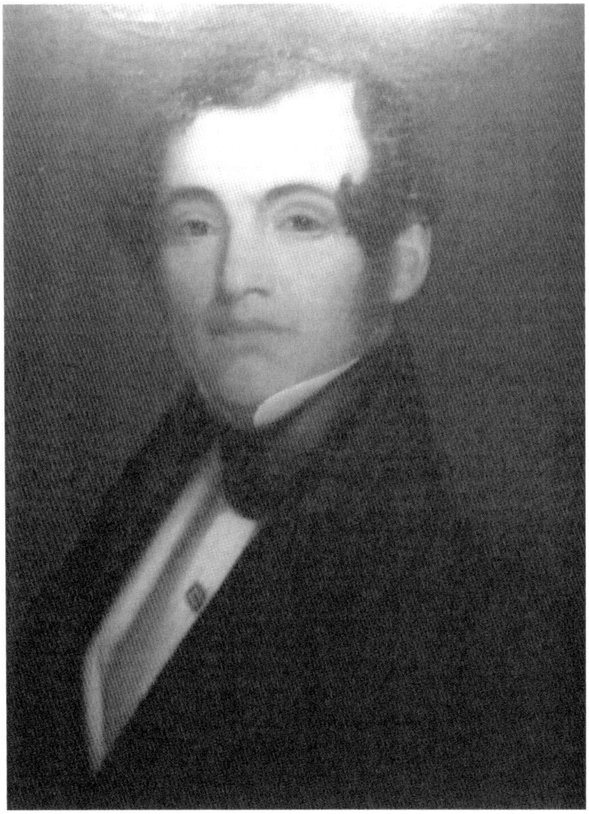

Capt. Richard Hennessy (1813–1858) and Family
The Hennessy house at 210 Webster Street was built in 1840, before East Boston homes had street numbers. Richard Hennessy, who came to the United States from Kilkenny, Ireland, in 1832, became an East Boston ferryboat captain and moved to the home in 1840 with his wife, Mary King. At the time, there was no Catholic church in East Boston, and the Hennessys had to take a ferry to the North End to attend church. In January 1857, at the age of 15, their eldest son, Richard, went to China as a cabin boy on Donald McKay's clipper ship the *Staghound*. He returned to East Boston and shipped out to India in March 1858. His diary reveals that seafaring was a hard life; he was homesick and regretted going to sea. He wrote that he could not wait to see his family and that, once home, he would never ship out again. Sadly, his father died of tuberculosis while he was away. Even more tragic, young Richard developed cholera in India and died in Calcutta on May 27, 1859. His body was thrown overboard, and the captain wrote a letter informing Mary Hennessy that her son had died. The Hennessy's youngest son, Lawrence, inherited the house and lived there with his wife, Ellen. He worked for a shipping company and, despite being born in Boston, faced anti-Irish discrimination by the English who dominated the shipping industry. Later, his son James Aloysius, who was a conductor on the narrow-gauge railroad to Winthrop, Lynn, and points north, occupied the house with his wife, Mary. Their son, James Lawrence, lived in the house with his wife, Mary Anderson, whom he married at the Assumption Church in 1944. Their daughter Jay Hennessy Benson now lives in the home. In her living room is a painting of her great-great grandfather, "Captain Dick," and photographs of generations of her relatives who lived in the home. She still has her great-great grandfather's old maps, her great-great uncle's diaries written from China and India, and the faded letter from the ship captain informing her great-great grandmother of the cabin boy Richard's death. Hennessy Benson's children and grandchildren stay with her during summers and vacations, representing seven generations of the family to occupy 210 Webster Street. (Courtesy of Jay Hennessy Benson.)

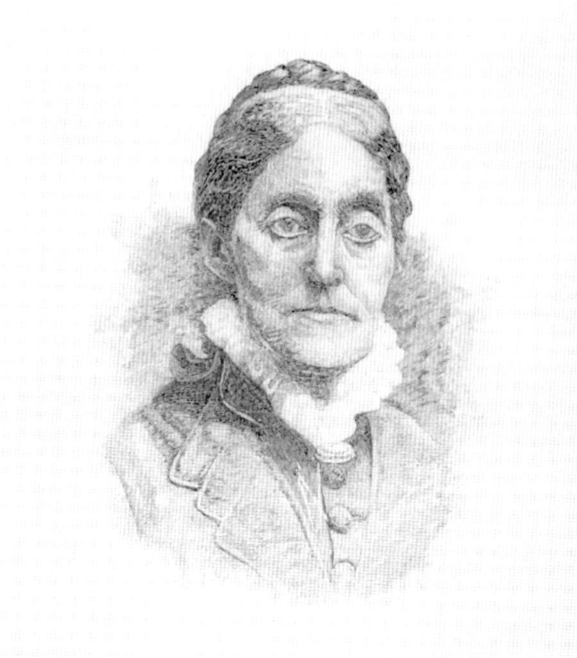

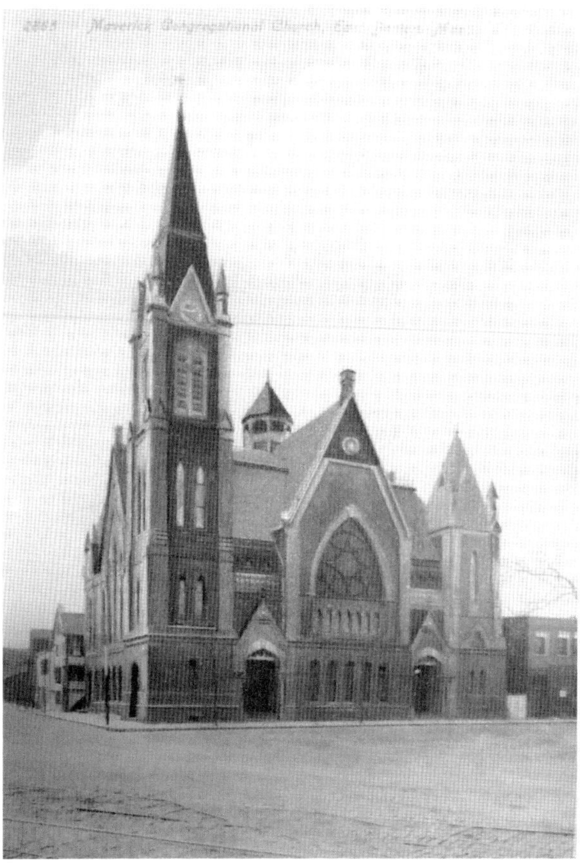

Armeda Gibbs (1807–1884)

Armeda Gibbs, the first Civil War nurse for the Union side, moved to East Boston around 1840, residing there until her death. An active member of Maverick Congregational Church, she taught Sunday school, helped the Maternal Association, and raised funds. She was a tireless missionary devoted to helping the poor, the sick, and the imprisoned throughout Boston. As an abolitionist, she aided escaped slaves who came North. When thousands of Union soldiers were wounded in the Civil War, Gibbs was the first woman recommended to serve as a nurse. The idea of sending females to the battlefield was strongly opposed by surgeons and army officers at Annapolis, but finally the experiment was approved. With her endless energy and skill, Gibbs won the hearts of all. Word was sent back to Boston, "If you have any more women like Miss Gibbs, send them down to us." (Top, courtesy of Michael Laurano; bottom, courtesy of BPL.)

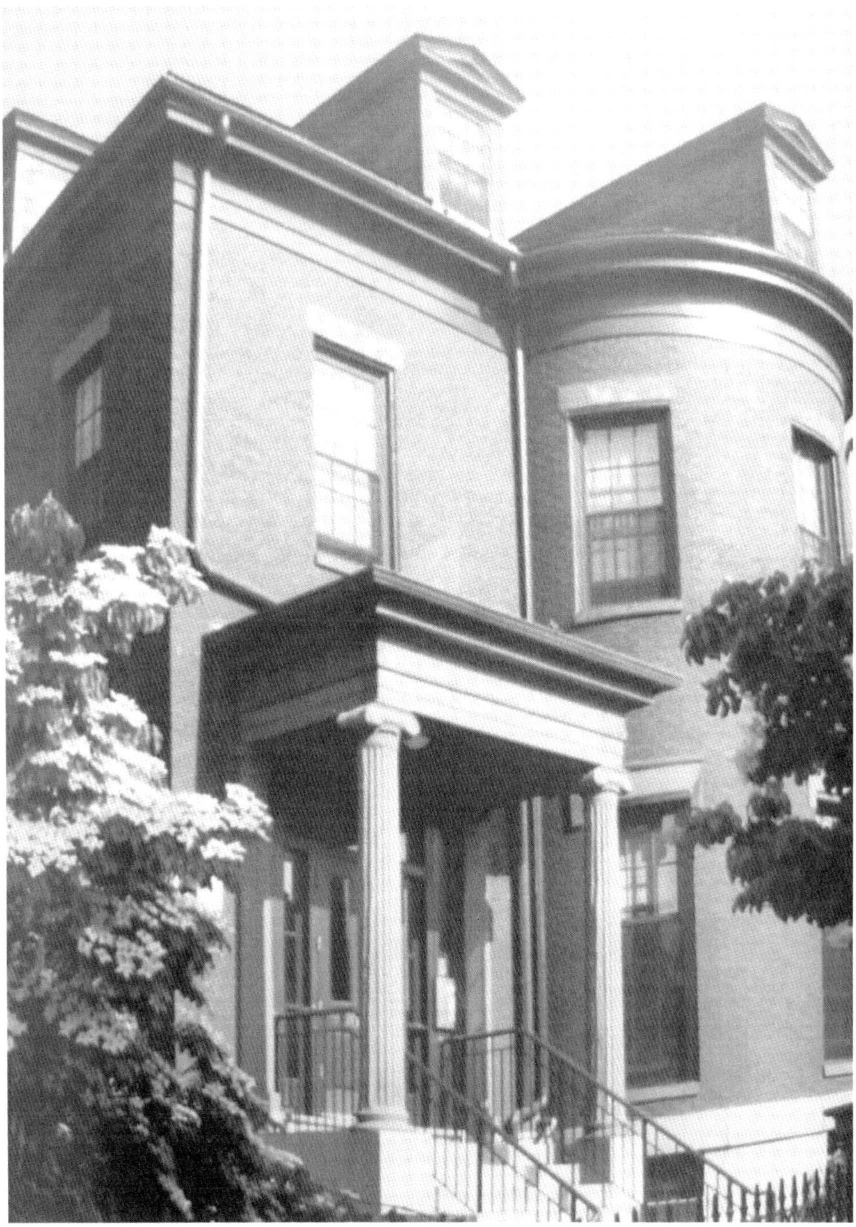

Noah Sturtevant (1800–1861)
In 1847, industrialist Noah Sturtevant and his wife, Angeline, built a brick mansion at 406 Meridian Street. They were one of East Boston's wealthiest couples, hosting opulent parties and balls. In the 1840s, Sturtevant opened a sperm oil, candle, and soap factory on Meridian Street, branching out to run a linseed oil plant that became one of the largest such manufacturers in the United States by 1849. Civic minded, he was the first person to propose and fund a tree-planting campaign in East Boston. In 1917, Boston's Trinity Church bought the Sturtevant home, and its rector, Philips Brooks, established it as the Trinity Neighborhood House—a settlement house serving immigrant families. In 1990, after it was damaged by fire, the house was purchased and converted into affordable housing by Neighborhood of Affordable Housing (NOAH). It is now listed in the National Register of Historic Places. (Courtesy of NOAH.)

Rev. Warren H. Cudworth (1825–1883)
After graduating from Harvard Divinity School in 1851 and his ordination in 1852, Rev. Warren Cudworth immediately moved to East Boston to fortify the community's Unitarian church. He transformed it from a struggling, small group with no minister to a flourishing congregation with a new building at 50 Meridian Street. In 1861, he became chaplain of the First Massachusetts Regiment of the Civil War, and in 1865 he published an account of his experience: *History of the 1st Regiment (Massachusetts Infantry)*. His book and the many personal letters he wrote from the war provide some of the most detailed historical accounts of the Civil War. On returning from the war, he lived and ministered in East Boston until his death. (Courtesy of Michael Laurano.)

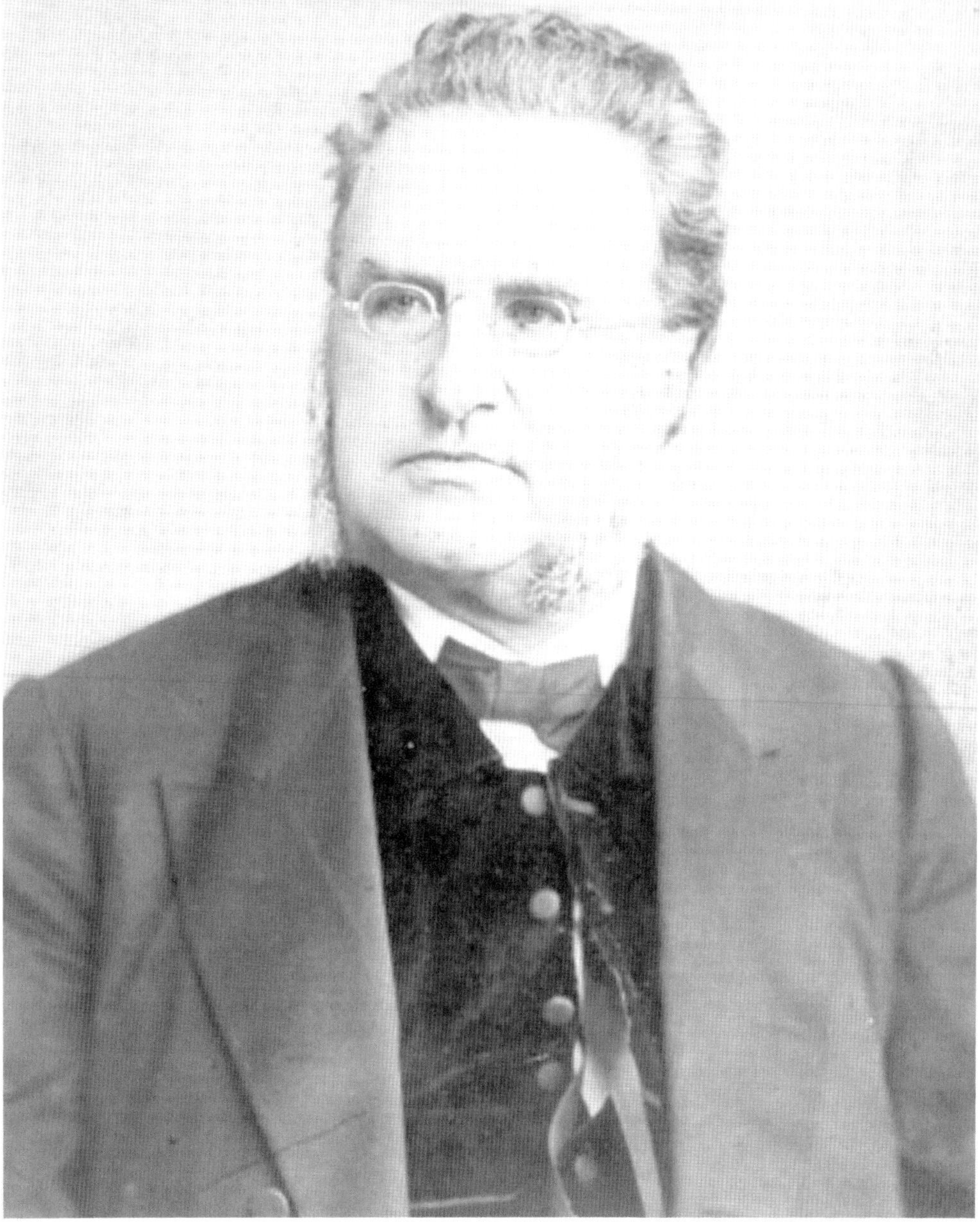

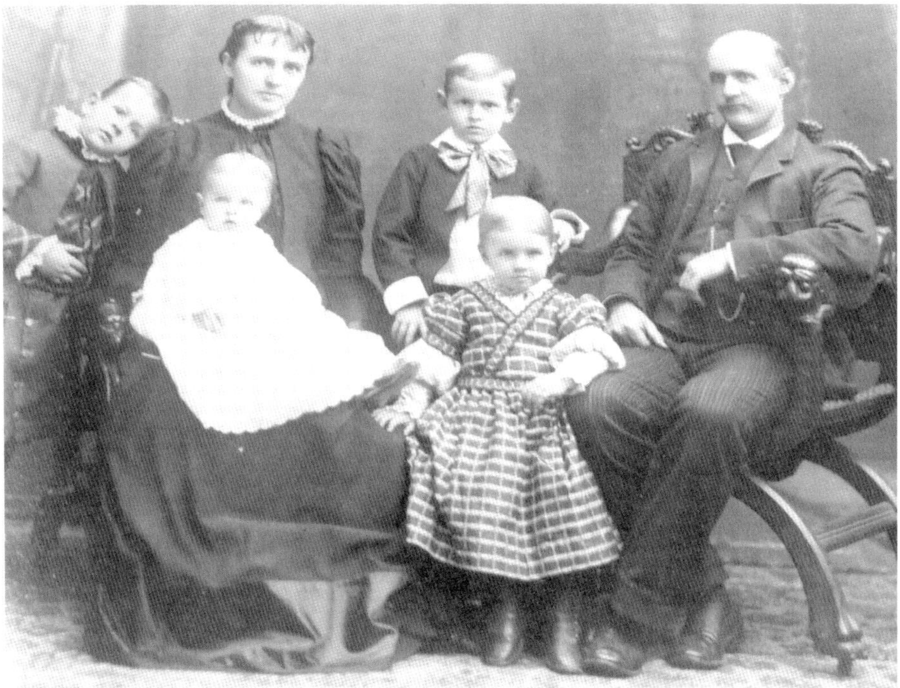

Judith Winsor Smith (1821–1921)

In 1842, Judith Winsor married Silvanus Smith, a shipbuilder in East Boston. In 1871, they built a home at 76 White Street (below), overlooking Border Street's shipyards, and lived there for the rest of their lives. Judith was active in social and political affairs and, in 1875, founded the Home Club of East Boston, the second women's club in Massachusetts. The group met twice monthly at her home. At the first meeting, attended by 30 women, the renowned feminist Julia Ward Howe (founder of the New England Woman Suffrage Association) spoke. Over the years, Judith worked with Julia Ward Howe, Lucy Stone, and other activists to gain women's suffrage and improve women's legal, social, and economic status. She was an officer in state and national women's suffrage associations and remained active in the movement until her death. She was also an ardent abolitionist. (Above, courtesy of MHS; below, courtesy of BPL.)

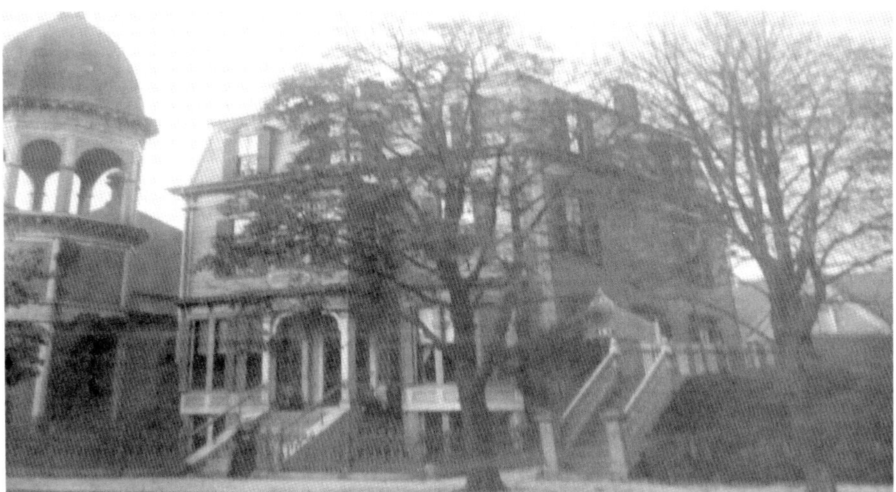

Donald McKay (1810–1880)

Born in Nova Scotia, shipbuilder Donald McKay (pictured on the cover) moved to East Boston in 1845. He opened the most modern shipyard in New England at the time on Border Street (below). Unlike other shipbuilders, McKay utilized a steam-powered sawmill, a lathe machine, and large derricks (lifting devices). This enabled him to build the largest and fastest ships in the world quickly, including the *Flying Cloud*, *Glory of the Seas*, *Staghound*, *Westward Ho*, and many others immortalized in books and paintings. McKay's unique designs allowed the ship's bow to cut through water with unprecedented speed. On her maiden voyage, the *Flying Cloud* made the quickest run from New York to San Francisco ever known. *New England Magazine* noted in 1894, "Such sailing as this astonished all nautical men and immediately gave a world-wide fame to East Boston." McKay's fame attracted more shipyards and naval industries to East Boston, including foundries, oil and gas works, spar makers, ship painters, sail makers, and marine railways. A contemporary observer noted, "There was no place in the United States or New England where there were so many provisions for ship building." This booming industry attracted new residents and new developments to East Boston, including food and clothing stores, doctors and apothecaries, coal and brick sellers, carpenters, carriage shops, portrait painters, schools, churches, and more, helping to transform the area from a rural retreat to a busy urban district. An important influence on McKay's career was his first wife, Albenia Boole, whom he married in 1833. Boole was the daughter and sister of talented shipbuilders and had lifelong exposure to ship construction. She was an expert drafter and ship designer who mentored McKay years before he opened his shipyard, sharing with him her vast knowledge of marine architecture. Family historian Richard McKay wrote, "She continually assisted him in his work. Night after night, together they toiled, planning and designing sailing craft." McKay's biographer noted that the McKays jointly completed early plans for a clipper ship. Sadly, Albenia died before her husband reached the pinnacle of his career. McKay built a mansion on top of Eagle Hill, where he could observe his Border Street shipyards. Famous people of the era visited him there, including Ralph Waldo Emerson and Henry Wadsworth Longfellow. The house, at 78–80 White Street, is listed in the National Register of Historic Places. (Courtesy of BPL.)

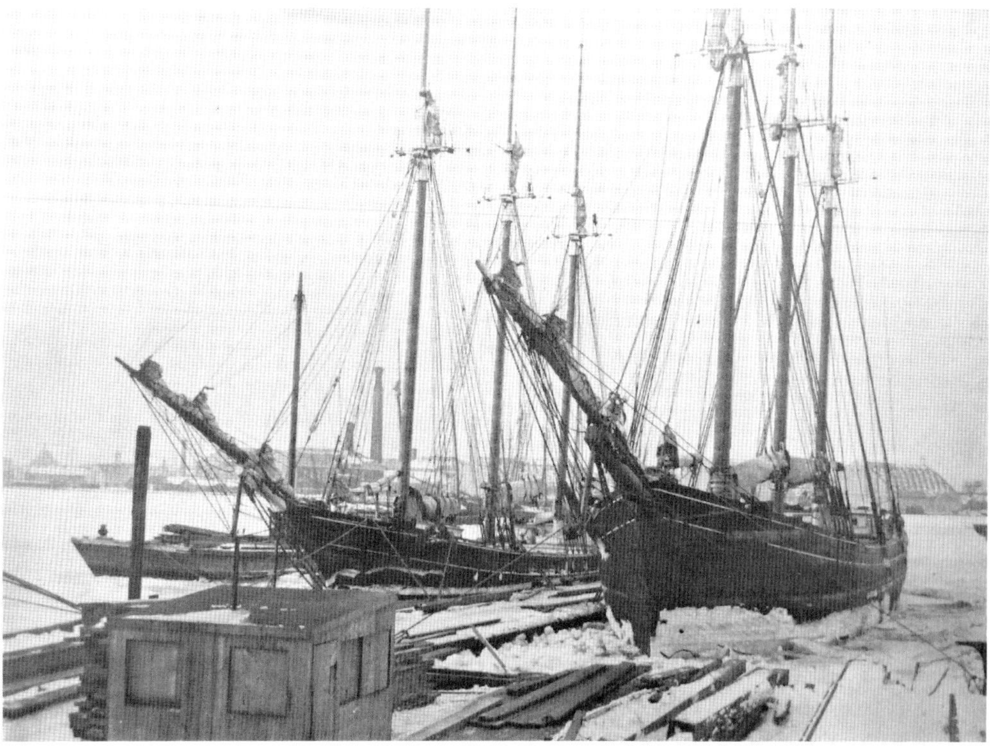

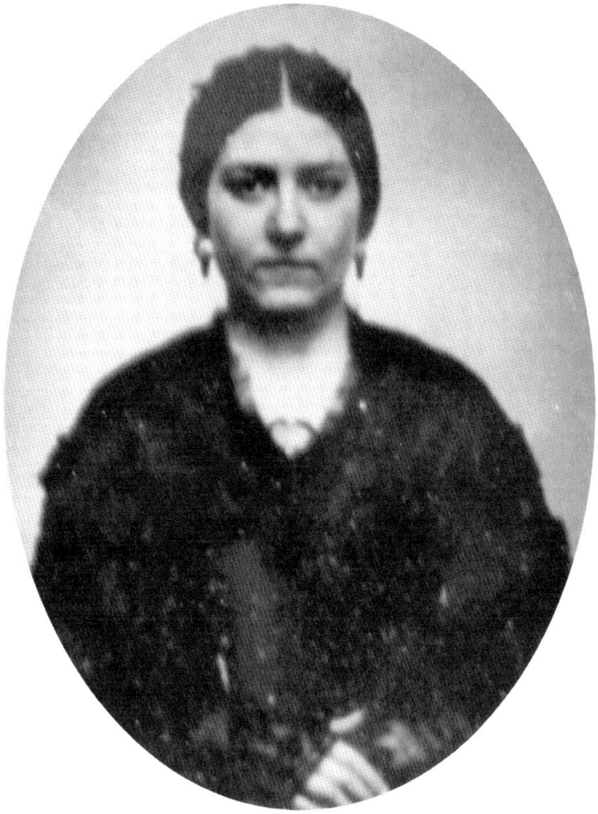

Mary Ann Brown Patten (1837–1861)
Mary Ann Brown grew up in a relatively well-off family in East Boston and was an educated woman, talented in mathematical calculations. Surrounded by ships all her life, she liked reading books on marine navigation. At the age of 16, she married ship captain Joshua Patten and went to sea with him, watching him work and assisting him when possible. It was not unusual for captains' wives to join their husbands at sea. What *was* unusual is that Mary became the first female commander of an American merchant vessel when she was 19 years old and six months pregnant. In 1856, Joshua Patten was asked to captain the clipper ship *Neptune's Car* from New York to San Francisco. While at sea on the first voyage, he noted in his diary that his wife was "uncommon handy about the ship . . . and would doubtless be of service if a man." He felt she could easily pass the examination for a master's certificate in navigation. On the second trip, July 1, 1856, the ship left New York in a race against two other clipper ships. Speed was economically critical to ship owners, who sometimes resorted to planting crewmembers on competing ships to sabotage a race. *Neptune's Car* apparently had such a saboteur in its first mate, Mr. Keeler, who was insubordinate and abusive, sneakily pulled in sails to slow down the ship, and slept while on watch. Soon after, Captain Patten fell ill with tuberculosis, becoming feverish and delirious. As Mary nursed him, Keeler tried to mutiny. Unwilling to jeopardize the ship's $300,000 cargo, Mary convinced the crew to remain loyal to her. Not in good health herself, she took control of the ship, set its course, and navigated it for 52 days around the dangerous waters of Cape Horn, arriving in San Francisco earlier than three other clipper ships that had left New York on the same day. Mary Patten became an instant news celebrity from coast to coast, winning a $1,000 gift from the insurance company that underwrote *Neptune's Car*. In a laudatory letter, the company wrote, "We know of no other instance on record where a woman has been called upon to assume command of a large and valuable vessel, and exercised proper control over a large number of seamen." Mary Patten was the inspiration for a novel by Douglas Kelley titled *The Captain's Wife*. (Author's collection.)

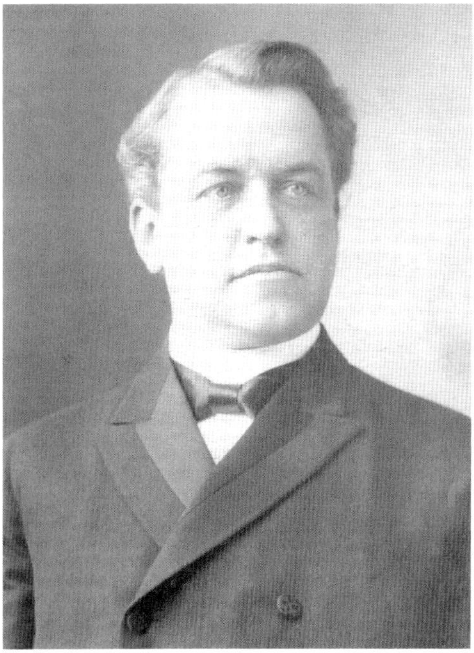

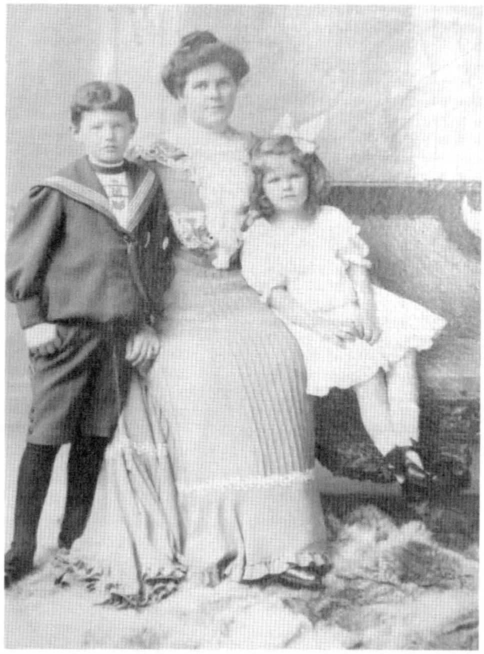

John Lewis Bates (1859–1946)

John Lewis Bates was the 41st governor of Massachusetts (1903–1905) and lieutenant governor from 1899 to 1902. A graduate of Boston Latin School and Boston University Law School, he represented East Boston for three terms in the House of Representatives, serving as speaker of the house from 1894 to 1899. Bates pushed to get the first underwater trolley tunnel built and was a trustee of Boston University, the Boston YMCA, and the Columbia Trust Company. The 1870 mansion at One Monmouth Square (below), where he lived with his wife, Clara, and four children, later became Strong Hospital and is now a rehabilitation home. (All, courtesy of BPL.)

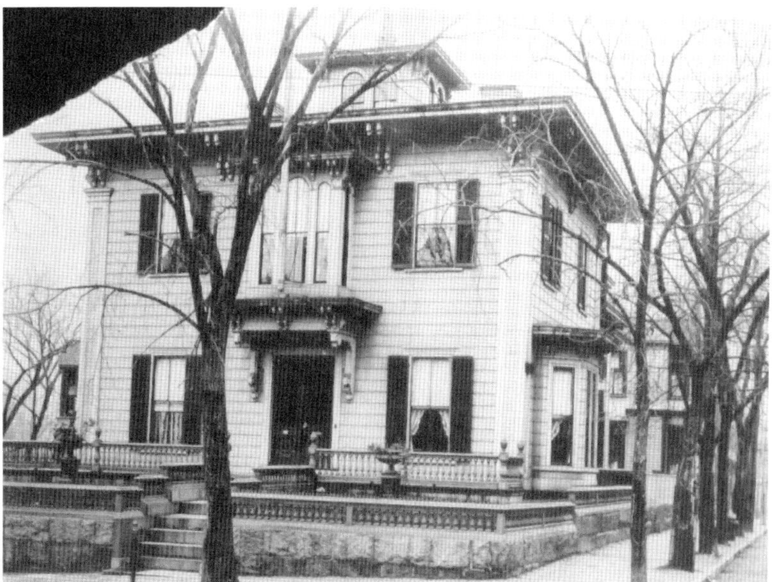

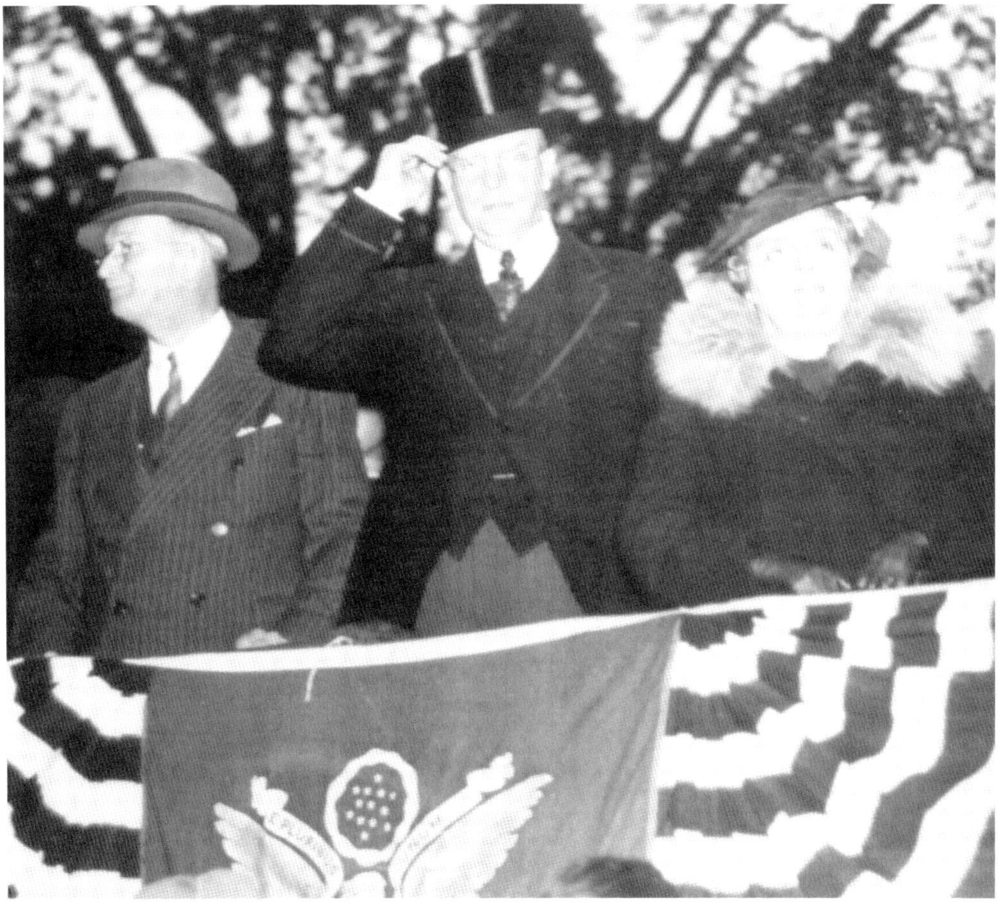

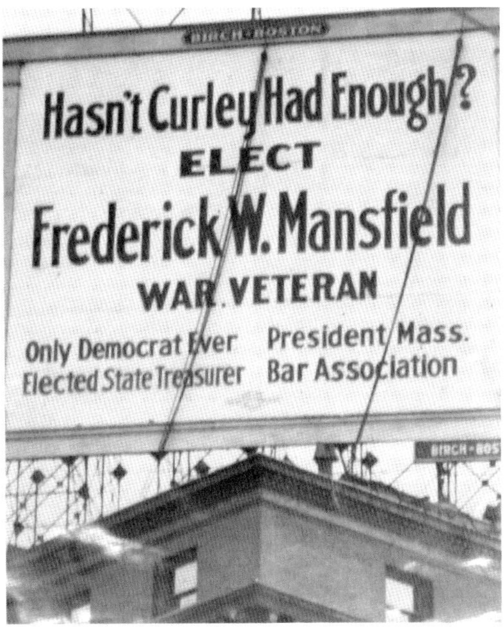

Frederick Mansfield (1877–1958)
Frederick Mansfield, the 46th mayor of Boston, attended East Boston High School and Boston University Law School before serving as mayor from 1934 to 1937. He led the city during the Great Depression, confronting poverty and rampant unemployment. Utilizing federal funds from the Works Progress Administration, he created jobs by extending subway routes, building roads, and upgrading parks. His administration expanded City Hospital, renovated Faneuil Hall, built seven new schools, and modernized the city's accounting and auditing systems. A man of progressive ideals, he advocated for low-income housing and a sales tax on non-necessities, both of which later became government standards. (Both, courtesy of BPL.)

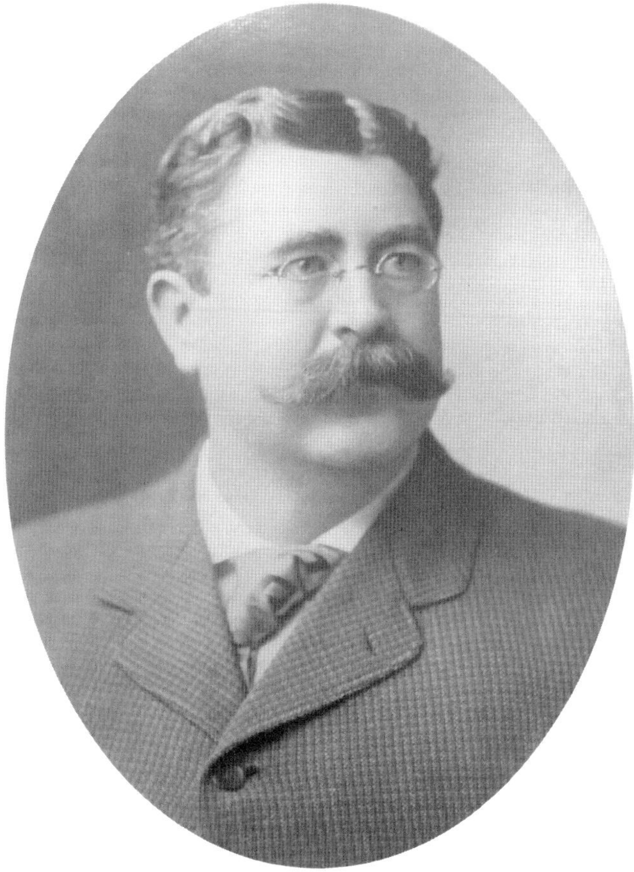

Patrick Joseph "P.J." Kennedy (1858–1929)

Patrick Joseph Kennedy, grandfather of Pres. John F. Kennedy, was the son of immigrants from County Wexford, Ireland. He was born in East Boston in 1858 in his family's modest home on Liverpool Street and was baptized at the Most Holy Redeemer Church, the religious and social center of East Boston's Irish community at the time. Quitting school to help support his family by working as a cooper and longshoreman on the Marginal Street waterfront, Kennedy eventually rose to become a prominent businessman. He married Mary Augusta Hickey in 1887 and bought a failing saloon in Haymarket Square, turning it into a thriving business. He then bought two saloons in East Boston that became highly popular gathering places where local residents shared their news and problems, asking Kennedy's advice and seeking his assistance. At the saloon, he received a constant stream of information from his customers and made useful connections. He offered loans, arranged job interviews, and made business deals. With the money he earned at his saloons, he invested in the Suffolk Coal Company. He also helped establish the Columbia Trust Bank at 20 Meridian Street in 1885 and the Sumner Savings Bank at 25 Meridian Street in 1897. In so doing, he penetrated a sacrosanct realm of Boston's Brahmins—the banking world. This set the scene for his son, Joseph, to later become president of the Columbia Trust Bank. The economic prosperity and clout P.J. Kennedy gained through his East Boston businesses positioned him to enter politics, and he served for three terms in the Massachusetts House of Representatives and was later elected to the Massachusetts Senate. Yet, his most enduring political power lay in his unofficial capacity as ward boss of East Boston's District 2 for more than 30 years. In the days before social-service agencies and government programs to help society's vulnerable, residents of working-class neighborhoods relied on the help of ward bosses to survive. The Patrick J. Kennedy School bears the name of this influential East Bostonian. (Courtesy of the JFK Library.)

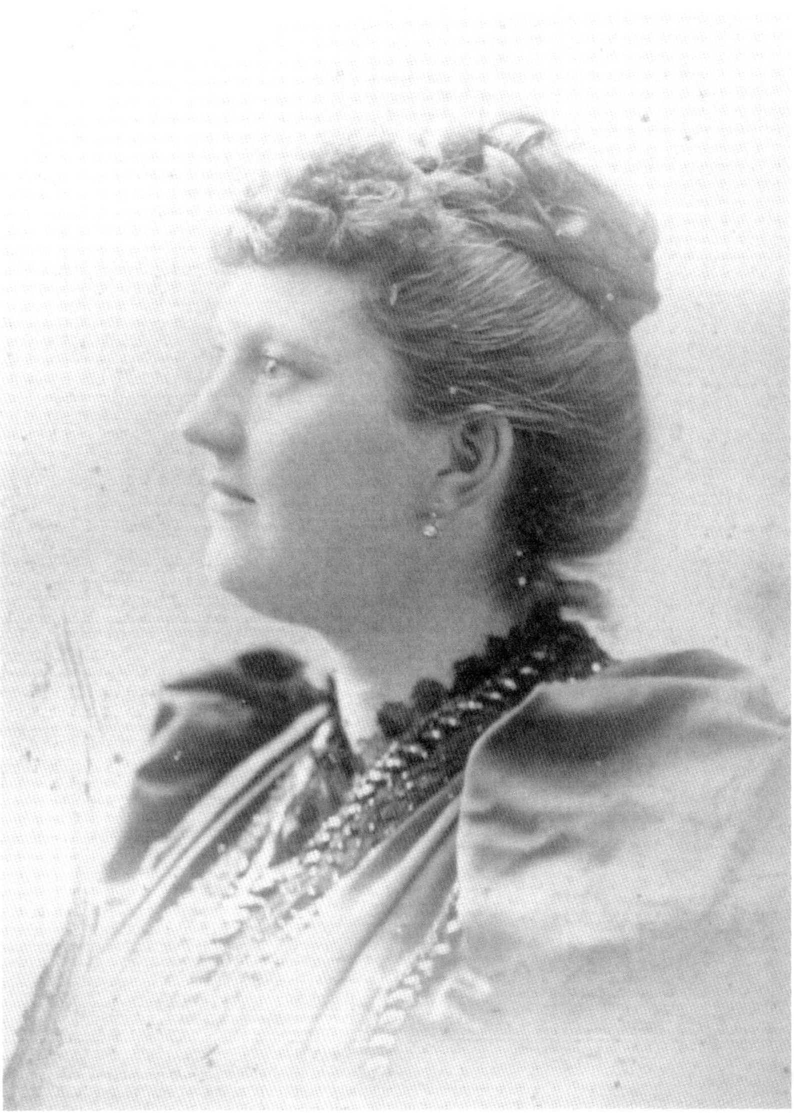

Mary Augusta (Hickey) Kennedy (1857–1923)
Mary Hickey, grandmother of Pres. John F. Kennedy, was born and raised in East Boston, the daughter of Irish immigrants from County Cork. Her father was a successful contractor, making the Hickeys members of East Boston's "lace curtain" Irish elite. Educated at Notre Dame Academy, Mary Hickey was a modern woman whose refined image appealed to her less educated husband, Patrick J. Kennedy. She read broadly, and her knowledge, wit, and optimism were vital sources of support for her husband and his endeavors. She greatly influenced her son, Joseph, encouraging him to strive for success within Boston's dominant Brahmin institutions. She purposely avoided the Irish tradition of naming a son after his father and grandfather, as she worried that the name Patrick would attract anti-Irish bigotry. Instead, she named her son the more neutral-sounding Joseph. Against the advice of local priests who felt Catholic youth should attend Catholic schools, Hickey encouraged her son to attend Boston Latin School and Harvard College so that he could better meld into Yankee society. She was an independent thinker who was active in woman's suffrage and other political concerns in East Boston throughout her life. (Courtesy of the JFK Library.)

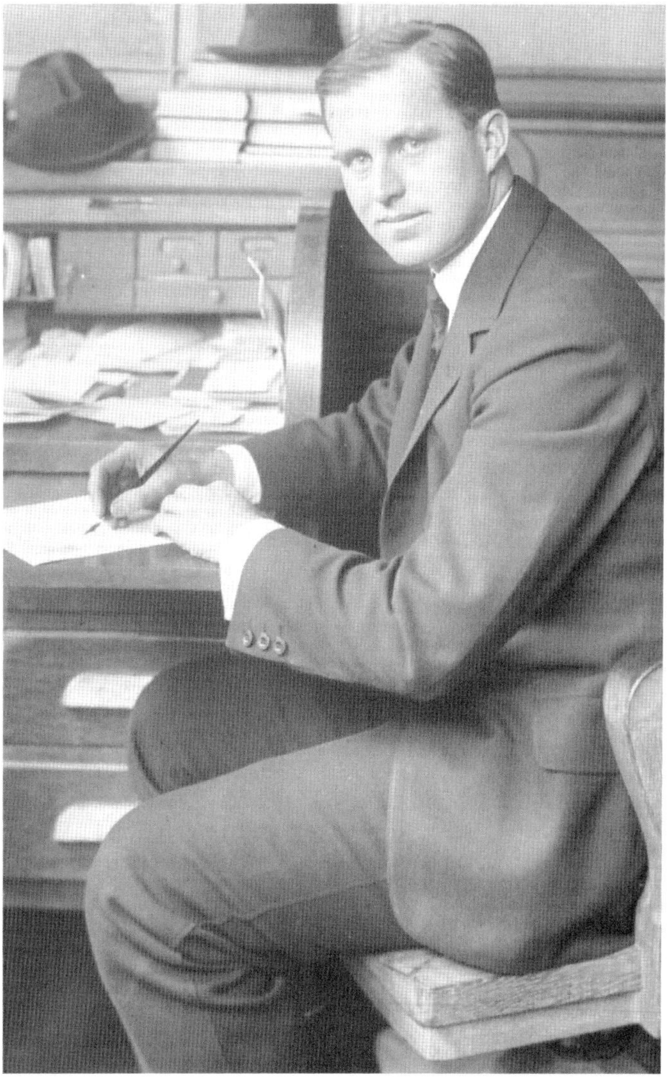

Joseph Patrick "J.P." Kennedy at Columbia Trust Bank (1888–1969)

In 1888, Joseph P. Kennedy was born to Mary and Patrick Kennedy at 151 Meridian Street in East Boston. He attended the Assumption Elementary School, graduated from Boston Latin School, and earned a bachelor of arts degree from Harvard College in 1912. Soon after, he became the assistant state bank examiner for Massachusetts, beginning a lucrative career in finance. By the age of 25, J.P. was president of the Columbia Trust Bank in East Boston, establishing himself as America's youngest bank president. He later branched out to hold investments and influential positions in the stock market, steel industry, real estate, liquor importing, Hollywood movie production, the Massachusetts Electric Company, the Securities and Exchange Commission, the US Maritime Commission, and various philanthropic organizations, along with being appointed by Pres. Franklin D. Roosevelt as the US ambassador to Britain. As the son of a wealthy and politically influential father, J.P. grew up in the same social circles as Rose Fitzgerald, the daughter of Boston mayor John "Honey Fitz" Fitzgerald. Their families sometimes summered together in Maine, and J.P. courted Rose seriously after graduating from college. They were married in 1914 and moved to Brookline, raising nine children, including John Fitzgerald Kennedy, the 35th president of the United States. (Courtesy of the JFK Library.)

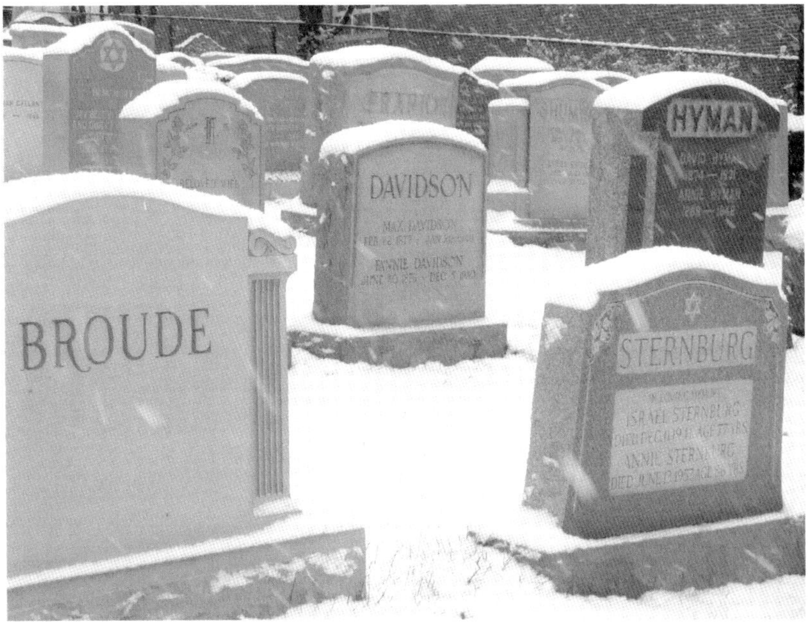

Ohabei Shalom Jewish Cemetery and Chapel
In 1844, a group of about 10 Jewish immigrant families purchased land at 147 Wordsworth Street to create Ohabei Shalom, the first Jewish cemetery in Massachusetts. In 1904, a Victorian Gothic chapel was built at the site—today the oldest surviving Jewish chapel in the state. By 1905, East Boston was the largest Jewish community in New England and some of Boston's oldest and most prestigious Jewish families have ancestors buried in the cemetery. Listed in the National Register of Historic Places, the chapel, which has been unoccupied for years, is being restored by the Jewish Cemetery Association of America in collaboration with the Massachusetts Immigrant and Refugee Advocacy Coalition to transform the building into an East Boston Immigration Center that will feature exhibits, lectures, and events related to the history of the area's Jewish and other immigrant populations. (Both, author's collection.)

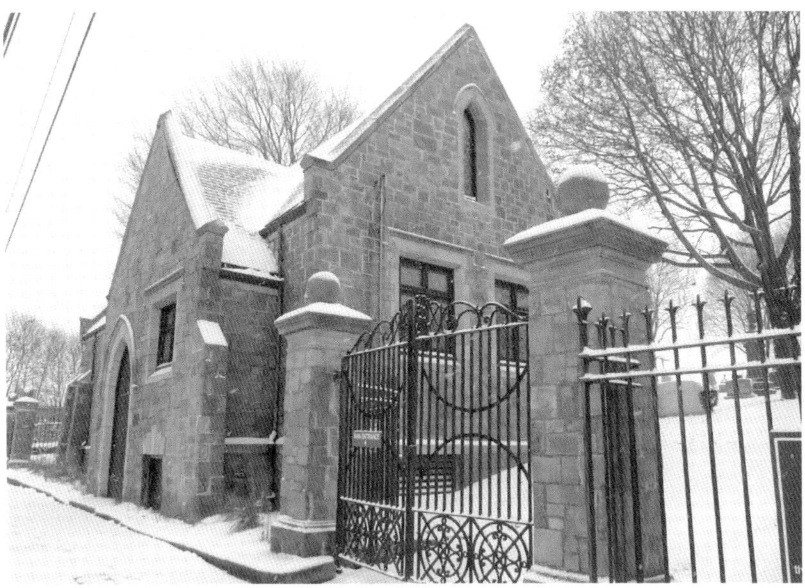

The Flynn-Greer Family

A lifelong East Boston resident with a love of historic homes, Christine Flynn became a television celebrity in 2006 when her home was featured on the PBS television show *This Old House*. During the renovation period, televised nationally, curious tourists and neighbors, including Mayor Menino, came to view the progress, and Flynn always invited them inside and gave them a tour. The Flynn family has lived in East Boston since the 1840s, when they left Ireland during the Great Famine. Flynn's great-grandfather Thomas Flynn was a Boston fireman for decades while her great-grandmother Ethel Roland Flynn was a talented milliner, creating stylish hats for East Boston's wealthy in the 1920s. She was selected for the honor of restoring the tattered flags in the Hall of Flags at the Massachusetts Statehouse. In 1914, Chris Flynn's maternal grandparents, Andrew Greer and Maggie Ryan Greer, built the house on St. Andrew Road where Flynn grew up and now lives. Andrew Greer was an East Boston ferryboat captain and his brother Frank Greer was the 1904 Olympic gold medalist in rowing. As a boy, Flynn's father, Tom Flynn, a Boston mailman for 44 years, was hired by East Boston Jewish families to light their stoves and lamps on Saturdays. As a senior citizen, he volunteered his time to speak at local schools, telling children stories of the old days in East Boston. Flynn's aunt, Grace Flynn, worked for decades as the much-loved secretary at Trinity Neighborhood House, while her mother, Mary Greer Flynn, was one of the first women in East Boston to have her own car (in 1913), at the age of 16. Christine Flynn has traveled the world as a professional trip director and is also a member of the L Street Brownies, the oldest "polar bear" swimming club in America. (Author's collection.)

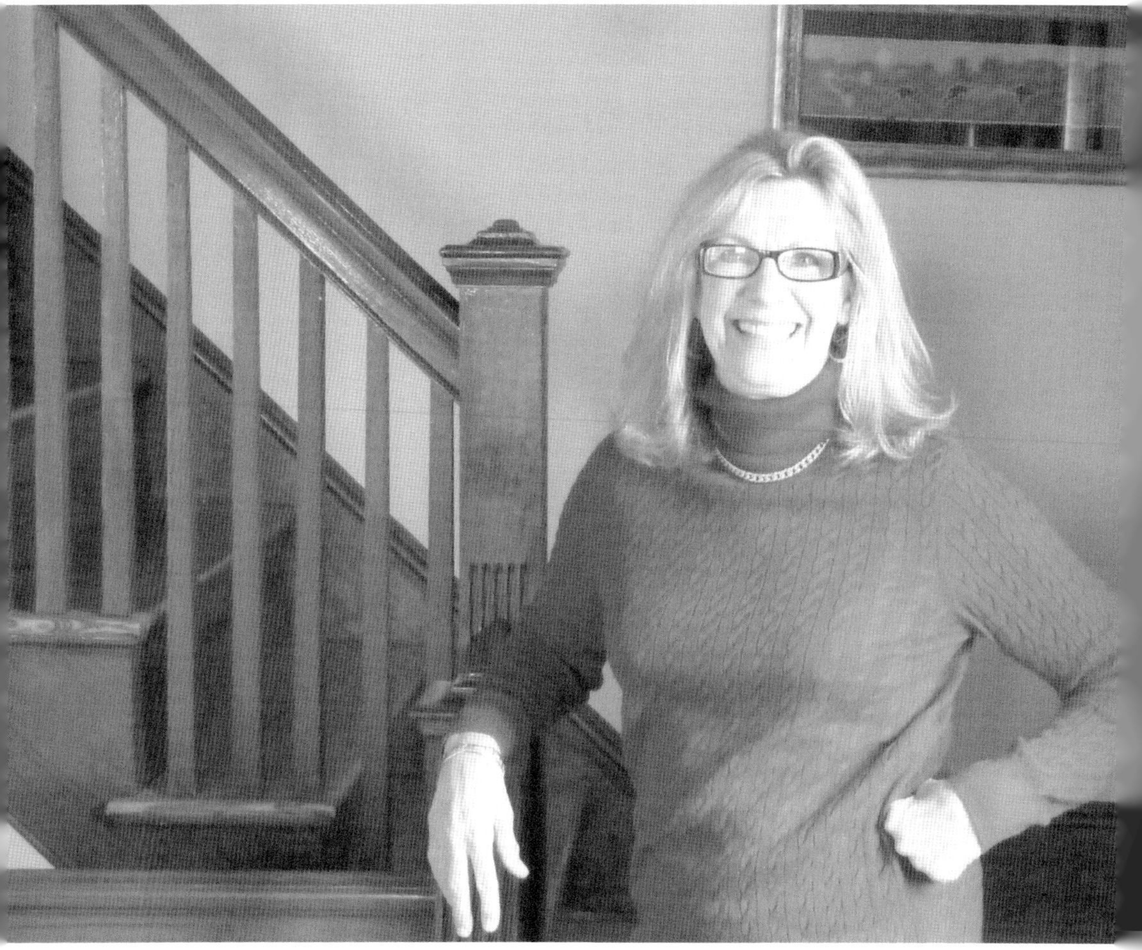

CHAPTER TWO

Community Leaders

East Boston has a long history of activism, inspired in no small part by its geography. "The island ward," as it was called in the 1800s, was cut off from city services and political decision making. This forced residents to form committees to lobby the city for basic services such as streetlights, fire hydrants, and fire engines. In 1859, reporting on "terrible conflagrations" in East Boston, the *Boston Journal* noted the island's "extreme vulnerability." Fires were frequent among its closely packed wooden homes heated by wood and coal. After midnight, when the ferries stopped running, there was no way to get fire engines across the harbor. In the 1840s and 1850s, East Bostonians petitioned the city multiple times to provide the community with a fire station and its own steam fire engine. In another example, East Bostonians worked together to get a bridge built between East Boston and Chelsea. They also united to oppose exploitative toll rates charged by the ferry companies. According to an 1860 *Boston Journal* article, the "whole community" of East Boston felt that "the people of the island ward are entitled to and shall have a fair and equitable rate of toll and not be left at the mercy of private corporations."

East Bostonians formed many voluntary associations to address community needs. These included groups that raised money to plant trees and advocate for the construction of parks. Part of a national movement to democratize leisure spaces, Wood Island Park opened in 1898. Designed by the father of American landscape architecture, Frederick Law Olmsted, it was part of his Emerald Necklace of Boston parks that included Franklin Park, the Arnold Arboretum, the Riverway, the Back Bay Fens, and the Jamaica Pond greenway. With rolling hills, graceful old trees, and miles of walking trails, it was the only major park in East Boston—75 acres where people of all ages, ethnicities, and social classes enjoyed swimming and picnic areas, tennis courts, baseball diamonds, football and volleyball fields, playgrounds and flower gardens, a gymnasium, a bathhouse, a field house, and a band shell.

This park gave rise to East Boston's most enduring activist struggle—opposition to the expansion of Logan Airport. When established in 1923, Boston Airport consisted of a cinder runway built on local tidal flats. As air travel grew increasingly popular, presidents, movie stars, and flight celebrities from Charles Lindbergh to Amelia Earhart landed in East Boston. Local residents would gather in the fields around the runway to watch the excitement, but the thrill subsided as the airport continued to expand, expropriating increasing quantities of East Boston land for runways, terminals, airplane hangars, fuel stations, access roads, parking lots, and affiliated projects. In 1949, residential and commercial areas of Porter and Gove Streets were demolished to build Boston's first expressway, conveying traffic from the Sumner Tunnel to the airport. By the mid-1960s, East Bostonians were besieged night and day with the roar of jets overhead, airport-related traffic on local streets, and fumes from planes and road vehicles.

The Massachusetts Port Authority (Massport) decided to expand the airport into Wood Island Park, and, in April 1967, Olmsted's opus was bulldozed. A year later, homes on Neptune Road were taken by eminent domain and bulldozed. Fr. John Nazzaro recalls, "I was there. George DiLorenzo jumped into a bulldozer to try to stop it. My father cried when they bulldozed Neptune Road. It was his biggest regret in life." These events galvanized community opposition to airport expansion. Lifelong resident Mary Ellen Welch explains, "To East Boston people, 'Remember Wood Island Park' is like 'Remember the Alamo.' It's a war cry. You don't let it happen again." Residents formed activist groups, organized street protests, waged lawsuits against Massport, and joined citywide coalitions working for fair transportation planning. Their activism set an important precedent in establishing the legal rights of community residents to have a voice in development projects affecting them. East Bostonians helped raise national awareness of the fact that airports, highways, oil-storage facilities, and other ventures bringing undesirable environmental impacts were disproportionately located in working-class, ethnic communities. This helped inspire the US Department of Transportation and other government agencies to embrace environmental justice, a concept that seeks to avoid disproportionately adverse health and environmental effects on low-income and minority populations and ensure that community residents get to participate in making decisions about development projects that affect them. This, in turn, led to today's laws that require public hearings, comment periods, and environmental-impact studies regarding development proposals. In 1981, East Boston was the first community in the country to create an airport-community agreement whereby the airport soundproofed schools and homes under flight paths and provided other forms of community mitigation—an example that has since been replicated by airport-abutting communities around the country.

By the 1970s, Logan Airport occupied two-thirds of East Boston's total landmass. Bremen Street was lined with airport rental-car parking lots. Condor Street and Chelsea Street housed massive oil-storage tanks. Marginal and Border Streets had dilapidated piers and abandoned industrial buildings, and East Boston had the least green space per capita of any Boston neighborhood except Chinatown. Former Boston transportation commissioner John Vitagliano notes, "No other community in Massachusetts has had as much property and land taken from it for the purpose of constructing regional transportation facilities as has East Boston." Determined to regain land for the community, residents formed neighborhood councils to transform the landscape. Progress was slow and they faced years of daunting economic and political obstacles, but, piece by piece, land was reclaimed. In the 1970s, residents prevented an abandoned drive-in movie site on Bennington Street from becoming an airport oil-storage facility. Today, it is Belle Isle Marsh Reservation, 152 acres of Boston's last remaining salt marsh. After years of meeting with oil-company executives, city and state officials, conservation groups, and the EPA, residents from the Chelsea Creek Action Group succeeded in getting the oil storage tanks on Condor Street removed. This land on the Chelsea Creek is now the Condor Street Urban Wilds. More than 15 years of meetings between residents and Massport resulted in the creation of the Harborwalk in Jeffries Point and the transformation of a decrepit pier on Marginal Street into Piers Park, now one of Boston's most beautiful parks. Pursuing the dream of a linked greenway of parks in East Boston, residents asked Conrail, owner of an abandoned railway corridor on Bremen Street, to donate the land. Nearly 20 years of resident advocacy, planning, and working together with elected officials, the Boston Natural Areas Fund, private foundations, and Massport resulted in the East Boston Greenway, a park with community gardens, playgrounds, and bike trails. East Bostonians continue to work together for family-friendly community development. In 2013, a multiracial interfaith coalition successfully organized the grassroots No Eastie Casino campaign to prevent Suffolk Downs from becoming a casino. Today, the observations of a 1905–1914 sociological study of East Boston still hold true: "The very isolation and provincialism of the island has turned out to be a source of strength. In no other portion of the city will one find anything like so well-knit and humanized a population and one so fitted to participate in local affairs."

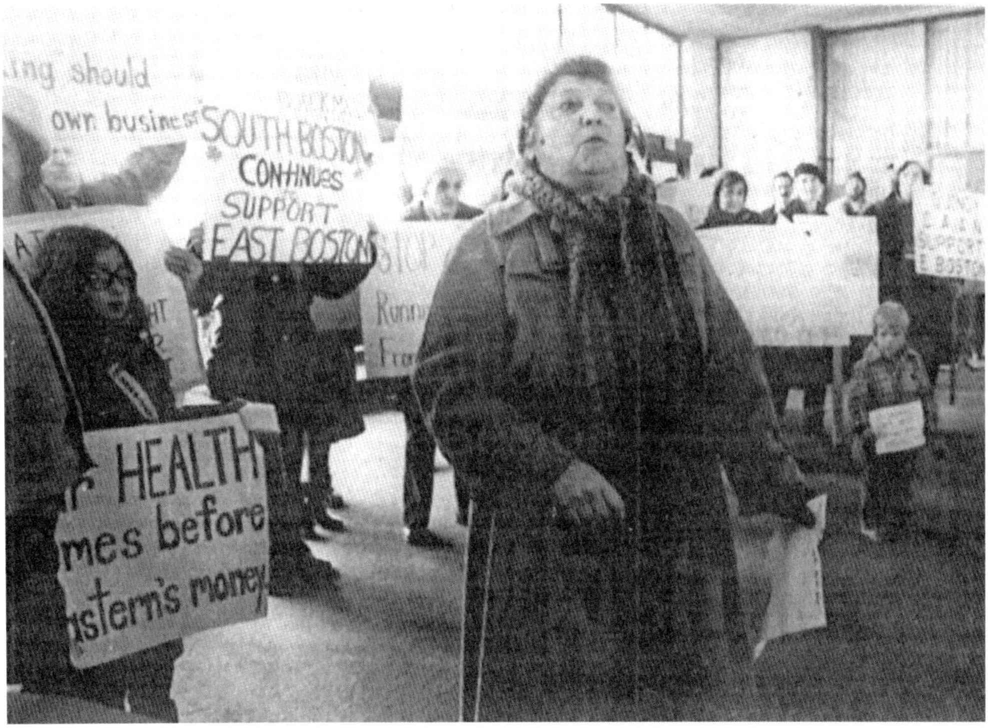

Anna DeFronzo (1907–1998)

Lifelong East Bostonian Anna DeFronzo was a leader of the Maverick Street Mothers, a political protest discussed in sociology books. Widowed at a young age, DeFronzo struggled to support her five children by working as a seamstress. She was known for her beautiful knitting and crocheting, always welcoming new babies in the neighborhood with handmade gifts. In her lifetime, she saw Logan Airport grow from a single runway into an international travel hub. Its growth brought daily noise, traffic, and air pollution to local residents. In 1968, as Massport converted Bird Island Flats into an air-cargo facility with an area for a short runway, dump trucks and other heavy vehicles began using densely populated Maverick Street as a shortcut from the airport. Their speed and weight shook homes, cracking foundations and windows. Residents complained that truck drivers were reckless toward pedestrians and the many children who played on Maverick Street. Yet, their grievances to city and state officials fell on deaf ears. DeFronzo, a respected community matriarch, gathered neighbors around her kitchen table to discuss the problem. Inspired by the nonviolent protests of Dr. Martin Luther King Jr. happening at that time, they resolved to take direct action by blocking Maverick Street traffic. The women of the neighborhood determined that they would lead the protest, fearing that males would more likely be arrested and lose their jobs. On September 28, 1968, dozens of mothers pushing baby carriages, grandmothers in their housedresses, career women coming home from work, and a few men bravely faced down angry truckers who warned them to clear the street. State police arrived and threatened to arrest them but were unsure of how to handle so many women and baby carriages. The protest became headline news, and Massport soon announced it would build an alternate truck route to Bird Island Flats on airport property. A gate was placed at the Maverick Street airport exit to prevent nonresident vehicles from using the street. DeFronzo, often accompanied by her daughter, Theresa "Chickie" Cipriano, was a lifelong activist and spokesperson for airport-related environmental concerns in East Boston and was known and respected by journalists, activists, and politicians across the state, including mayors and governors. For this reason, the senior center on Maverick Street bears her name. From DeFronzo's small kitchen emerged a movement of East Boston environmental activism that continues today. (Courtesy of EBCN archives.)

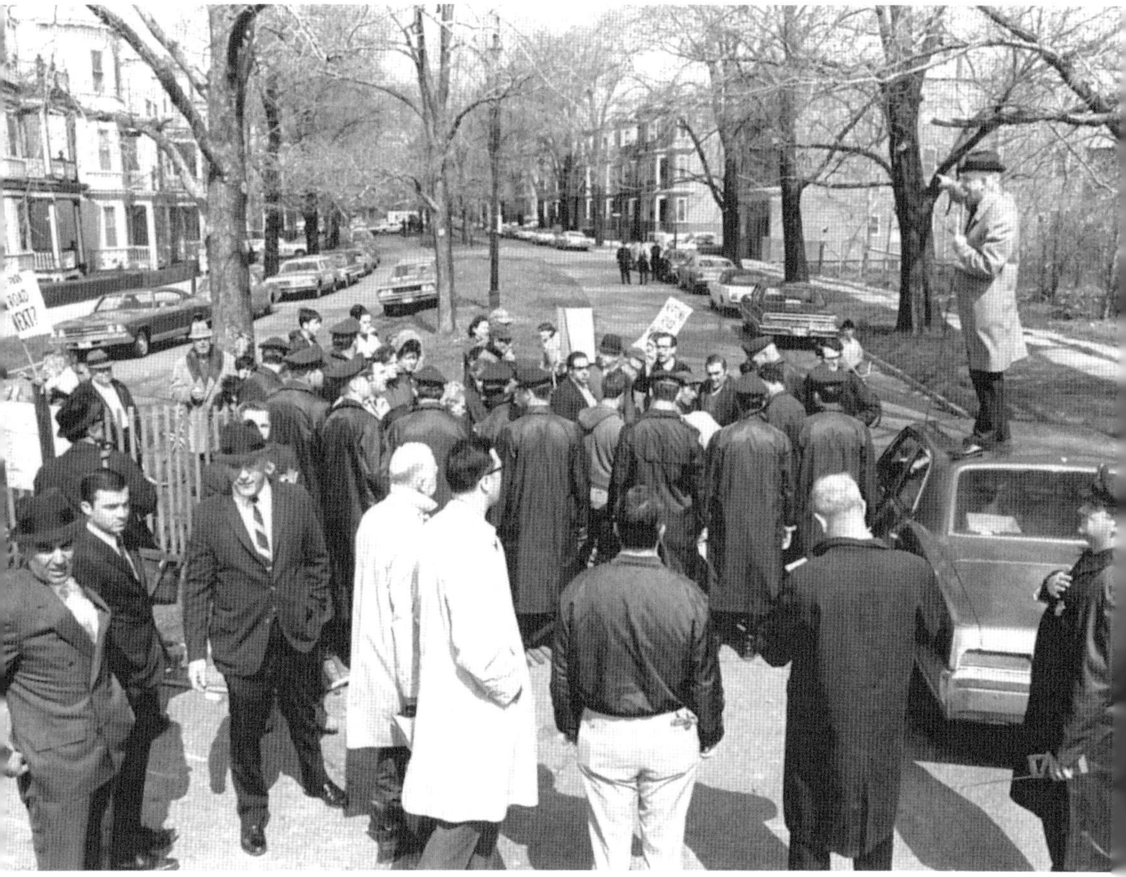

George DiLorenzo (1919–2004) (ABOVE AND OPPOSITE PAGE)
Former East Boston state representative George DiLorenzo was born and raised in Maverick Square and never lost touch with his working-class roots. He proudly called himself a "dump rat," referring to the fact that the apartments on Cottage Street where he grew up were built on a former garbage dump. A graduate of Suffolk University, DiLorenzo worked as a teacher and social worker and was an advocate for mentally handicapped children. As a state representative from 1965 to 1970 and 1973 to 1974 (the years of court-ordered school desegregation in Boston), he was a vocal critic of busing. But, he is most remembered by East Bostonians as an adversary of Logan Airport. In 1968, he marched with the Maverick Street Mothers, blocking Maverick Street with a sit-in to prevent airport construction trucks from using local streets. The next year, with East Bostonians indignant over the razing of Wood Island Park and the loss of other local land to airport expansion, DiLorenzo helped lead the unsuccessful battle to save Neptune Road, a tree-lined residential street that was the former entrance to Wood Island Park. When residents of Neptune Road and a connecting section of Prescott Street were informed that their homes would be taken by eminent domain, many refused to vacate. As they wrote letters and called city and state officials for help, state police began forcibly removing resisters. (Miss Loschi, an elderly woman in a wheelchair, refused to leave her home and was carried out by the police.) George DiLorenzo gathered on Neptune Road with fellow East Bostonians to try to stop the takeover. The image of him holding a bullhorn to rally protesters remains in many people's memories today. While the homes on Neptune Road are no longer there, DiLorenzo is remembered as a legendary fighter for the community. The George DiLorenzo playground in Bremen Street Park is named in his honor. (All, author's collection.)

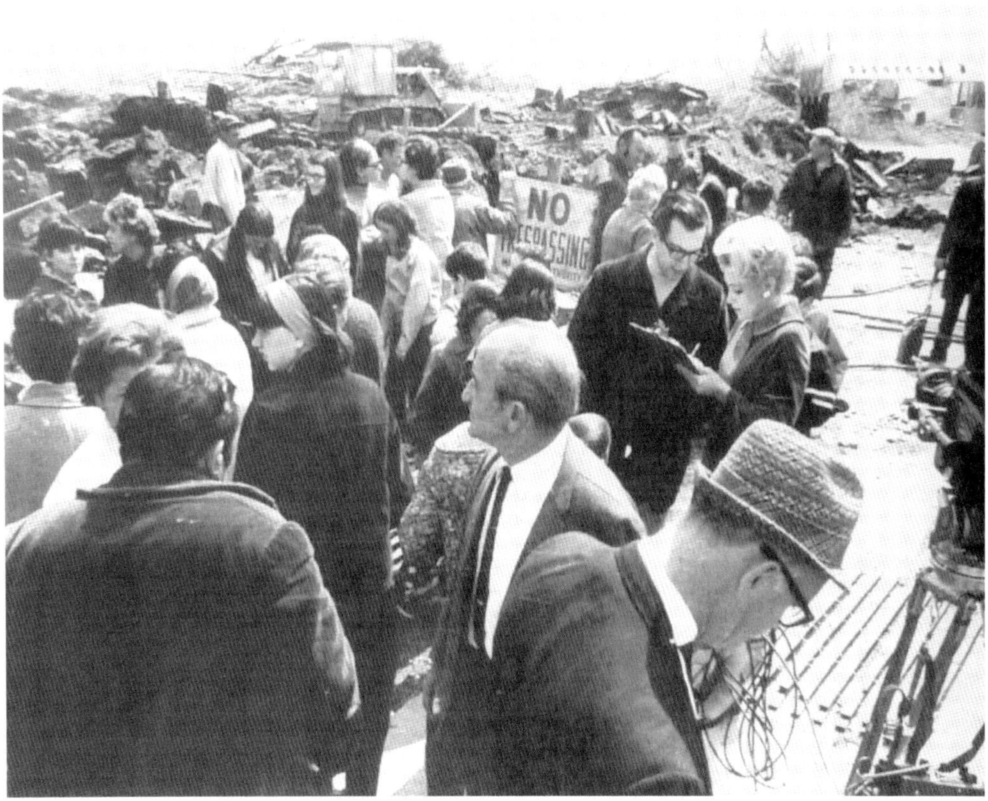
NO
TRESPASSING

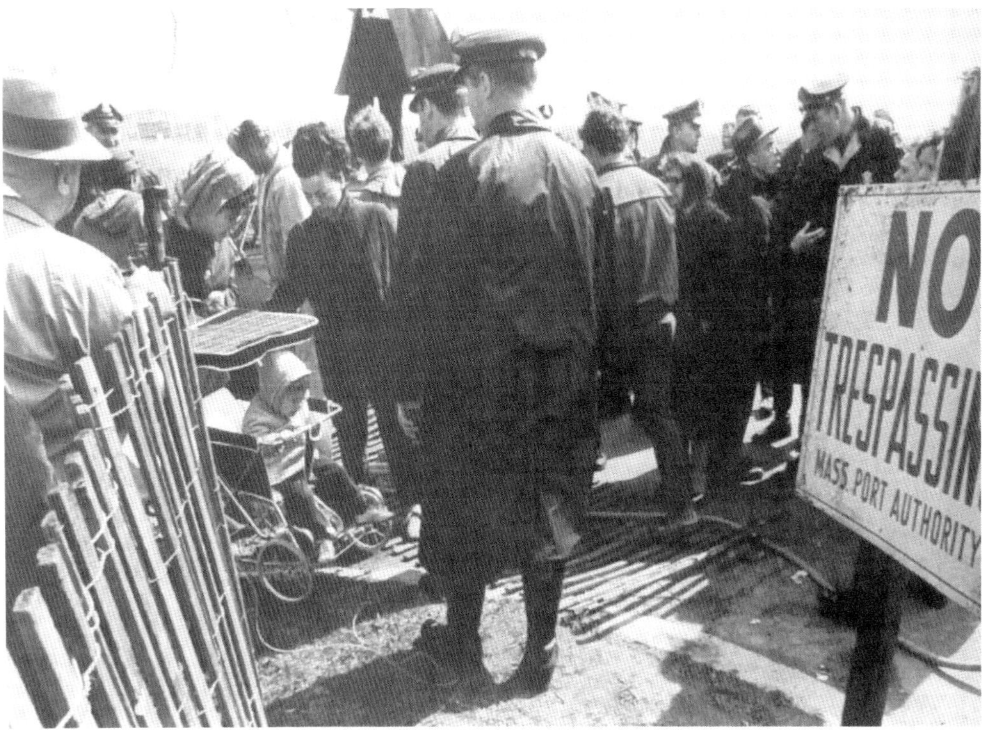
NO
TRESPASSIN
MASS. PORT AUTHORITY

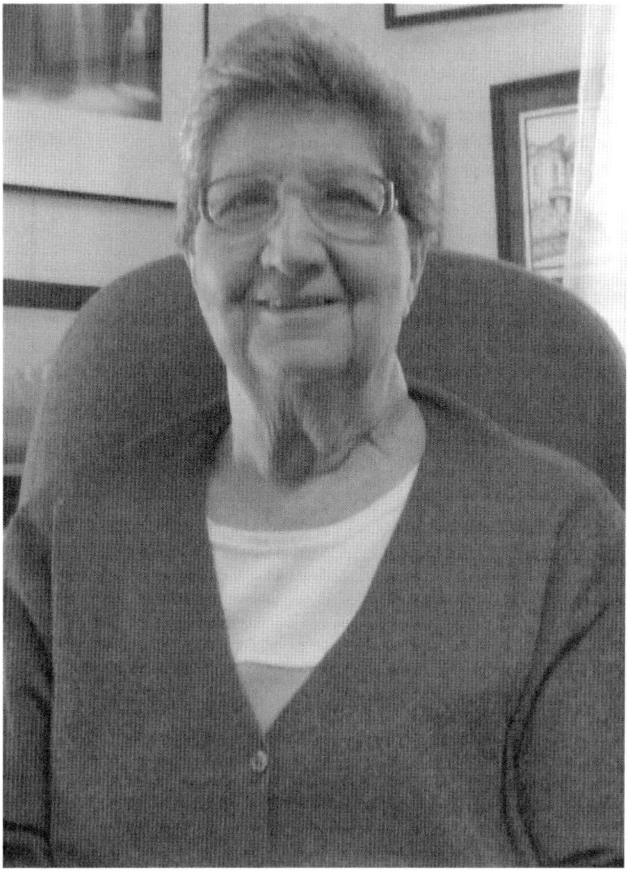

Evelyn Morash

Evelyn Caucci was born in East Boston in 1929 to immigrant parents from Roccasecca, Italy. She married Arthur Morash when she was 19, and as a young mother, she volunteered at Trinity House and was a Girl Scout leader. In 1960, she worked on the citywide census, making friends with Bostonians of diverse races. Feeling that the public schools her five children attended were underperforming, Morash joined School Volunteers for Boston and CDAC, a citywide coalition of parents, teachers, and concerned citizens working to improve the Boston public schools. One of her proudest achievements was her advocacy work to ensure that every East Boston school had a library. When Boston public schools were desegregated in the 1970s, Morash was one of a minority of parents in the neighborhood to publicly support desegregation and the busing of students across the city to integrate schools. Her support of the ideals of busing and her willingness to send her own children to schools in African American neighborhoods brought threats and violence from some neighbors, who spray-painted her home and threw stones at her windows. Rather than intimidate her, this made Morash more determined to stand up for her beliefs. After serving on a citywide desegregation planning committee, she was appointed to the State Board of Education by Gov. Michael Dukakis. Morash was a working mother before it was the norm: "People thought all I did was volunteer, but I also worked full-time!" On Sunday nights, she would cook a big dinner, and her home became a weekly gathering spot for young local activists who saw Morash as a motherly mentor. An early proponent of multilingual services and cultural diversity, Morash was also active in planning the Umana Barnes Middle School and volunteered for years on the boards of the East Boston Social Centers and the East Boston Neighborhood Health Center. Known for bringing her neighbors homegrown vegetables, fresh baked goods, or books she wants to share, Morash has spent more than eight decades exemplifying the ideals of engaged citizenship. (Author's collection.)

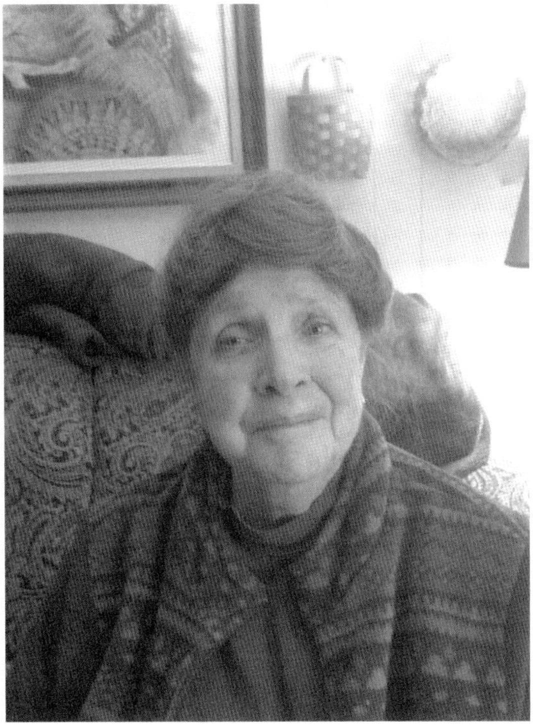

Mary Ellen Welch
A fourth-generation East Bostonian, Mary Ellen Welch grew up on Webster Street and graduated from Emmanuel College. While a teenager in the 1950s, she worked as a "soda jerk" at Woodbury's Pharmacy in Maverick Square and was a member of the Assumption Cadets drill team. A second-grade teacher for 47 years, Welch was beloved by generations of students for her patient and creative teaching style, which incorporated multicultural music and art at her own expense, at a time when public schools lacked funds for art and music programming. A strong proponent of racial and gender equality, Welch attended the 1963 Civil Rights March in Washington, DC, led by Dr. Martin Luther King Jr. and later volunteered as campaign manager for African American mayoral candidate Mel King. She has been a community activist in East Boston for more than 55 years, working to improve public schools, increase affordable housing, strengthen community-based health and social services, attract positive community development, and mitigate the environmental impacts of living next to an airport. She served for many years as the president of Airport Impact Relief Inc., the Jeffries Point Neighborhood Association, and NOAH. She was also an active board member of the East Boston Ecumenical Community Council, the Land Use Council, the Neighborhood Health Center, Friends of Belle Island Marsh, the Harborside Community Council, and other boards, often serving as chairperson. A self-educated expert on the technical, legal, and regulatory aspects of airports, Welch has been a prominent advocate for the soundproofing of East Boston homes, schools, and other public buildings located under flight paths, as well as for additional forms of community mitigation from Massport. These have included funding for local youth and senior programs and the construction of new parks to compensate for the loss of Wood Island Park. Armed with her famous homemade cookies, Welch has spent her life speaking out at city, state, and local meetings and public hearings to ensure that East Boston's dream of parks such as Piers Park on the waterfront, the Urban Wilds on Chelsea Creek, and the Bremen Street Greenway became realities. In her retirement, she continues to be a full-time activist for green space and quality-of-life improvements, participating in meetings and advocating for East Boston with handwritten letters that she mails daily to government officials and elected leaders, including President Obama. (Courtesy of Gary McMullen.)

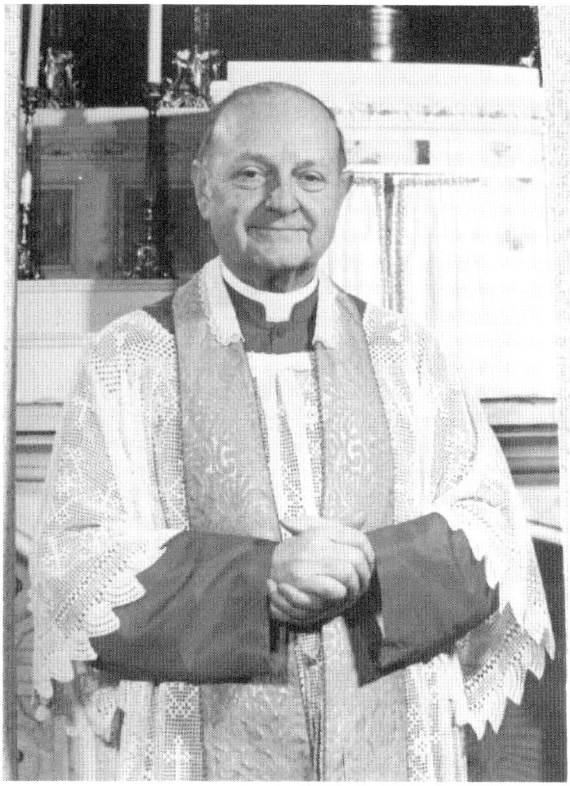

Msgr. Mimie Pitaro (1916–1995)
Mimie Pitaro served from 1964 to 1973 as minister of the Most Holy Redeemer Parish and was the first priest ever elected as a state representative in the United States. Growing up in an Italian immigrant family in the conservative 1950s, where he was taught to respect authority, the mild-mannered Roman Catholic priest seemed unlikely to become a political activist. When racial tensions erupted in the late 1960s in the Maverick public housing projects, Pitaro encouraged residents to treat each other with respect. Growing up hearing the anti-Italian slurs "dago" and "guinea," Pitaro understood what it felt like to be a minority. He spoke against bigotry, but anger in East Boston grew at the prospect of a federally mandated busing program to desegregate the public schools. Reflecting larger violent battles around desegregation that were happening throughout Boston's working-class neighborhoods, conflicting factions developed in East Boston—those supporting desegregation and those against it. A proponent of racial equality and desegregation, Pitaro received hate mail and even death threats from some local residents, while he was admired as a brave leader by others. He formed an ecumenical parish council that advocated for racial harmony and focused on improving public services to address the poverty and institutional neglect facing East Boston. Calling for better communication between City Hall and East Boston, the parish council was a key force in inspiring Mayor Kevin White to establish Boston's first Little City Hall in 1968—an office trailer located in Maverick Square. Managed by Frederick Salvucci, who was fluent in Italian and later became Massachusetts state secretary of transportation, Little City Hall was a place where East Bostonians could take care of city-related paperwork without having to travel downtown. In an era when large portions of the population were monolingual Italians, residents could bring their concerns directly to the mayor's staff, speaking in Italian if needed. Perhaps because he had seen his former parish in the South End demolished by urban renewal, Pitaro was an outspoken critic of Logan Airport expansion and its impacts on the community. Wanting East Boston to have more effective representation at the state level, he ran for and won a seat in the Massachusetts House of Representatives in 1971. (Courtesy of Mary Ellen Welch.)

Dr. Edith G. DeAngelis

Educator, activist, and neighborhood historian Edith DeAngelis lived most of her 86 years on Meridian Street. Her grandparents were the first Italian family to buy a home on Eagle Hill, populated at the time by Irish and Jewish families. "The Irish treated us badly. But, there was a lovely Irish neighbor, Mrs. Kerr, who was kind to us and scolded the others for how badly they treated us." DeAngelis graduated from East Boston High School and earned a master's and doctorate from Boston University. Volunteering at Trinity House at the age of 10, she always cared about recreational opportunities for youth and dedicated her life to fighting for green space. "East Boston was destined to be an airport. The politicians weren't helping us. They sold us down the river. So, we had to do it ourselves." As president of the East Boston Recreation, Master Planning, Land Use Advisory Council in the late 1960s, DeAngelis led East Boston's early master-planning process. "The Parish Council with Msgr. Mimie Pitaro and Judge Ferrino was how it all started," she says. Over the years, DeAngelis volunteered on more neighborhood committees than can be listed. She was a key activist in stopping Belle Isle Marsh from becoming an oil refinery and in getting the Condor Street oil tanks removed to convert the land into the Urban Wilds. She often attended meetings every night of the week regarding various land-use projects that became today's East Boston Health Center, Paris Street Pool, Harborside Community Center, Lopresti Park, Porzio Park, Piers Park, and Greenway. One of her longest projects was the Eagle Hill Memorial Community Garden on Border Street: "It took 29 years of fighting to get that." Today, DeAngelis is proud of being one of the midwives of East Boston's rebirth. "It makes me feel wonderful when I look at Piers Park and the Greenway and see children playing there." But, she is most proud of a scholarship fund she established with her sisters to honor her parents, Amelia and Henry DeAngelis, and aunt Edith Colantuono. In the past 20 years, the fund has awarded 100 scholarships to East Boston students and volunteers. DeAngelis (right) is pictured here with her sister Florence D'Avella, another lifelong East Boston volunteer who was a beloved "lunch mother" at the O'Donnell School for many years. (Courtesy of Edith DeAngelis.)

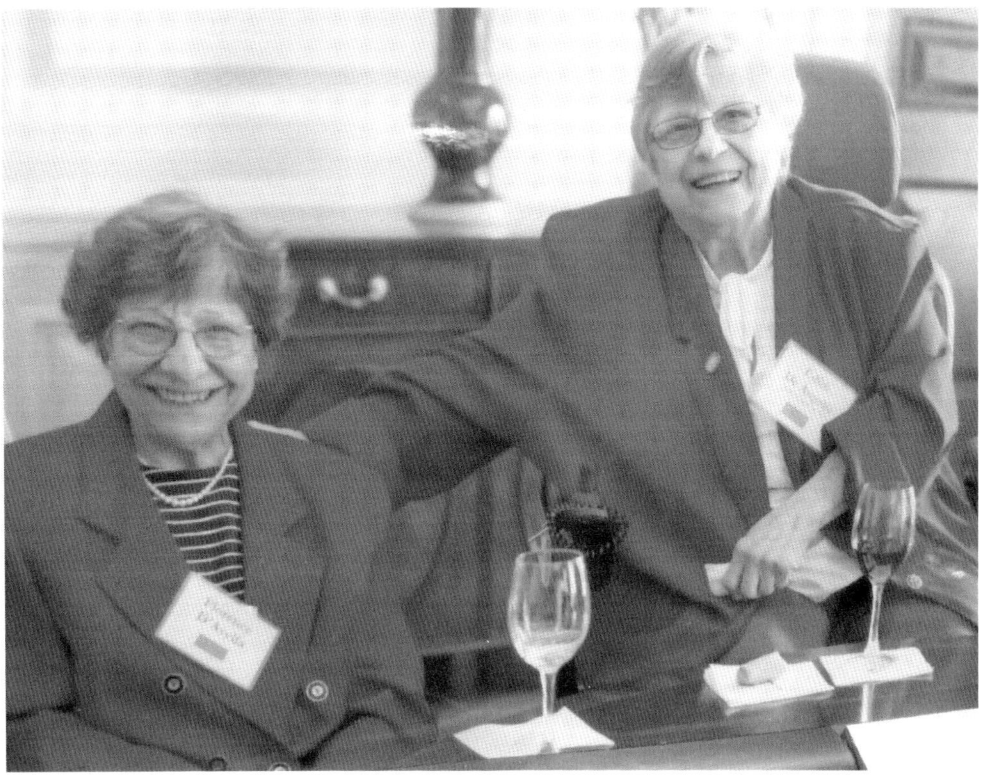

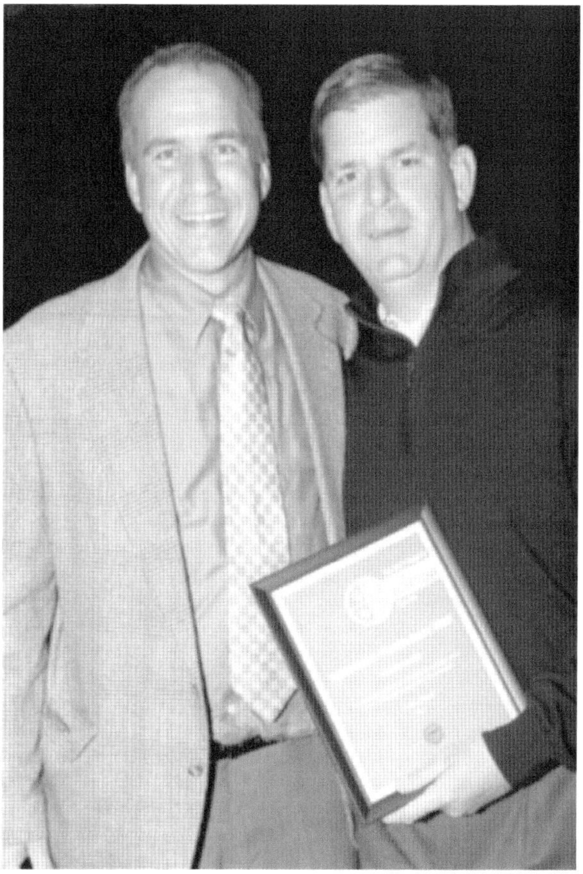

Christopher Marchi

East Bostonian Chris Marchi (left) grew up playing in vacant lots littered with broken glass, trash, and weeds. His elementary schoolyard at the O'Donnell was an expanse of cracked asphalt. As a teen at Boston Latin School, studying with peers from across the city, he saw how social class differences shaped neighborhood landscapes. In the 1990s, he worked in the City of Boston's public works department, helping start the city's curbside recycling program. When he married, he chose to raise his family on the same block of Saratoga Street where he lived as a child and became even more involved with local environmental issues. As a volunteer, he conducted litter research on Eagle Hill, inviting local children to collect and analyze litter on their streets. He spearheaded an anti-litter campaign focused on prevention, which increased the number of trash receptacles on Eagle Hill. As vice president of Airport Impact Relief (AIR Inc.), he worked with fellow members to mitigate harmful airport impacts. As a member of the Friends of Belle Isle Marsh and the East Boston Greenway Council, Marchi worked vigorously to get the Greenway extended from Bremen Street toward Constitution Beach, going door to door to talk with neighbors about the project. When first told a Greenway extension would be impossible, he created a video, which went viral, helping people envision what such an extension could look like. As a volunteer, he designed and conducted comprehensive neighborhood surveys and focus groups regarding the relationship of green space to community health and safety. His research illustrated the feasibility of extending the Greenway Connector and garnered political support for the idea. Marchi is also the founder of East Boston Environmental, an umbrella group that connects local activists. For his leadership on behalf of environmental issues in East Boston, he received the 2013 Man of the Year Award from the *East Boston Times*, as well as the City of Boston's 2014 Greenovate Award from Mayor Martin Walsh (pictured). (Courtesy of John Lynds.)

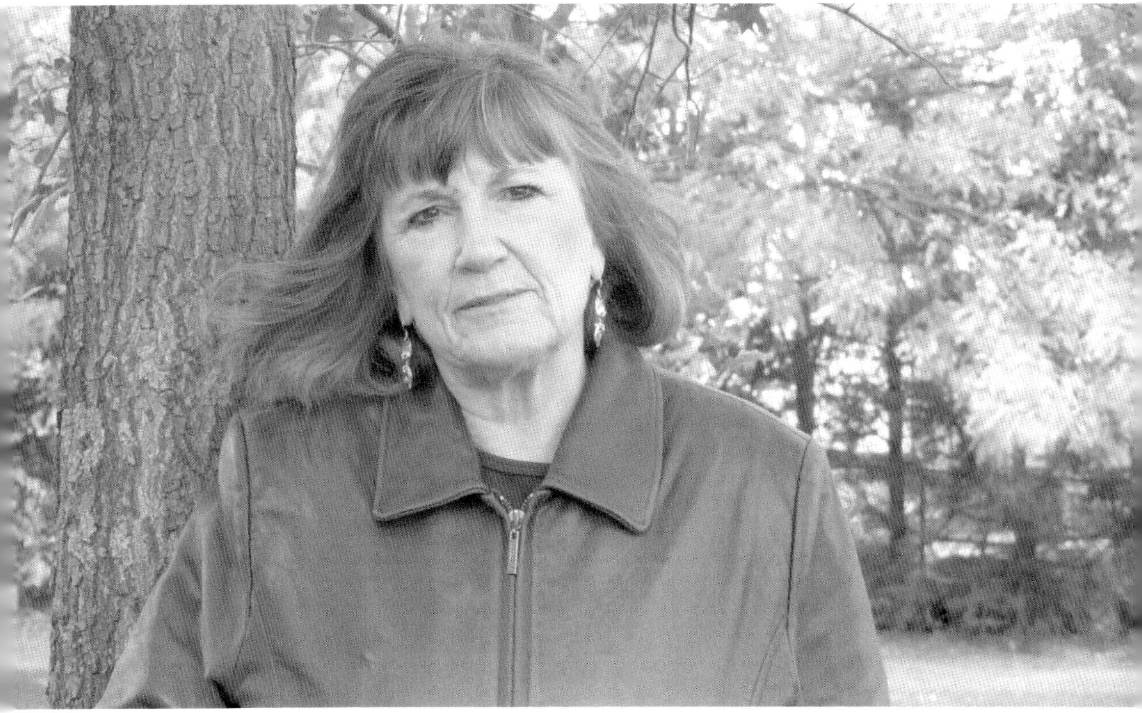

Gail Miller

Gail Miller moved to East Boston in 1981 because it was convenient for her job at one of the airlines. She liked the strong sense of community and began volunteering on local environmental issues. She has been active for years with the Friends of Belle Island Marsh and worked to help bring about the Condor Street Urban Wilds and the East Boston Greenway. "I never did anything alone. My foremothers, Edith DeAngelis, Mary Ellen Welch and others started before I came here and I've always worked with other people." These included members of the Chelsea Creek Action Committee, the East Boston and Chelsea Collaborative, AIR Inc., and other resident groups. In 2011, Miller was a leader in the fight to oppose plans to build an ethanol blending plant across from Suffolk Downs. "Global Petroleum wanted to carry ethanol by train from Albany to East Boston. This flammable liquid would be transported on 60-car trains, using commuter rails in the wee hours of the morning while people slept," she explains. Given the significant number of accidents and explosions that have occurred transporting ethanol in other areas, Miller began an education campaign. "This required a regional approach, because it affected Cambridge, Somerville, Everett, Revere, Chelsea and other towns with commuter rails. It was a big campaign and we were able to get support in the city and the legislature, winning a temporary moratorium on the project." Since Hurricane Sandy, Miller has been active in climate-change education, helping fellow East Bostonians, many of whom live in flood zones, be better prepared for future super storms. Regarding East Boston's environmental activists, she observes, "All of us are older and we look behind and don't see too many people following. I'm hoping more younger people will feel passionately about these issues and carry on the work." (Courtesy of Barbara Bishop.)

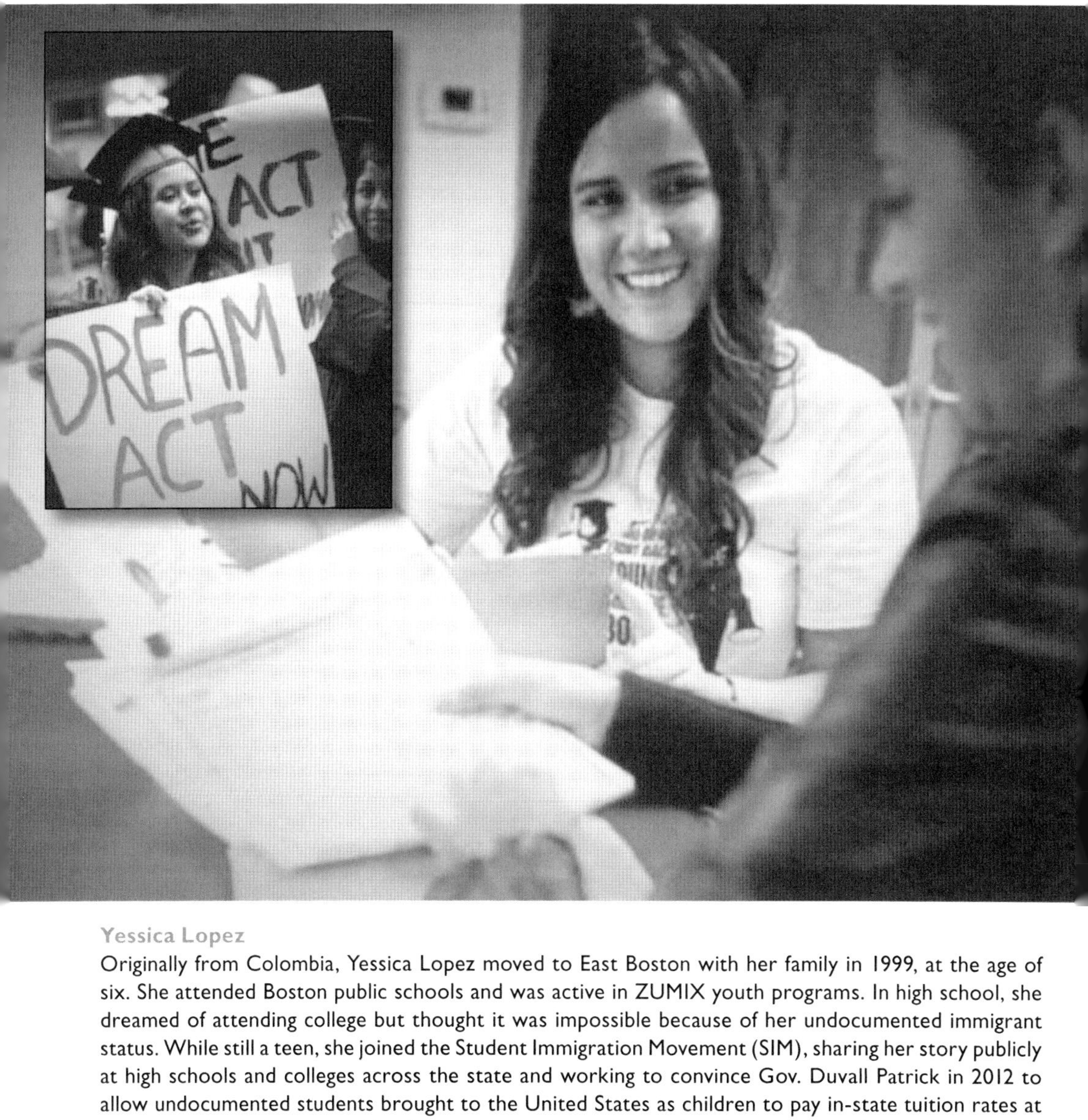

Yessica Lopez
Originally from Colombia, Yessica Lopez moved to East Boston with her family in 1999, at the age of six. She attended Boston public schools and was active in ZUMIX youth programs. In high school, she dreamed of attending college but thought it was impossible because of her undocumented immigrant status. While still a teen, she joined the Student Immigration Movement (SIM), sharing her story publicly at high schools and colleges across the state and working to convince Gov. Duvall Patrick in 2012 to allow undocumented students brought to the United States as children to pay in-state tuition rates at state schools. She is now the East Boston regional coordinator for SIM, working to help undocumented students attend college and achieve paths to US citizenship. Currently enrolled at Bridgewater State University, she has a medical interpreter certificate and is studying to become a social worker. (Courtesy of Yessica Lopez and SIM.)

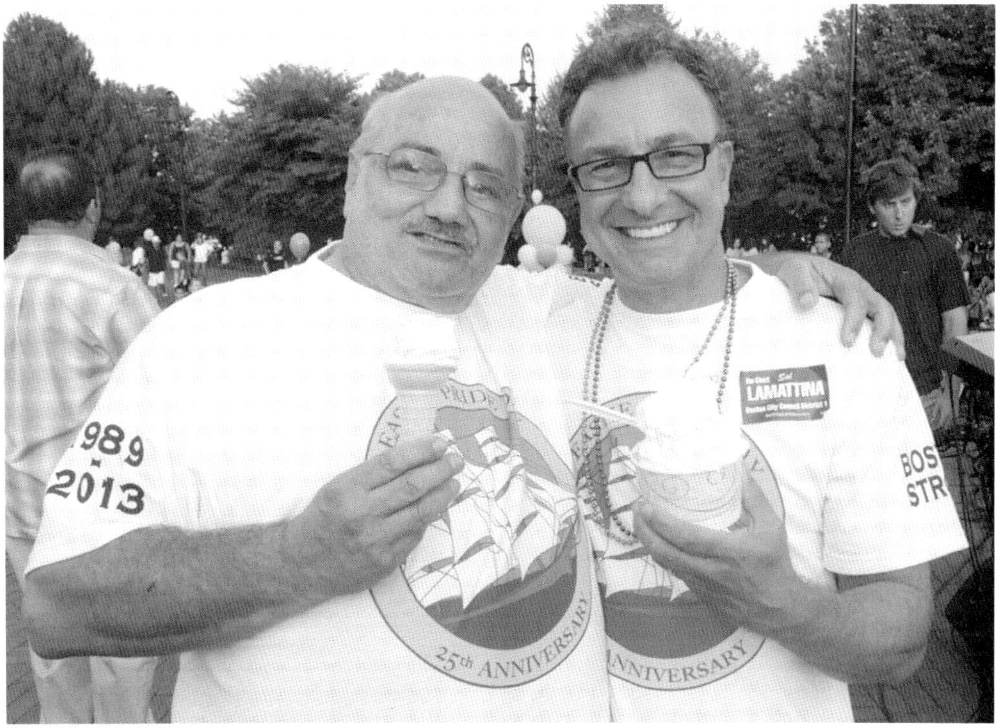

Anthony J. Albano (1948–2014)

Anthony Albano (left), a man both tough and compassionate, worked at East Boston High School for decades and was like a father to generations of students. He did anything to help children, including scolding them, getting them jobs, or giving them money to buy prom dresses or rent tuxedos. He was also extremely active in local politics. When he passed away in October 2014, more than 6,000 people came to his funeral—a testament to the impact he had on so many lives. (Courtesy of John Lynds.)

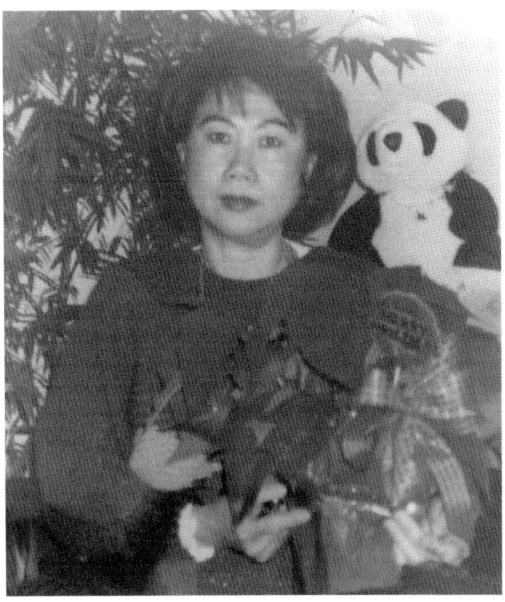

Quyen Tran

Natives of Saigon, Vietnam, Quyen Tran and her husband came to East Boston in 1980 as refugees from the Vietnam War. "We escaped by boat to Malaysia, where we lived in a refugee camp until we came to the US." A teacher in Vietnam, Tran got a job as a Vietnamese health educator at South Cove Community Health Center and later worked at the East Boston Ecumenical Community Council for 13 years as a community organizer with East Boston's Vietnamese community, which numbered more than 3,000 in the 1990s. For many years, she was an active leader of East Boston's Vietnamese Association. Tran raised her family in Maverick Square and now lives in Orient Heights. (Courtesy of Quyen Tran.)

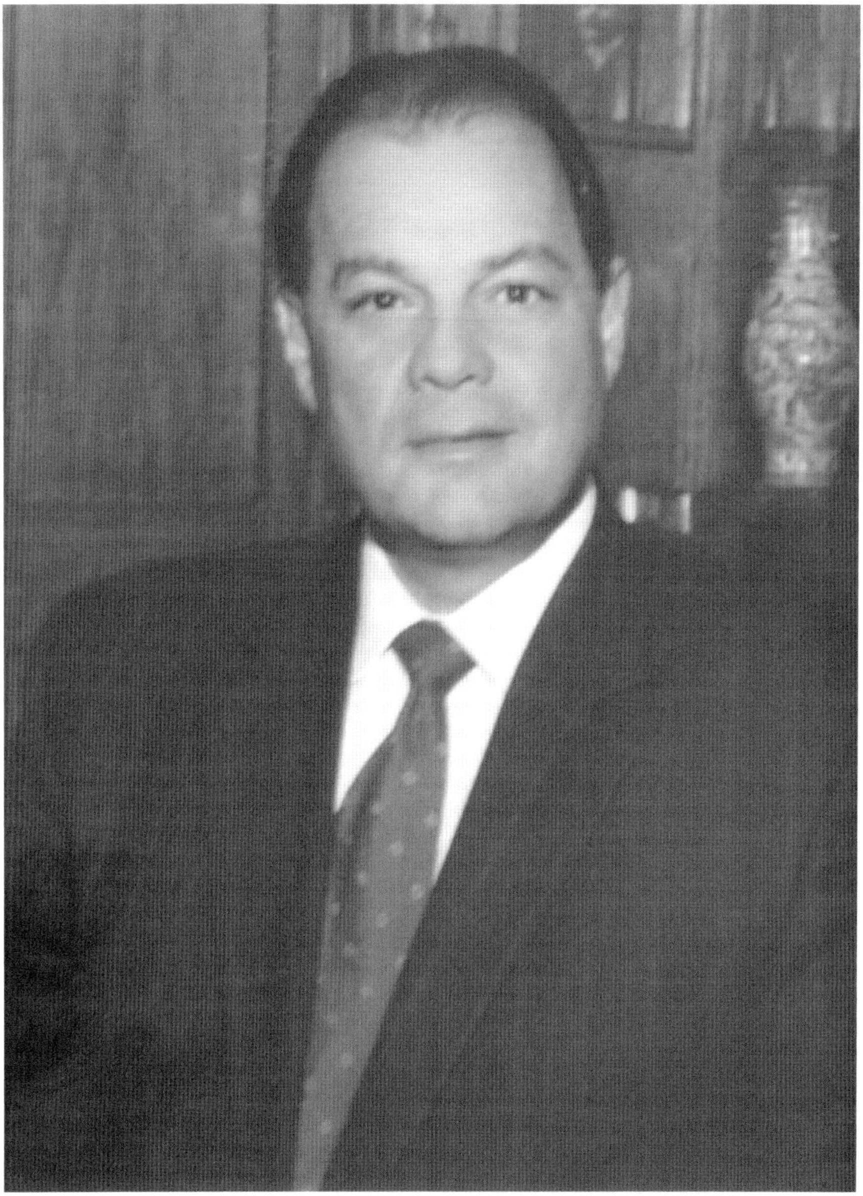

Robert Travaglini

Former president of the Massachusetts State Senate Robert Travaglini grew up at 81 Horace Street, graduating from Dominic Savio High School and Boston State University. His father died when he was quite young, but Travaglini was mentored by Tony Marmo and Frank Ciampa, who were active in East Boston politics and recreational sports. As a teen working at the Porrazzo Rink's summer program, he realized he loved public service and knew he would someday run for office. He was elected to the Boston City Council from 1984 to 1992 and then to the Massachusetts State Senate from 1992 to 2007. As state senate president from 2003 to 2007, Travaglini presided over major legislative accomplishments such as the 2007 landmark healthcare-reform bill and legislation regarding stem-cell research and same-sex marriage. He retired from the senate in 2007 to start his own consulting company. (Courtesy of Robert Travaglini.)

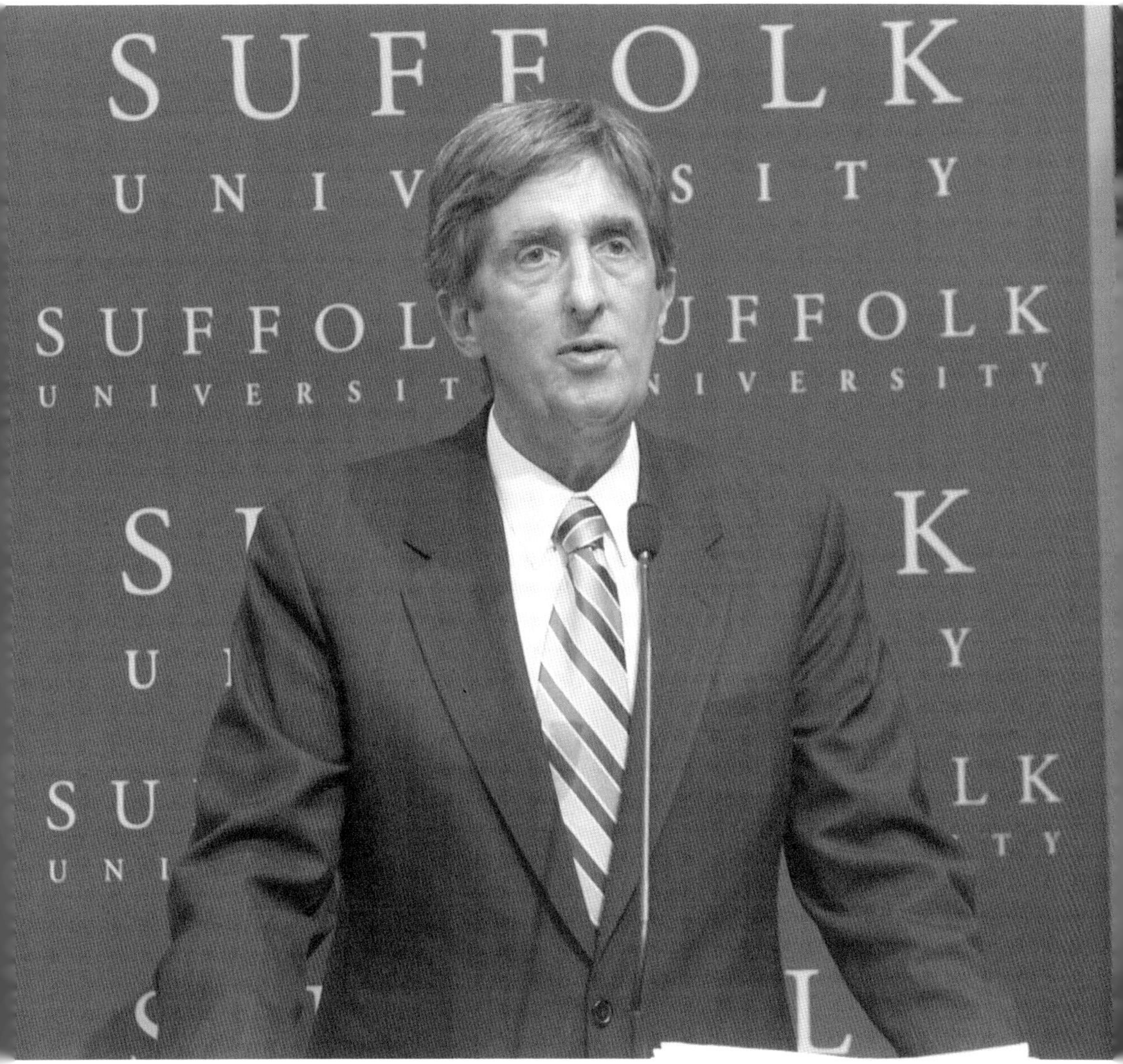

John Nucci

John Nucci is a lifelong resident of East Boston whose grandparents came from Mineo, Sicily, in 1922. After graduating from Boston Latin School and Boston College, he worked counseling troubled teens and coaching youth sports. Youth work led him to run for Boston School Committee, on which he served for six years. He was later the first Italian American from East Boston elected to the Boston City Council. He also worked as the director of community coordination at the anti-poverty program Action for Boston Community Development. After 11 years as clerk of the Suffolk County Criminal Court and 17 years teaching public administration part-time at Suffolk University, he is now vice president of external affairs at Suffolk University. (Courtesy of John Nucci.)

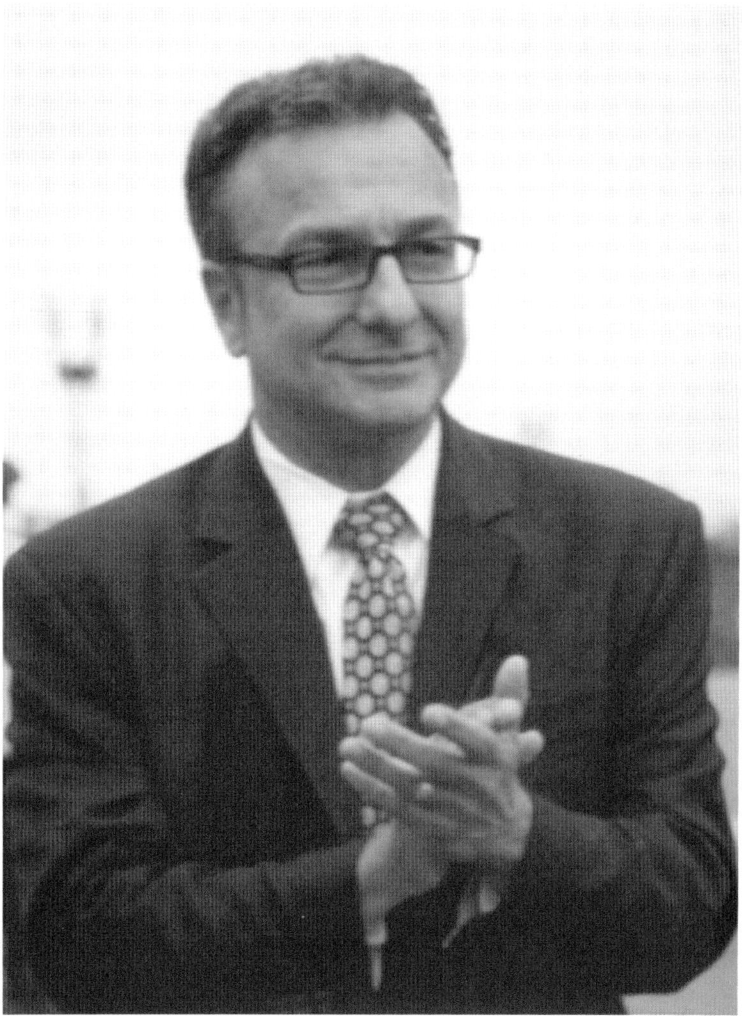

Salvatore "Sal" LaMattina

City councilor Sal LaMattina's family came to East Boston from Naples and Sicily in 1911, settling in what used to be called The Marsh neighborhood—an area bordered by Porter, Chelsea, Gove, and Paris Streets. He grew up in a two-decker house in Drake Place (off of Chelsea Street), with his grandparents living upstairs. Like many old homes in East Boston at the time, there was no bathroom in the apartment. The toilet was in a closet in the hall, and his grandfather installed a cold-water shower in the basement. "In the winter, we took hot showers at the Paris Street Bath House." LaMattina attended the Alighieri, Lyman, and McKay Elementary Schools and remembers getting homemade donuts after school at Olympia's Bakery, located in the cellar of a local house. His family shopped at Lacy's and Ladinsky's department stores, where the proprietors knew customers by name. President of the student council, LaMattina graduated from East Boston High in 1978 and attended the University of Massachusetts at Amherst, majoring in political science. "I knew from a young age that I wanted to get into politics." From 1984 to 1987, he worked at the Crossroads Shelter, helping homeless families find apartments. From 1992 to 2001, he was the assistant director for Boston's Central Artery Project and later worked as the director of operations for Boston's department of transportation. He was elected to the Boston City Council in 2006 and has worked to expand local parks, develop the waterfront, and prevent ethanol trains from coming to East Boston. (Courtesy of Sal LaMattina.)

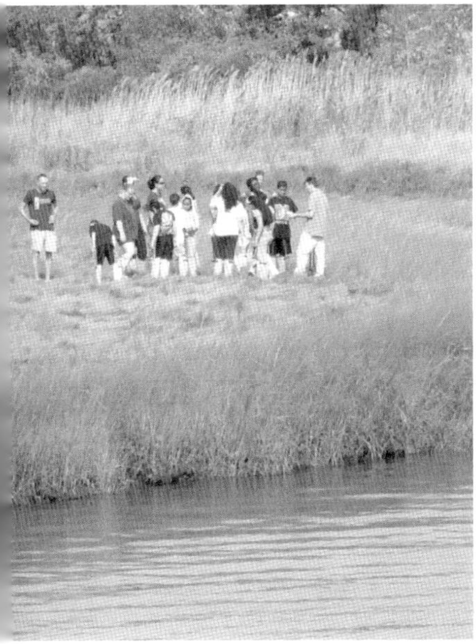

Friends of Belle Isle Marsh

The Friends of Belle Isle Marsh, a nonprofit grassroots environmental organization, was formed in the early 1980s to help preserve Boston's largest remaining salt marsh, publicize its importance as a regional natural resource, and plan fun and educational marsh activities. (Courtesy of Barbara Bishop.)

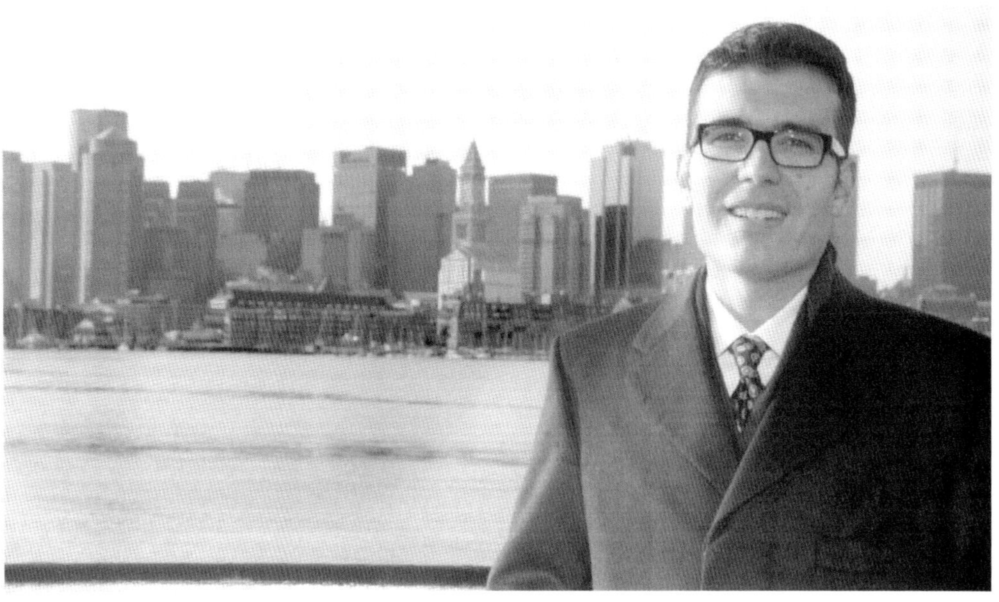

Ernani DeAraujo

Ernani DeAraujo's Brazilian father and Colombian mother settled in East Boston in the 1970s. When DeAraujo was a year old, his father passed away and his mother, devastated, moved with her son to live with family on Saratoga Street. That night, there was a gas explosion, and the house burned down, although residents escaped unharmed. DeAraujo grew up on Horace Street, playing at the Orient Heights Community Center. He attended East Boston Head Start and the Bradley and Umana Barnes Schools, later graduating from Boston Latin School and Harvard University. After earning a law degree, he became the East Boston Community Liaison for Mayor Menino. He is now general counsel and compliance manager for the East Boston Health Center. DeAraujo mentors local youth and cofounded, with Adrian Madaro, the Mario Umana Public Service Fellowship, which gives students at East Boston High School paid internships in government service. (Courtesy of Ernani DeAraujo.)

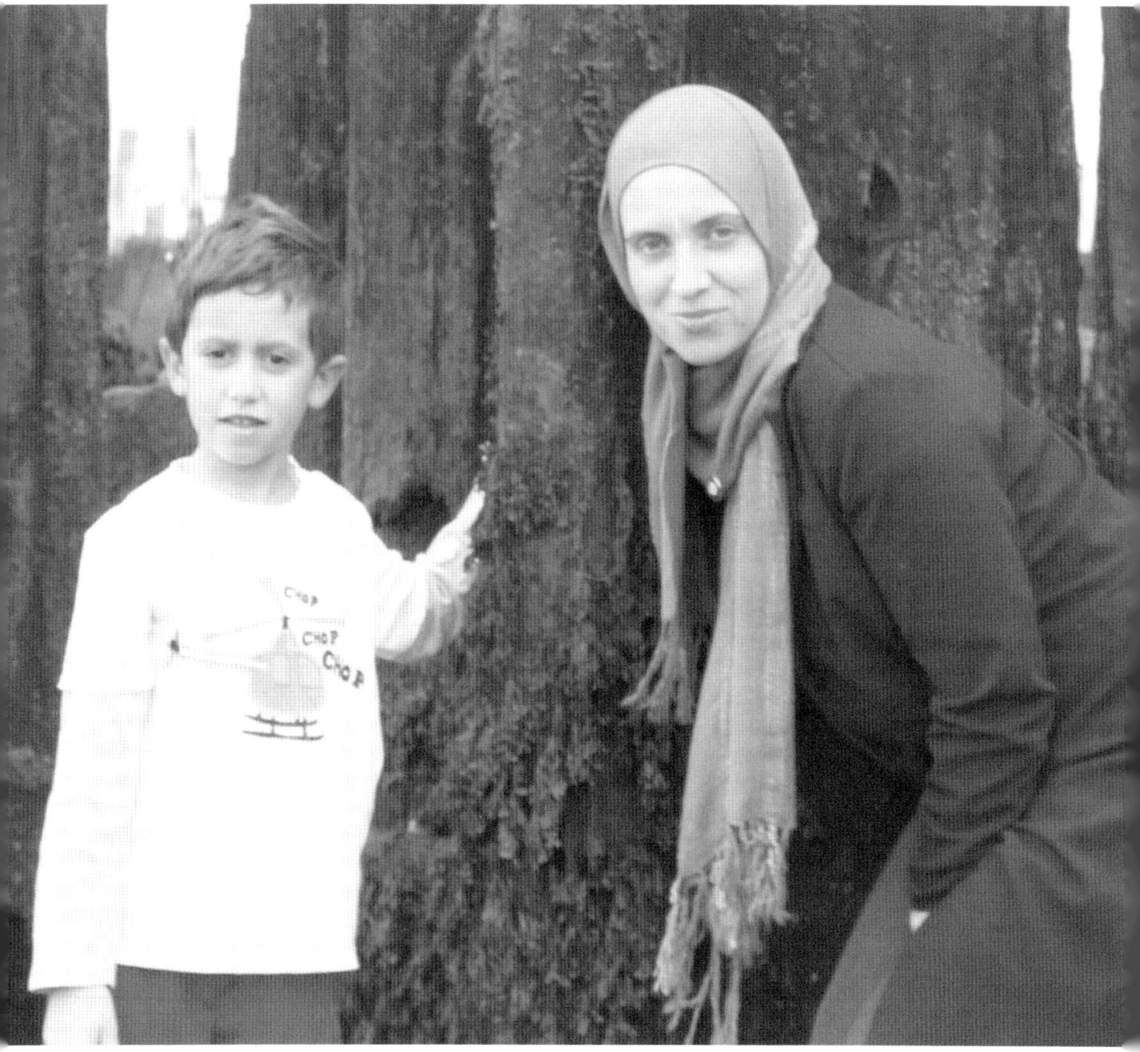

Magdalena Ayed

A Latina and Muslim, Magdalena Ayed has dedicated herself to organizing Latino, Middle Eastern, and other residents of Maverick Landing, the housing development where she lives. After three shootings occurred in her neighborhood, she volunteered nearly full-time to start a new Maverick residents' association, coordinating with local agencies and neighborhood groups. Concerned with environmental issues, she also volunteered with the Chelsea Creek Action Group and NOAH, where she now works as a community organizer. Speaking Spanish, English, Arabic, Italian, and Eritrean, Ayed has united diverse Maverick residents since 2005 to improve housing, social services, safety, and green space. (Courtesy of Magdalena Ayed.)

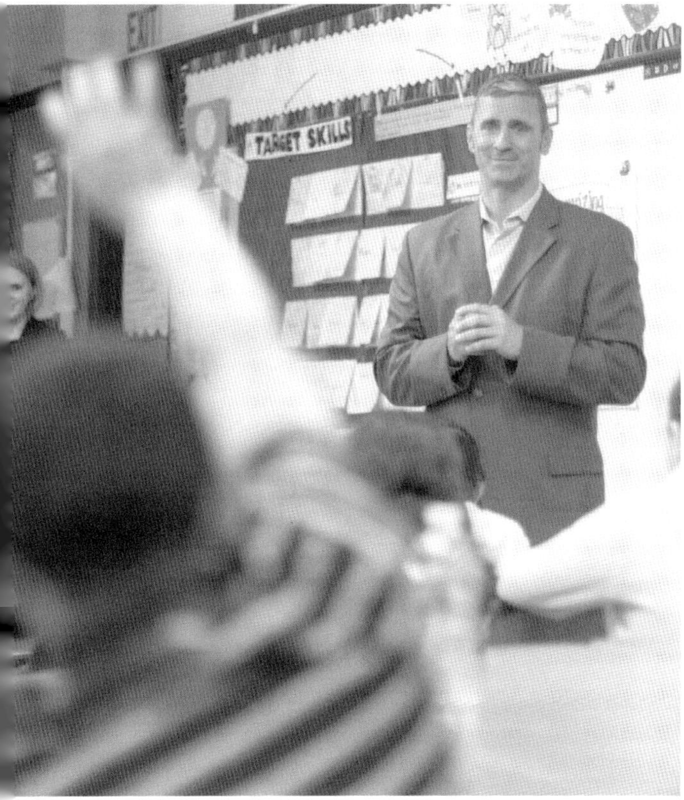

Carlo Basile
Carlo Basile grew up on Havre Street and was active in youth recreational programs as a teen. While serving as East Boston's state representative from 2007 to 2014, he was a strong advocate for senior citizens and youth recreational opportunities. As chair of the committee on veteran affairs, he worked to pass legislation to greatly expand benefits for Massachusetts veterans. In January 2015, Basile vacated his House seat to accept a position as chief secretary to Gov. Charlie Baker. (Courtesy of Carlo Basile.)

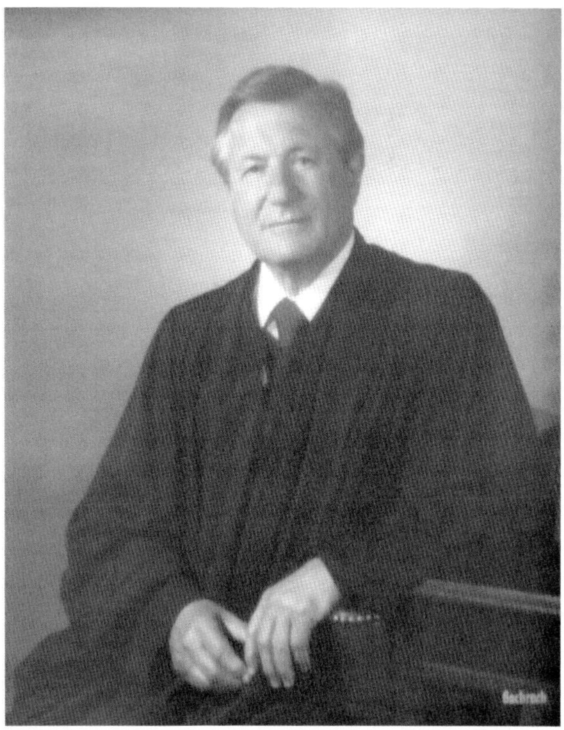

Judge Mario Umana (1914–2005)
With a blue-collar background and Ivy-League education, Mario Umana was a powerful figure in East Boston politics for decades. He served for four years in the state house of representatives and 20 years in the state senate before wrapping up his career as a municipal court judge. Mario Umana Academy is named for him. (Courtesy of Mario Umana Academy.)

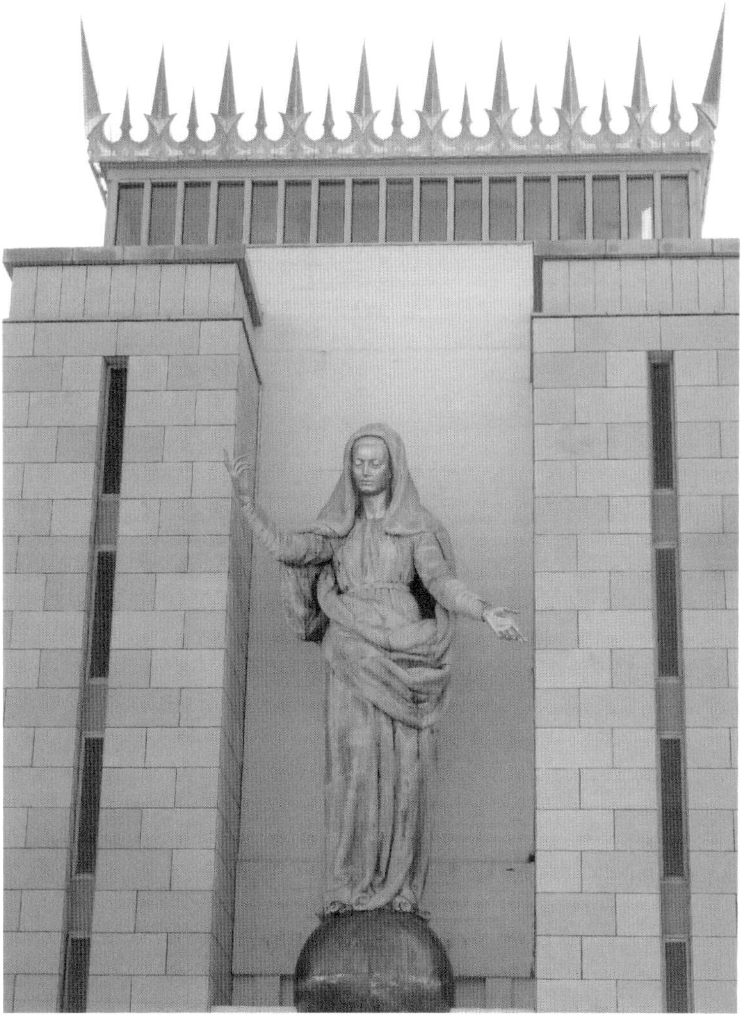

La Madonna

For many East Bostonians, La Madonna is a family member or good neighbor overlooking the city from her home at 150 Orient Avenue. One of Boston's most visible landmarks from air, land, and sea, it is the largest statue of the Virgin Mary in the Eastern United States. *Madonna Queen of the Universe* (her official name) has a heartwarming history of interfaith solidarity. This 35-foot statue of bronze and copper was created by Jewish sculptor Arrigo Minerbi as a gift for the Roman Catholic order of Don Orione. In 1940, when the Nazis invaded Italy and arrested thousands of Italian Jews, transporting them to concentration camps, only a few hundred survived the Holocaust. The Don Orione priests, whose mission is to help orphans and the poor, protected Minerbi from the Nazis, hiding him among them disguised as "Fr. Della Porto." After the war, Minerbi created the Madonna as a gift for the Order of Don Orione to express his gratitude. The statue was placed on the hill of Monte Mario, overlooking Rome. In 1949, the Don Orione fathers came to East Boston to establish a nursing home for elderly Italians, and Minerbi created an exact replica of the Madonna for them. In 1954, the statue was transported from Italy to East Boston and unveiled before a crowd of 10,000. Local residents enthusiastically collected money to build the giant foundation on which the statue stands, with a golden crown-like top. Since then, thousands each year have made religious pilgrimages to the Madonna Queen National Shrine, but one does not have to be religious to admire her beauty, history, and spectacular views of the city. (Author's collection.)

CHAPTER THREE

Creative Minds

Historically, East Boston is a place where creativity has flourished, from the artistry of shipbuilding to the community's diverse architecture (Georgian, Federal, Greek Revival, Victorian, Queen Anne, Italianate, and more) and the concerts and theatrical performances held in Pythian Hall, Lyceum Hall, and other famed performance spaces. Throughout the 1800s and early 1900s, East Boston had numerous portrait and photography studios, but as the neighborhood grew less affluent, the studios closed or relocated downtown. In the 1970s, thousands of middle-class families left Boston for the suburbs, triggering institutional disinvestment in the city's ethnic neighborhoods. Streets filled with potholes. Parks became littered with trash, glass, and used drug needles. Public schools had broken windows, exposed asbestos pipes, and peeling lead paint. Scores of homes and storefronts in East Boston were boarded up—often victims of arson for insurance scams. Despite this, many long-term residents stayed in East Boston, determined to address its problems. As Eleanor K. Welch, who moved to Webster Street in 1912, noted in a 1976 interview, "The greatest percentage of residents have never lived anywhere else. They have no desire to live elsewhere. Our homes are our castles."

East Boston's low rents in the 1970s and 1980s made it an attractive site for struggling artists, musicians, writers, and other creative individuals who appreciated the ethnic flavor of the community. With its Italian religious feast days, backyard family parties, and lively street culture—where people sat on the front stoops on warm nights chatting with neighbors and watching children play—East Boston provided great inspirational material. One aspiring actor and writer was Frank Renzulli, who grew up in the Maverick public housing projects in the 1960s and 1970s, when Maverick Square was considered the most crime-ridden area of East Boston. The square's many bars, rundown boardinghouses, and abandoned buildings were the backdrop for drunken brawls, street fights, shootings, and occasional murders. But, "the Projects" harbored a tight-knit community with its own traditions and laws, where lifetime friendships were formed, and fierce loyalty was expected. "Our whole world was the projects," says Renzulli. "At that time, there were a lot of Italians living there, along with some Irish and blacks. The common denominator was being on the lower rung of the socioeconomic ladder." Renzulli later used his knowledge of this world to write teleplays for *The Sopranos*, hailed as one of the greatest television shows of all time.

For residents with a flair for writing, photography, or graphic design (including Maxine Tassinari-Teixeira, Ginny St. Cyr, Carmela Ciccone, Billy Morris, Patty Morash, Marie DiFlumeri, Joanne Ciccarello, and many others), the *East Boston Community News* (EBCN) became their vehicle of self-expression. While East Boston had two weekly newspapers in 1880, the *Argus* and the *Advocate*, and three newspapers by 1930, the *Argus-Advocate*, the *East Boston Free Press*, and the *East Boston Leader*, by 1970, there was only one. The EBCN arose out of residents' desire not to be a one-paper town and to see a variety of perspectives expressed on issues such as transportation planning, economic development, women's rights, race relations, school desegregation, airport expansion, and other controversial issues of the day. The paper's nearly all-volunteer staff was comprised of community residents and journalism interns from local universities, many of whom went on to have prestigious careers in the fields of journalism and media. Known for hard-hitting investigative reporting and resident columnists' reflections on life in East Boston, the paper published bilingual news reports, a section of poetry and short stories by children, and award-winning photographs. The EBCN was one of the first community newspapers in Massachusetts, and, as it grew, it supported other fledging community newspapers in the region by offering advice and loaning out its printing equipment.

Music was historically a big part of life for East Boston's ethnic families, whether they came from Portugal, the Cape Verde Islands, Italy, or elsewhere. George Gloss, an elderly Jewish man who grew up on Border Street in the 1910s, fondly recalled hearing the sounds of his Italian neighbors singing and playing accordion at night when he was a boy. One young musician who grew up in East Boston around the same time as Gloss was Generoso Graziano or "Jerry Gray," who composed and arranged music for Artie Shaw and Glenn Miller. Isabel (Neves) Nicks, who grew up on Trenton Street in the 1940s and whose parents came from Cape Verde at the turn of the 20th century, notes, "Music was very important in our home. My father played traditional Cape Verdean music on the violin and the viola, a 12-string Portuguese guitar. Everyone in our family played instruments or sang." In this musical climate, her two older brothers, Paul and John Neves, learned to play piano, violin, and bass, later becoming prominent jazz musicians who played with luminaries such as Stan Getz and Herb Pomeroy. Music continues to be an important part of East Boston, where Latin American songs are often heard in homes, restaurants, and cultural festivals, and East Bostonians of all ethnicities take music lessons and enjoy diverse concerts offered by the arts organization ZUMIX. From the late 1990s onward, many different kinds of artists have moved to East Boston, repurposing former industrial sites such as the Atlantic Works Studios and Gallery at 80 Border Street, which is now home to the East Boston Artists Group, and HarborArts on Marginal Street, which has transformed the working waterfront into an outdoor exhibit of monumental art. These and other artists routinely organize open-studio events, art festivals, and other activities that foster cultural understanding and creative expression.

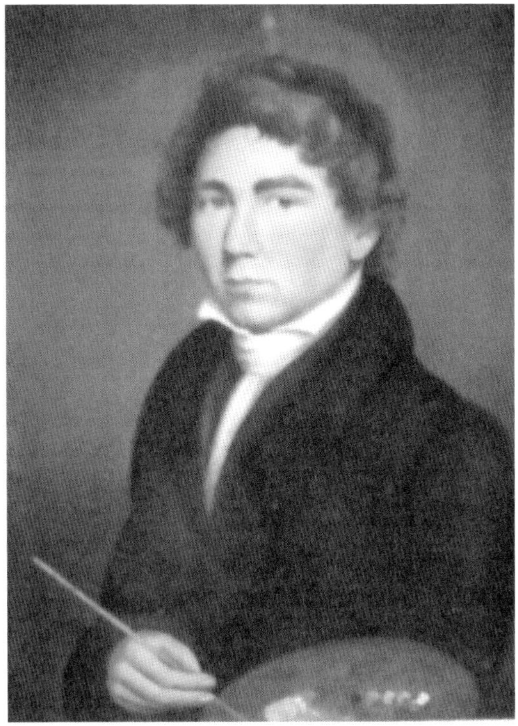

William Matthew Prior (1806–1873)
In 1840, William Prior, a prominent artist known for portraits of families and children, moved to 36 Trenton Street, where he had his studio. He painted 1,500 portraits, some of which now hang in Boston's Museum of Fine Arts, the National Gallery, and other museums. Prior was a prominent abolitionist and one of the few Anglo artists of his time to paint African Americans in a dignified and respectful manner. (Author's collection.)

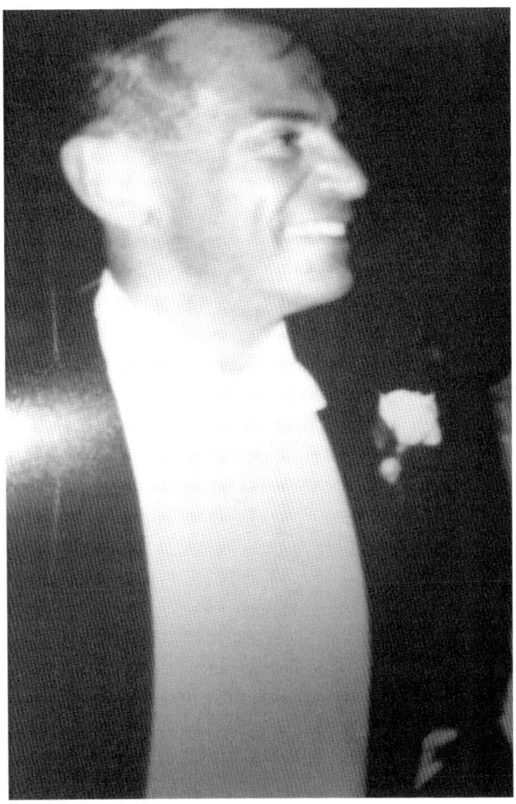

Alfred Fiandaca (1941–2013)
As a little boy growing up on Maverick Street in East Boston, Alfred Fiandaca liked to sew costumes for his puppets. At nine, he was cutting patterns alongside his father, a tailor, and at 21, he had his own clothing salon in East Boston. For more than 40 years, he had a studio on Newbury Street and was considered Boston's foremost fashion designer. With upscale fashion salons throughout the United States and in Europe, his innovative designs were worn by Audrey Hepburn, Julie Andrews, Joan Kennedy, Nancy Reagan, and Ann Romney, among other socialites. Fiandaca descended from a line of tailors reaching back to his great-grandfather in Italy and his mother, who was a second-generation seamstress. (Courtesy of Michelle and Theodora Fiandaca.)

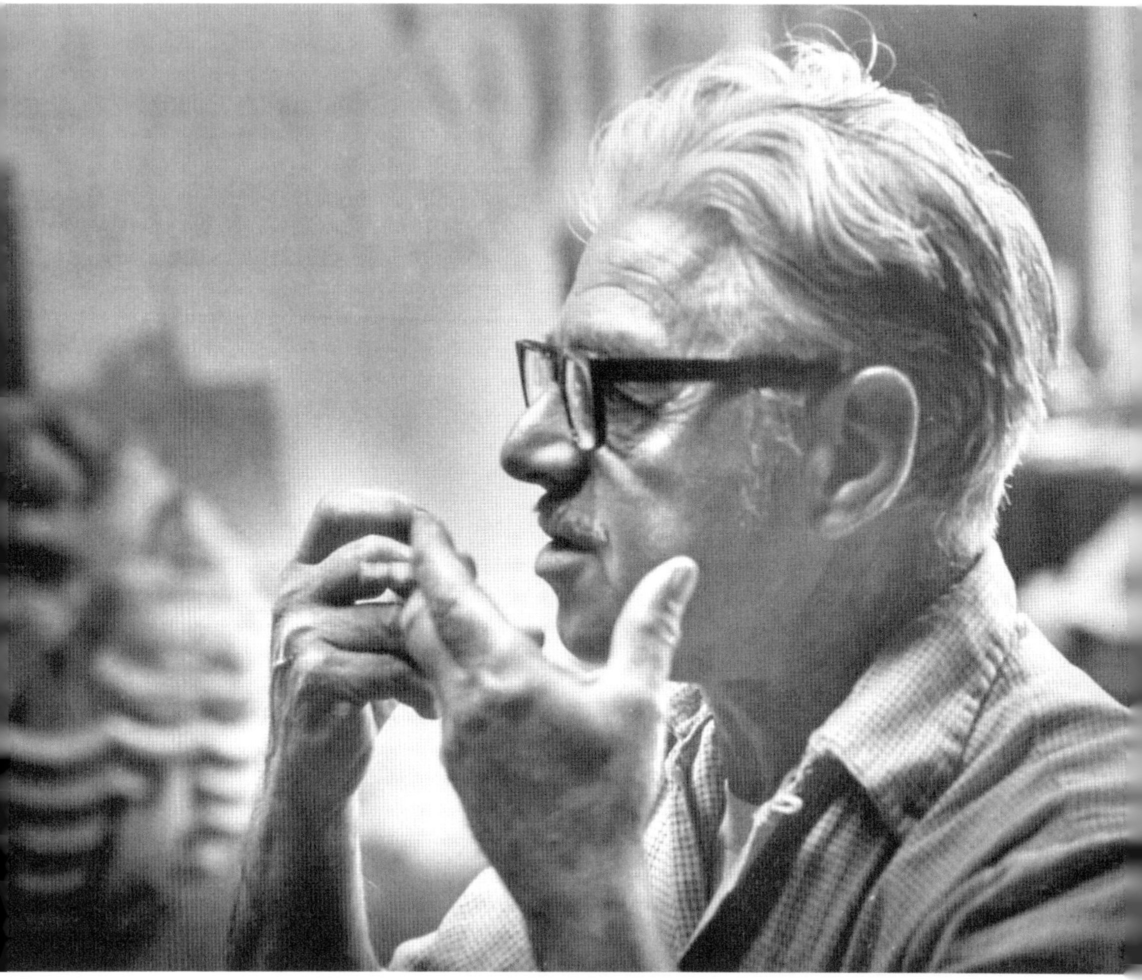

Theodore "Ted" Cotillo Barbarossa (1906–1992)

A prominent sculptor who worked in bronze and stone, Ted Barbarossa grew up in East Boston and had a studio on Border Street. Inspired by Italian stone-carving and plaster-casting traditions, he studied at the Massachusetts College of Art and Yale University. Bostonians know him best for his five carved stone panels on the façade of Boston's Museum of Science. His sculptures adorn churches, museums, and public buildings throughout the East Coast, including the Cathedral of St. John the Divine in New York and the Washington National Cathedral in DC. As part of President Roosevelt's WPA New Deal art initiative, Barbarossa created relief sculptures on post offices and other federal buildings depicting national ideals such as industry, education, and agriculture. His work has been exhibited in many museums and his bas-relief *The History of East Boston* decorates the façade of the Heritage Apartments in Maverick Square. (Courtesy of Susi Barbarossa.)

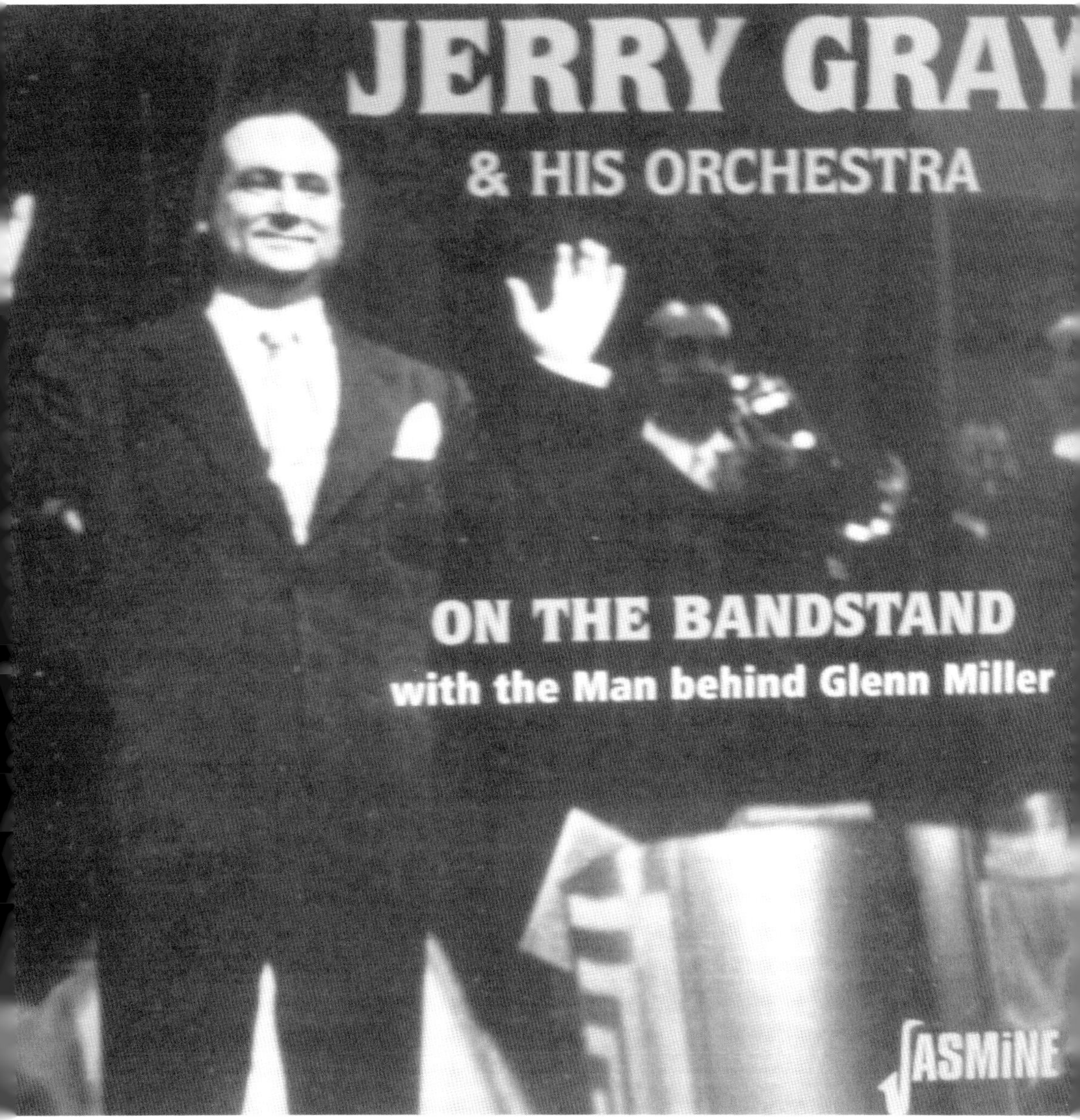

Jerry Gray (1915–1976)
Growing up in East Boston, Generoso Graziano was a child prodigy on the violin. He joined the Artie Shaw band while still a teenager, taking the stage name Jerry Gray. He was the arranger for Shaw from 1936 to 1939, arranging "Begin the Beguine" and "Softly as in a Morning Sunrise." He was later the arranger for Glenn Miller from 1939 to 1944, composing and arranging "A String of Pearls," "Pennsylvania 6-5000," "Moonlight Cocktail," and other classics. According to music historian Richard Vacca, "Gray was the architect of the Glenn Miller sound." (Courtesy of Jasmine Records.)

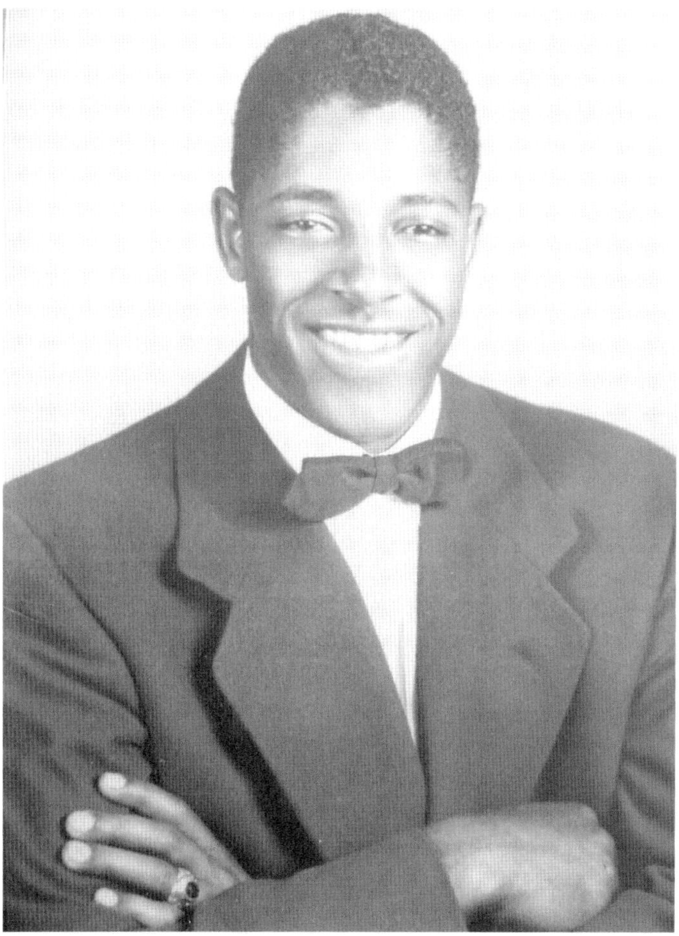

John Oliveira Neves (1931–1988)

Jazz bassist John Neves grew up on 66 Trenton Street as one of 10 children. In the late 1800s, his parents migrated from Cape Verde, an area with a long maritime history. They settled in East Boston, where his father worked as a seaman. John spent his boyhood playing baseball in the City Yards, and graduated from East Boston High in 1949, where he was a star athlete in basketball, football, and baseball. Dreaming of a career in baseball, he played with the Cleveland Indians farm team, but his prospects were shattered when he hurt his back in the Korean War. Neves, who grew up playing violin, taught himself to play the upright bass and was soon playing at Stables and Storyville in Copley Square, Lulu White's in the South End, Club 47 in Harvard Square, the Merry-Go-Round in the Copley-Plaza Hotel, and Zachary's in the Colonnade Hotel, sometimes joined by his brother, pianist Paul Neves. John performed and recorded more than 30 records with jazz icons Stan Getz, Maynard Ferguson, Marian McPartland, George Shearing, and Gerry Mulligan at the biggest jazz venues in the United States, including the Blue Note, Birdland, Webster Hall, RCA Studios, Capitol Studios, and the Newport Jazz Festival. His longest engagement was as bassist for the Herb Pomeroy Orchestra (1954–1983). Neves taught bass at Berklee College of Music for 13 years, where he was a favorite among the students. In an interview with the *Boston Globe*, Herb Pomeroy called Neves "one of the great jazz bass players, despite the fact he never achieved the celebrity of a Ray Brown, Red Mitchell or a Paul Chambers." A modest, soft-spoken man not given to self-promotion, Neves was sought out by the biggest names in jazz, although his own name was not widely known to the general public. Both Neves brothers have been nominated to the New England Jazz Hall of Fame. (Courtesy of Isabel Nicks.)

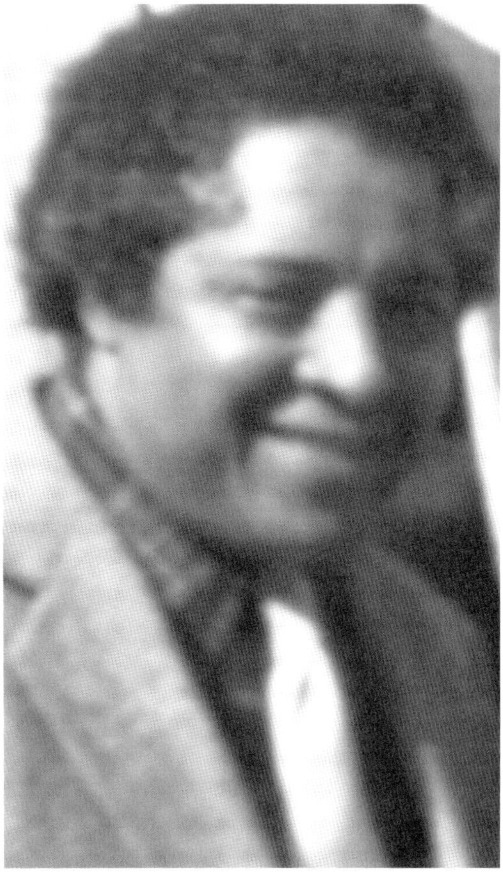

Paul Oliveira Neves (1930–1981)
Paul Neves was an exceptional pianist who, with his brother John, was part of the exciting 1950s Boston jazz milieu. Neves was also active in the Seattle and New York jazz scenes, working frequently with Coleman Hawkins and playing in the first *Jazz On Broadway* concert series in 1964. He accompanied renowned saxophonist Lucky Thompson on the album *New York City 1964–1965*, "spurring Thompson to new heights with his emphatic comping and solos," writes jazz journalist Doug Ramsey. In 1964, Neves played piano on the album *Spellbound* with bassist Ahmed Abdul-Malik, one of the first US musicians to incorporate African, Middle Eastern, and Indian influences into jazz. He and Neves shared a deep respect and admiration for musicians in developing countries, who were largely ignored by the music industry at the time. Neves worked to raise the profile of Afro-Caribbean musicians during the years he played at luxury resorts and nightclubs in Puerto Rico. He found an opportunity when he was hired by Laurance S. Rockefeller to play at the famous Dorado Beach Resort, a playground for the rich and famous. Neves's sister Isabel Nicks recalls, "Paul met many amazing Puerto Rican musicians and it upset him that none of the big clubs would hire them. All the resorts imported US bands and the local musicians couldn't get work. Paul told Rockefeller he felt this was wrong." Rockefeller took note, says Nicks, inviting Neves to tour various Caribbean countries, assess the quality of local musicians, and prepare a report, which Neves did. He moved permanently to Puerto Rico, where he founded the Caribbean Jazz Workshop, an organization that provided opportunities for local musicians to practice jazz. Considered a major jazz pioneer in Puerto Rico, Paul Neves was an inspirational figure in the performance, promotion, and teaching of modern jazz on the island. He died in San Juan in 1981, with jazz critics lamenting that he did not receive the credit he deserved during his lifetime. (Courtesy of Isabel Nicks.)

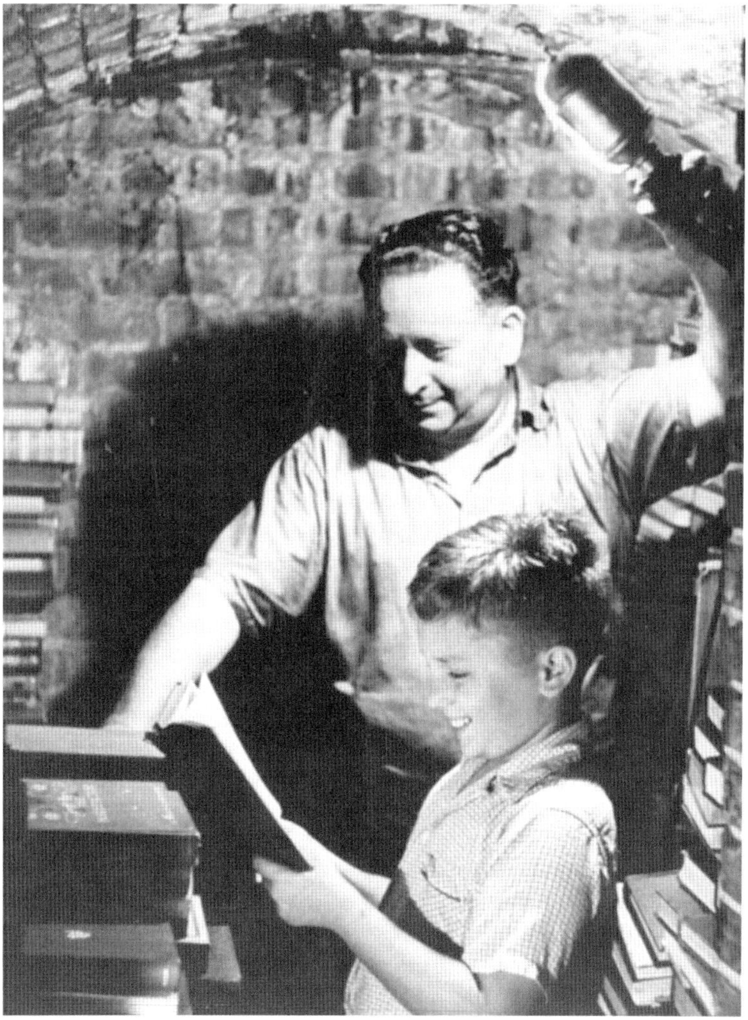

George Gloss (1912–1985)

George Gloss, longtime proprietor of Boston's Brattle Book Shop, one of the country's oldest and largest antiquarian bookstores, grew up on 42 Border Street. His Russian Jewish parents ran a little store that he likened to a "Dickens curiosity shop" that sold clothes, thread, tobacco, hooks, needles, and other items useful to seamen, carpenters, and ironworkers on the docks. In an interview for the Boston 200 Neighborhood History Series in 1976, Gloss recalls summer life in East Boston: "I remember sleeping on the roof. We would hear all the sounds of our Italian neighbors—accordion players and singing, the sounds of the water, the foghorns and the ships in the harbor. And, at the end of the street was the ferry. I would ride it for a penny." When he was five years old, Gloss acquired a library card from the Meridian Street library and fell in love with books; he would bring home as many books each week as he was allowed to check out. Mary Cronin, the librarian, "told us all the children's classics, the great fairy tales, all the mythology of Greece and Rome. The books illustrated by N.C. Wyeth, Maxfield Parish, Dulac. This had a great impression on me. It made me the storyteller of the neighborhood. I sat on the doorsteps with the tougher boys and I'd tell them stories and, as I was small, they would protect me." Gloss felt that his childhood in East Boston "led me up to being the proprietor of the oldest continuous bookstore in America," which he began running in 1949. Originally established in 1825, the store is now operated by Gloss's son Ken, pictured here with his father. (Courtesy of Ken Gloss.)

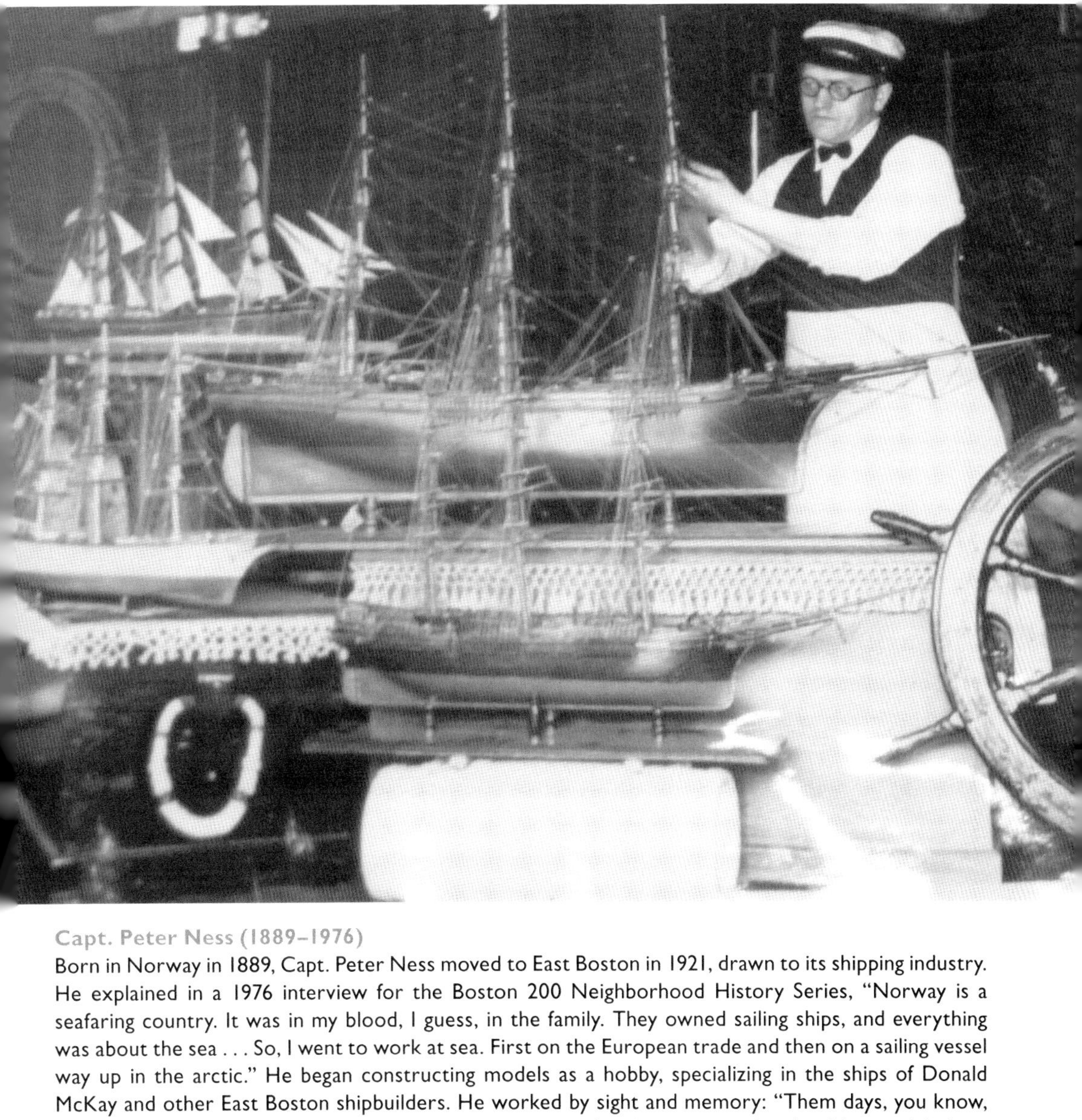

Capt. Peter Ness (1889–1976)
Born in Norway in 1889, Capt. Peter Ness moved to East Boston in 1921, drawn to its shipping industry. He explained in a 1976 interview for the Boston 200 Neighborhood History Series, "Norway is a seafaring country. It was in my blood, I guess, in the family. They owned sailing ships, and everything was about the sea . . . So, I went to work at sea. First on the European trade and then on a sailing vessel way up in the arctic." He began constructing models as a hobby, specializing in the ships of Donald McKay and other East Boston shipbuilders. He worked by sight and memory: "Them days, you know, there were no blueprints." Ness gained national renown for the intricate details of his model ships, which became highly prized works of art that are now on display in the Smithsonian, the MIT Museum, Boston's Museum of Science, and other museums. (Courtesy of BPL.)

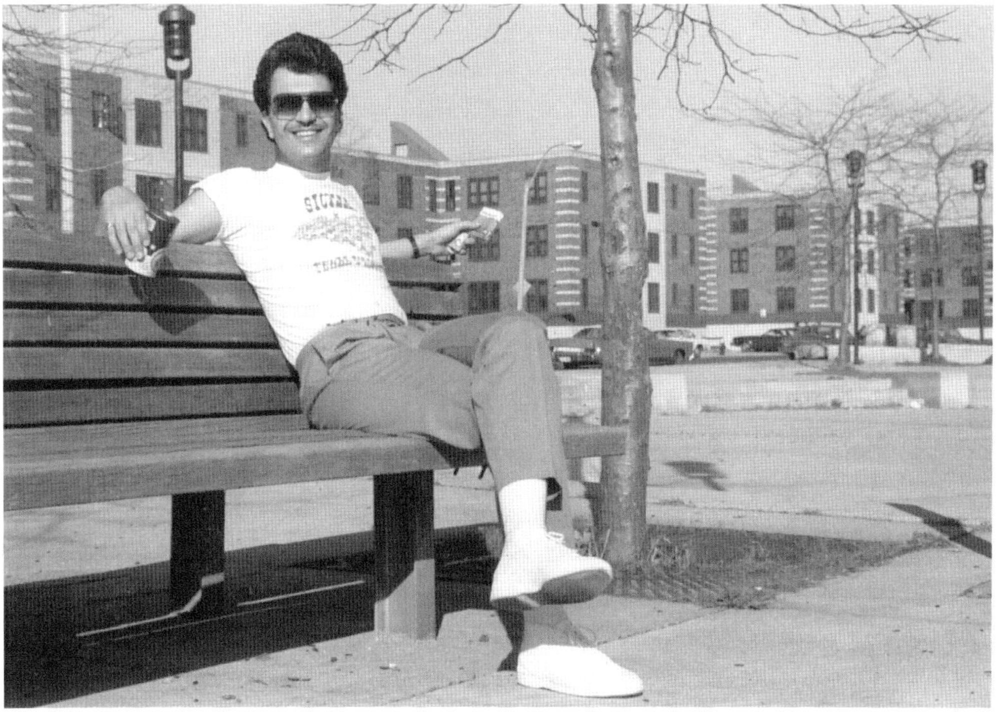

Frank Renzulli

Before Frank Renzulli became an Emmy-nominated writer and producer, winning the Golden Globe award for excellence in film and television, he grew up in the Maverick public housing projects. As a boy, he used to sing at family parties and began performing at bars in Maverick Square at age 14. He graduated from East Boston High School in 1975, wanting to be a singer. "College was never talked about in my world. It was never even a consideration." After unsuccessfully trying to convince Renzulli to become a plumber or electrician, his guidance counselor found a vocal-training program in Kenmore Square. The advertised vocal training turned out to be for acting rather than singing, but Renzulli decided to give the program a try. There, he caught the acting bug and became captivated by the plays of Tennessee Williams, Edward Albee, David Mamet, and Arthur Miller. He later moved to New York, where he met people of diverse social classes, sexualities, and ethnicities. "I lived my whole life by the rules of Maverick Projects. They were harsh rules, dangerous rules. In New York I learned other ways of doing things." After landing his first speaking role in Woody Allen's *Broadway Danny Rose*, he moved to Los Angeles. Through a fortuitous East Boston connection, the brother-in-law of a friend from Frankfort Street was Hollywood director Steve Miner. Miner offered Renzulli a part in *The Wonder Years* and encouraged him to write about East Boston. Renzulli wrote a pilot called *Maverick Square* and pitched it to Les Moonves (now president of CBS). "I didn't have an agent. I didn't even know what pitching was. But, I realized that pitching is what Italians do best. We tell stories." He was offered a development deal and wrote screenplays for 10 years until TV producer David Chase approached him with an idea about a mafia boss in therapy. "David had virtually no knowledge of the organized crime world," recalls Renzulli. "He didn't know the rules of the game or the subtleties of that world. The characters seemed one-dimensional." Renzulli joined the writing team of *The Sopranos* and generated the complex, multifaceted characters that became the show's hallmark. "I would only do it honestly and with love. The people I was drawing on were people I loved. Very complicated, colorful people that I had intimate knowledge of." (Courtesy of Jean Reisman and Frank Renzulli.)

Mossik Hacobian and Joan Ohanian

Born in Iran to Armenian parents, Mossik Hacobian and his family moved to Brooklyn in 1958, where he attended public schools and studied architecture at Columbia University. In 1968, he was active in student demonstrations to protest Columbia's expansion into Harlem, which was displacing longtime residents. Later, he received a draft notice for the Vietnam War and filed as a conscientious objector. Required by the draft board to do volunteer service, Hacobian found a job in East Boston as a community organizer for the IMPACT program. In this position, he helped establish the East Boston CDC and the *East Boston Community News*. In 1971, he and three friends (Larry Braman, Phil Giffee, and Bob Nakashian) bought a house on 112 Trenton Street and formed a housing commune of seven residents. Artist Joan Ohanian, his wife, joined them in 1972. "We shared everything. Cooking, cleaning, repairs and household purchases. We had one checking account for seven people! Everyone told us the neighbors would never accept a commune, but they did," says Hacobian. "We were like a family and still are. But, as people got married and had kids, we outgrew the space. Joan and I had our first child there in 1973 and then moved to our present home on Eutaw Street in 1976, where we raised our two sons." Seeing many abandoned buildings in East Boston at the time, Hacobian and Braman bought three other houses at auction and renovated them for affordable housing. In 1977, Hacobian was hired as a housing rehabilitation specialist at Urban Edge, a CDC in Jamaica Plain. Later becoming the CDC's director, he said, "The experience I had in East Boston rehabbing and financing affordable units prepared me for the job." After working at Urban Edge for 33 years, he became executive director of Higher Ground, a nonprofit focused on improving public education. Ohanian, originally from Belmont, Massachusetts, had culture shock when she moved to East Boston. "It was hard to adapt. I wasn't sure I could do it. But, I started appreciating different things here that I didn't experience growing up. I developed a broader view. I started to learn Italian and converse with shopkeepers. I met other artists and eventually went to Italy seven times to paint." As an artist, she loves East Boston's natural light, which she compares to the light of Provincetown, Massachusetts. "It's wonderful light for a painter!" (Author's collection.)

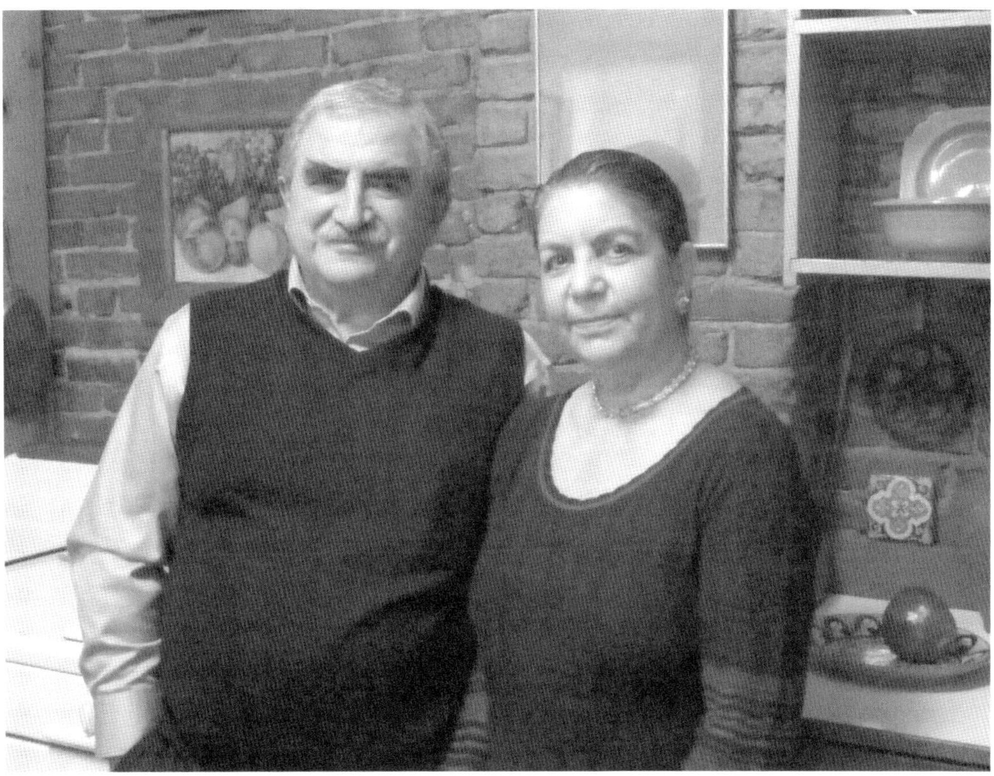

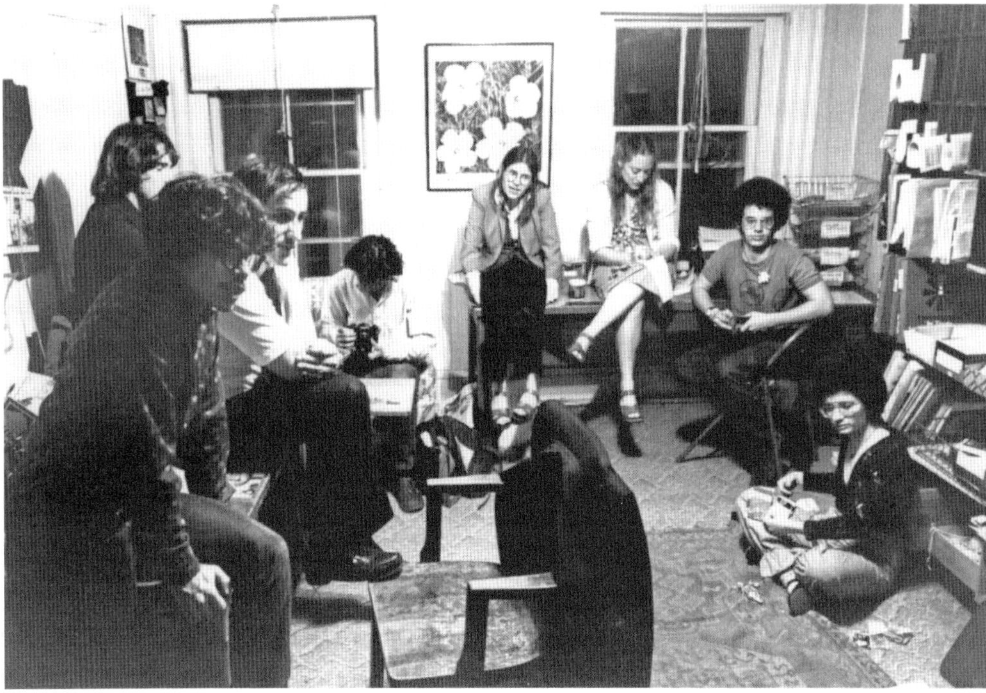

East Boston Community News (EBCN)
The EBCN was established in 1970, when Mossik Hacobian was hired to work as a community organizer for the IMPACT program in East Boston. Funded by the Federal Office of Economic Opportunity as part of Lyndon B. Johnson's War on Poverty, Hacobian's job was to start a community development corporation in East Boston to address community needs. A resident planning committee was formed and Hacobian went door to door asking East Bostonians what the community needed. People mentioned a movie theater, elderly housing (resulting in the eventual construction of the Heritage Apartments), and a community newspaper. While East Boston had two weekly newspapers in 1880 and three by 1930, in 1970, there was only one. "At the time, the only paper in town was completely uncritical of Logan Airport expansion. Massport could pay to publish favorable front page stories," recalls Hacobian. With initial funding from IMPACT, residents started publishing the *Impact Newsletter*, which soon became the *East Boston Community News*—specializing in hard-hitting investigative reporting. Funded by a spare-change jar in the office and annual members who donated $25 to $50 yearly for printing costs, the paper was published twice monthly. The first issues were laid out from the IMPACT office, then from the Most Holy Redeemer rectory, and then from the basement of Marie DiFlumeri's house on Sumner Street, until office space was rented on Meridian Street. "At first, we had no advertisements," notes Hacobian, "but we realized we couldn't stay afloat. After much debate, we decided to take ads. But, ads were hard to get because many local stores did business with Massport and didn't want to be associated with us. We got some grants and luckily had a lot of good talent for free." Never shying away from controversial issues, the paper won many supporters and some enemies along the way. Former staffer Joe Conason recalls, "Someone attempted to firebomb our office on Meridian Street, without success. Someone threw red paint on the office windows. And a local would-be politician warned me that my personal safety might be in jeopardy." While talented reporters and editors came and went, production manager Bob Nakashian quietly worked behind the scenes as a jack-of-all-trades for nearly 20 years, until the paper closed in 1989. Back issues of the paper are now archived at Northeastern University's Snell Library. (Courtesy of Bob Nakashian and EBCN Memory Book.)

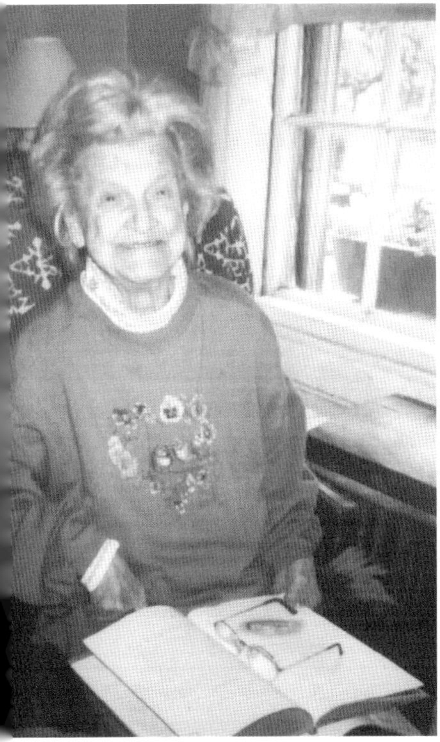

Eleanor K. Stafford Welch (1910–1998)

Schoolteacher, local church organist, and lifelong Jeffries Point resident Eleanor Welch was a popular columnist for the *East Boston Community News*. Interlacing her reflections of life in Jeffries Point with references from classical literature, politics, and history, she shunned typewriters and handwrote articles at her kitchen table while neighbors dropped in to share news and chat. Her kitchen was always abuzz with lively political conversations, and she was widely respected as a fierce defender of East Boston. The Welch family has resided at 212 Webster Street since 1912, including Welch's father, Charles Stafford, a ferryboat captain who was born in East Boston in 1865, and her grandmother Ellen Kelly Sullivan, who adventured to California during the Gold Rush and sailed back to East Boston with gold coins hidden in her hairdo so she would not be robbed. Today, Welch's son Charles Welch lives in the home with his family. In an example of the traditional closeness of East Boston neighbors, the Welches have been friends with the Hennessys in the adjoining house (210 Webster Street) for four generations. Before the days of telephones, the families used to knock on the dividing wall between their homes to signal each other. (Left, courtesy of Mary Ellen Welch; below, author's collection.)

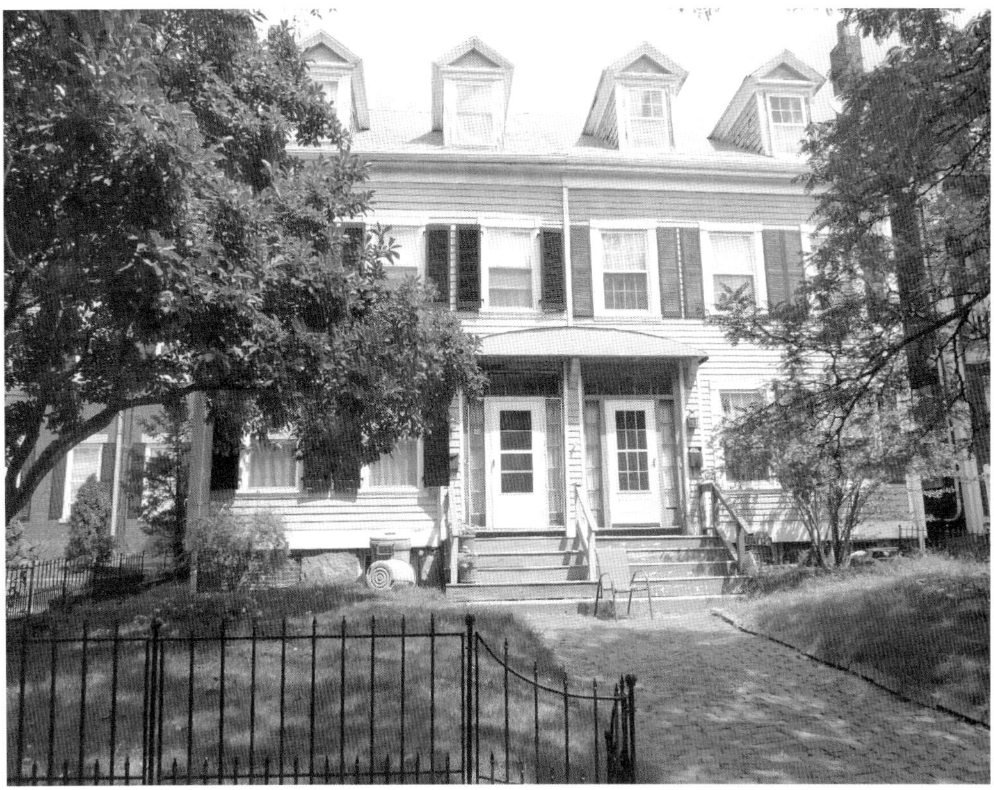

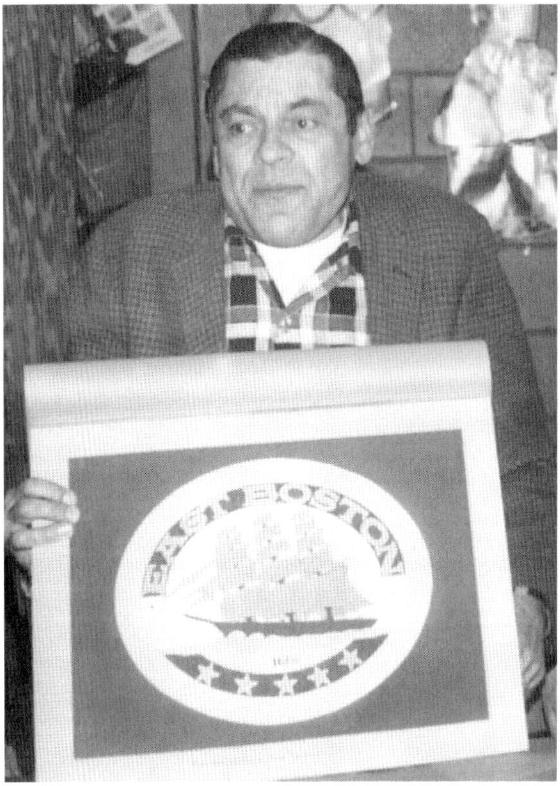

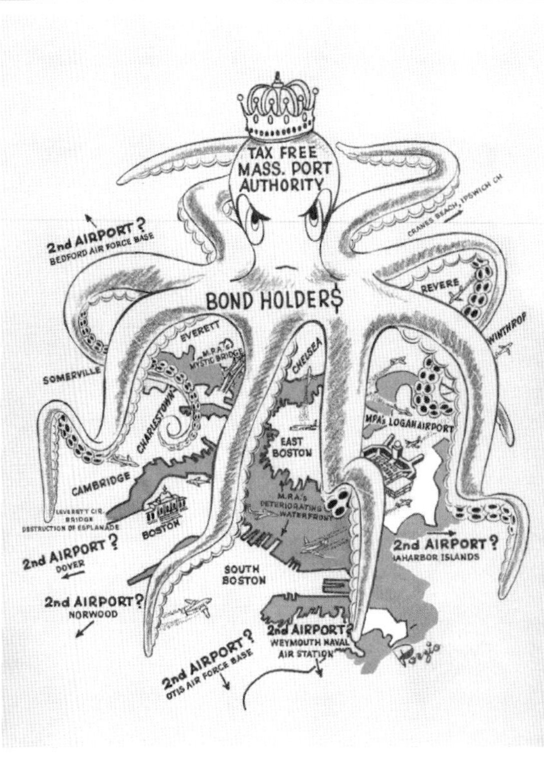

Joe Porzio (1918–1979)

Joe Porzio was a talented graphic artist whose political cartoons appeared regularly in the *East Boston Community News*. He was a modest, unassuming man, and most East Bostonians did not know that his work also appeared in the *New York Times* and the *Saturday Evening Post*. Dedicated to his family and church, Porzio was very active in struggles to halt Logan Airport expansion. He was a member of the Massachusetts Air Pollution and Noise Abatement Committee and chair of the East Boston Neighborhood Council, often taking unpaid time off from his job as a commercial artist to represent East Boston at airport-related State House and City Hall hearings. Eleanor K. Welch wrote of him, "His fervor far exceeded that of the paid lobbyists present at the same meetings" as he spoke on behalf of his neighbors. Porzio Park is named in his honor. (Top, courtesy of Mary Ellen Welch; bottom, courtesy of Bob Nakashian.)

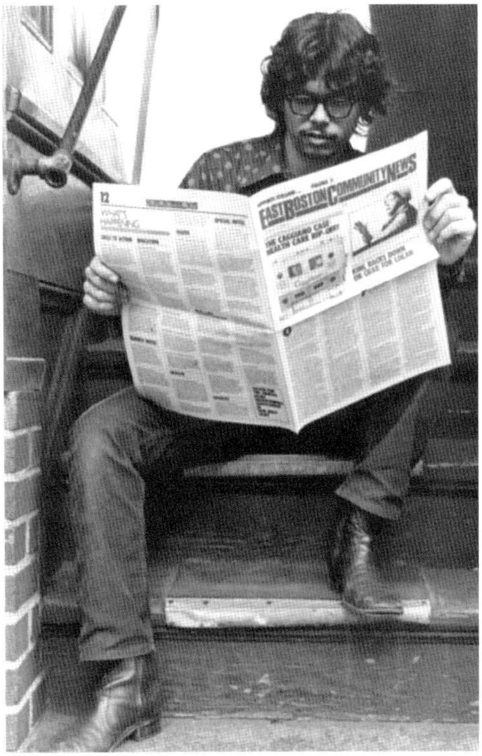

Michael Rezendes

Pulitzer prize–winning journalist Mike Rezendes lived in East Boston in the 1970s and 1980s, writing for the *East Boston Community News*. Reporting for the paper for several years before becoming its editor in 1983, he covered East Boston politics, particularly airport issues. In the process, he developed intimate knowledge of the workings of local, state, and federal agencies and established source contacts that few reporters at big city papers had. This led to his hiring as a political reporter for the *Boston Phoenix*, followed by jobs at the *San Jose Mercury News*, the *Washington Post*, and the *Boston Globe*. At the *Globe*, he was the lead reporter in a 2002 series revealing the Catholic Church's cover-up of sexual abuse committed for decades by Boston clergy. The story of the investigation of this scandal by Rezendes and his colleagues on the *Globe* spotlight team became a Hollywood movie called *Spotlight*. (Left, courtesy of Renée Loth and Bob Nakashian; below, author's collection.)

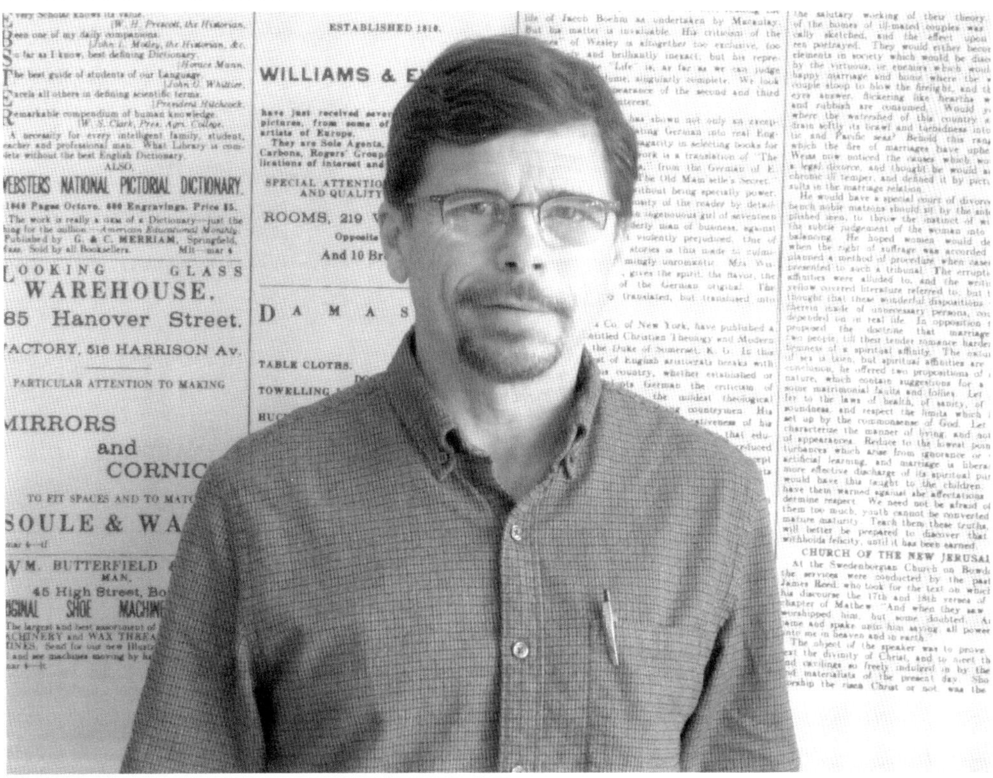

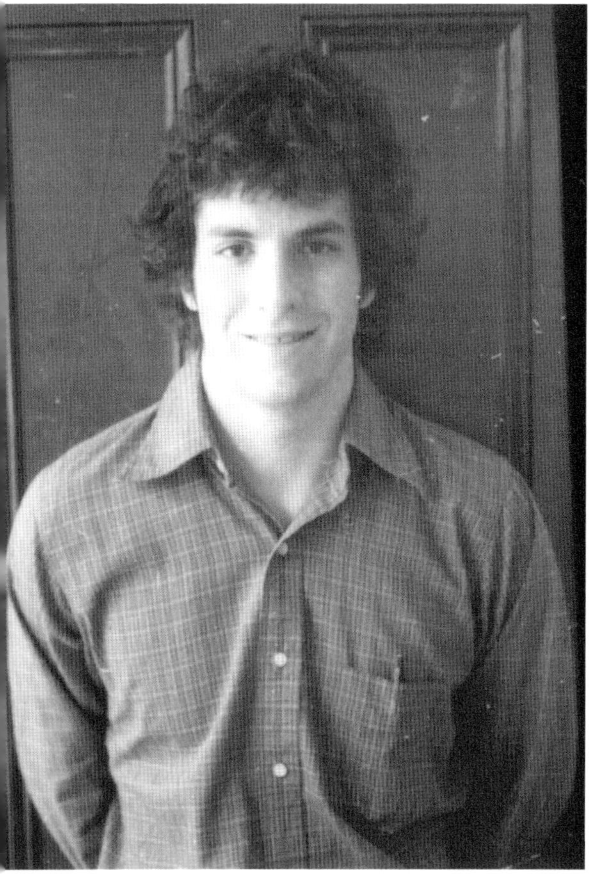

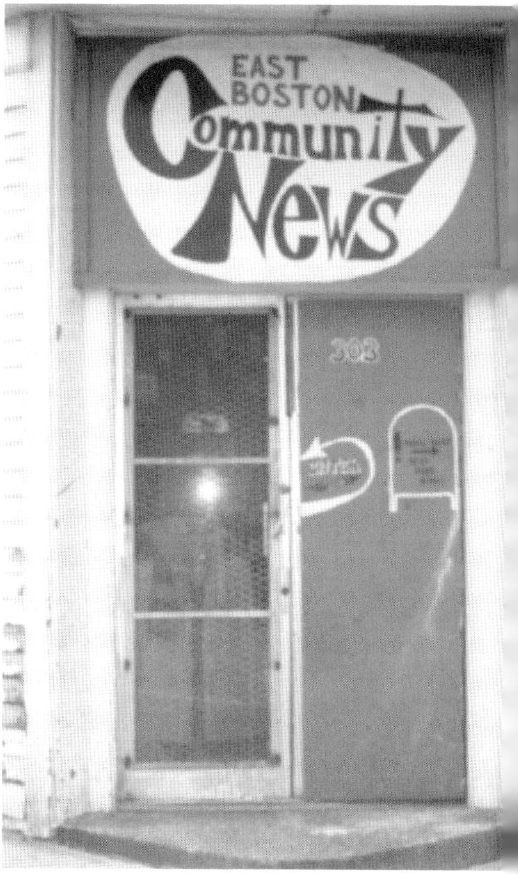

Joe Conason

While a senior at Brandeis University, Joe Conason volunteered with the *East Boston Community News* in the 1970s and liked the neighborhood so much that he moved to Lamson Street. After graduation, he worked at the paper full-time. "The country was in a deep recession. For a 21-year old aspiring reporter, this low-paid job represented an incredible opportunity." Working with Bob Nakashian and a small staff of volunteers, Conason wrote and edited articles, designed and sold advertisements, did layout, proofread, and delivered papers in a rusting deathtrap of a van. "In the process, I received an extraordinary education." He reported on community development, local corruption, school desegregation, and East Boston's struggles against airport expansion. The investigative stories he wrote eventually led him to a full-time job at the *Boston Phoenix*. Conason went on to become a reporter for the *New York Observer*, Salon.com, and Truthdig.com, and is now the editor-in-chief of the *National Memo*. "East Boston gave me a sense of purpose and belonging that I grew to cherish. Very few experiences have been as important in shaping my life and outlook, not only about issues of economic and environmental justice, but about democracy, citizenship, community, and journalism." (Both, courtesy of Bob Nakashian.)

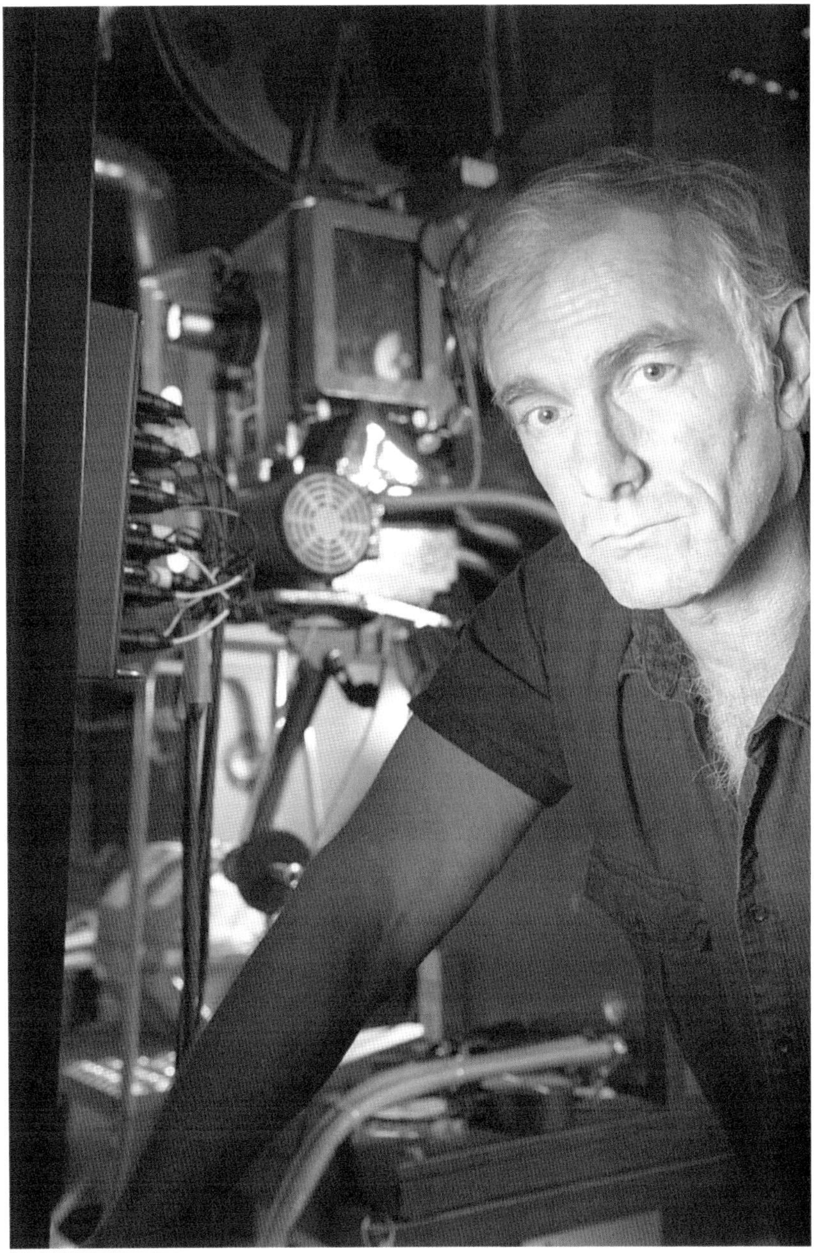

John Sayles
John Sayles is an Academy Award–nominated independent-film director and screenwriter whose films include *Passion Fish*, *Lone Star*, *Casa de los Babys*, *The Secret of Roan Inish*, and *Go for Sisters*. As a young writer, he lived in East Boston from 1973 to 1978, where he got ideas for characters and themes. He wrote his first novel living on Maverick Street "sitting next to the only source of heat, which was a vent in the side of the stove." He wrote his second novel on Haynes Street, with scenes inspired by local saint's day festas and a nearby Italian sausage factory. "What I liked best about East Boston was its real sense of being a neighborhood, accessible to the 'big city' but much quieter and laid back." (Courtesy of Ric Kallaher.)

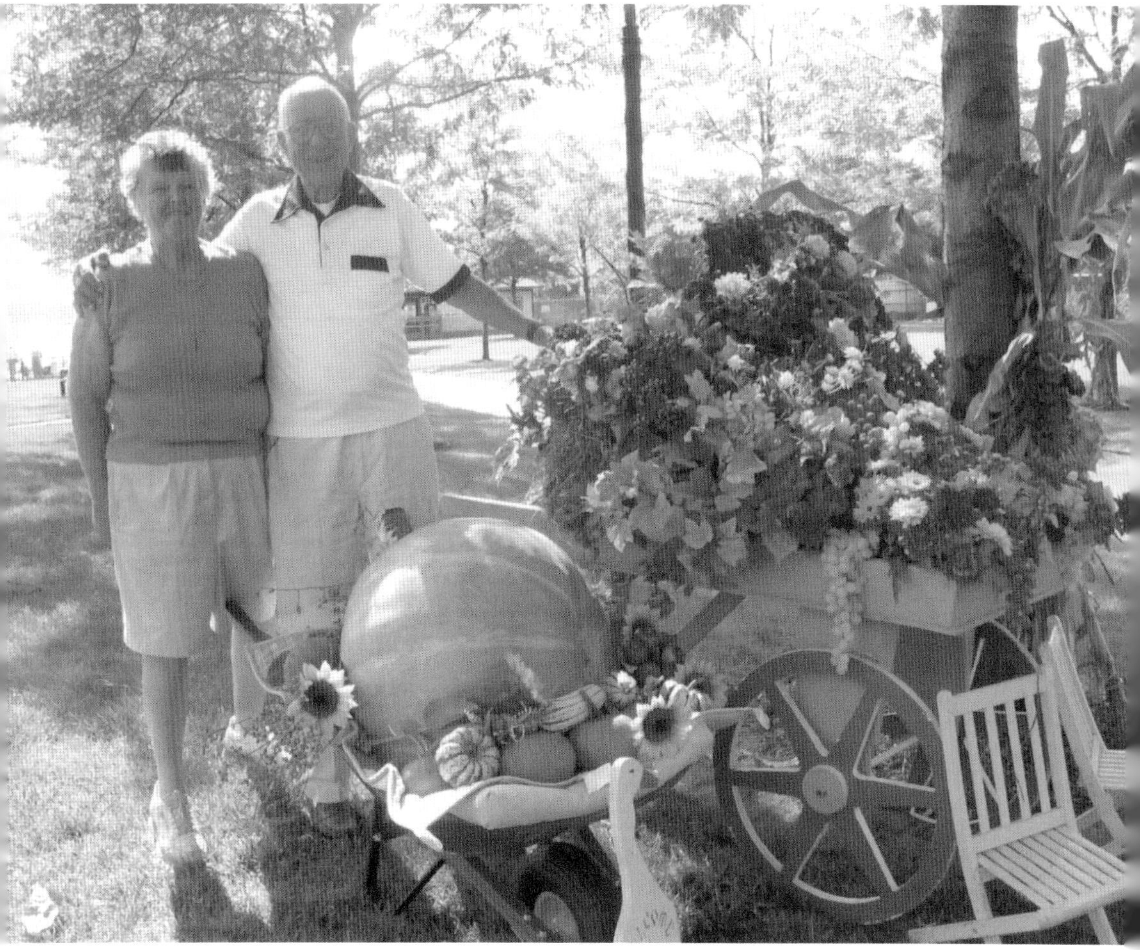

Fran Rowan

Fran Rowan was drawn to art as a child, creating pictures with melted crayons, seeds, and whatever else struck her fancy. Over time, she experimented with papermaking, bookbinding, photography, and jewelry. An enthusiastic supporter of East Boston artists, regularly purchasing and promoting their work, she was instrumental in repurposing the Atlantic Iron Works site at 80 Border Street for use as a collaborative artists' space. She has spent years supporting other worthy projects, including local health facilities and the youth arts organization ZUMIX. A major project of Rowan's was the 1971 establishment of Meridian House, a substance-abuse recovery program at 408 Meridian Street. Reacting to an epidemic of drug abuse in East Boston at the time, she convinced local residents, initially against the idea, to support it. She served on the board for decades and in 2003 spearheaded fundraising to renovate the 1878 Victorian Gothic home, which was renamed the Fran Rowan Meridian House in her honor in 2010. (Courtesy of Madeleine Steczynski.)

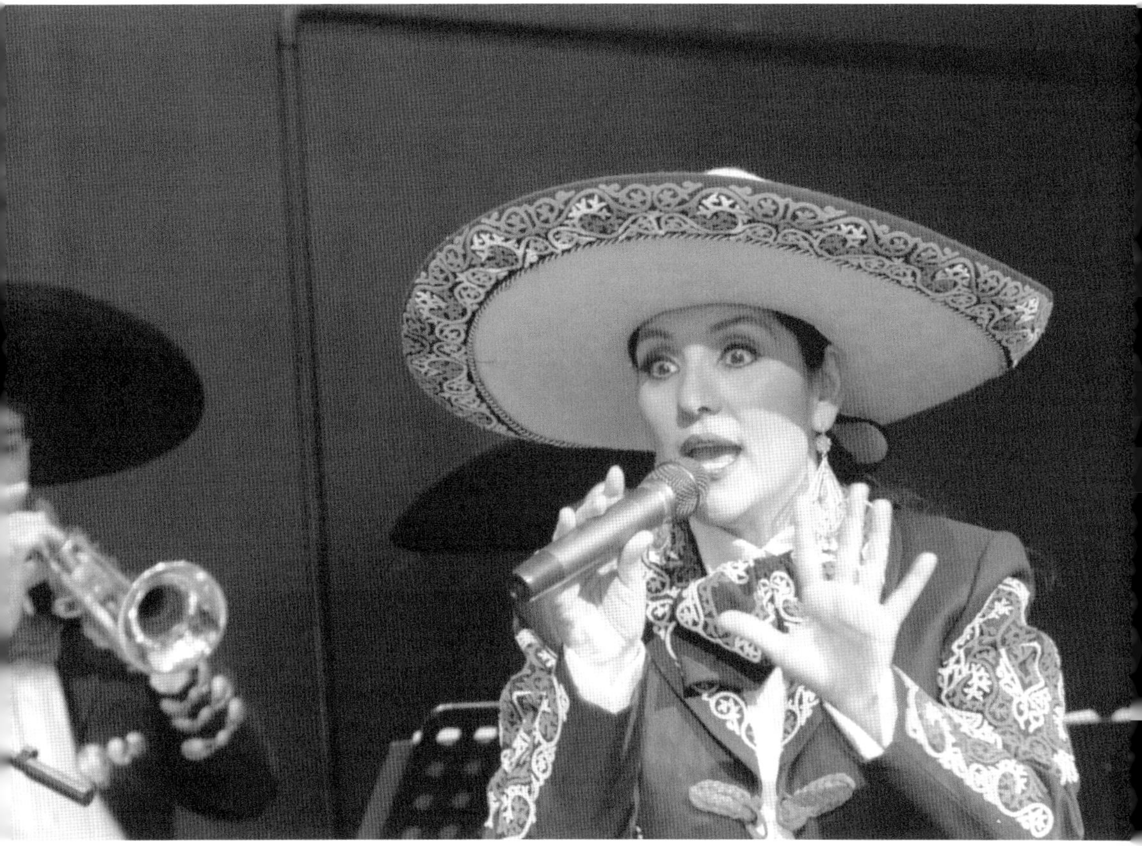

Veronica Robles
Hailing from Mexico City, Mexico, Veronica Robles began singing mariachi music as a teenager, later performing in Mexico and the United States. She started working in East Boston in 2000 when the chamber of commerce invited her to organize Latino cultural performances for the annual Columbus Day Parade. Since then, she has taught Latin American–folkloric dance to East Boston youth and is the director of the Veronica Robles Cultural Center on McClellan Highway. She still sings professionally and hosts a weekly Latino television variety show on *Telemundo.* (Courtesy of Veronica Robles.)

Joe Harvard

Raised Joseph Alia Incagnoli Jr. in Jeffries Point, "Joe Harvard" was a Harvard-educated archaeologist before making a career as a musician, producer-engineer, and indie-music pioneer. He cofounded Fort Apache Recording (1985), which produced the music of Natalie Merchant, Juliana Hatfield, the Pixies, Radiohead, the Lemonheads, and other indie music icons. He also founded Helldorado Productions (1988), New York City's Tribal Soundz (1999), and Asbury's Cranial Mass Productions (2008). He won the WFNX/Boston Phoenix Best Local Producer title (1989), New York's prestigious Moth StorySLAM Championship (2001), and Asbury Music Awards for Top Americana Band (2009), Top Multi-Instrumentalist (2010), and Top Avant-Garde Act (2010). He now lives in Asbury Park, New Jersey, performing and teaching free music classes to low-income youth. (Courtesy of Kristen Driscoll.)

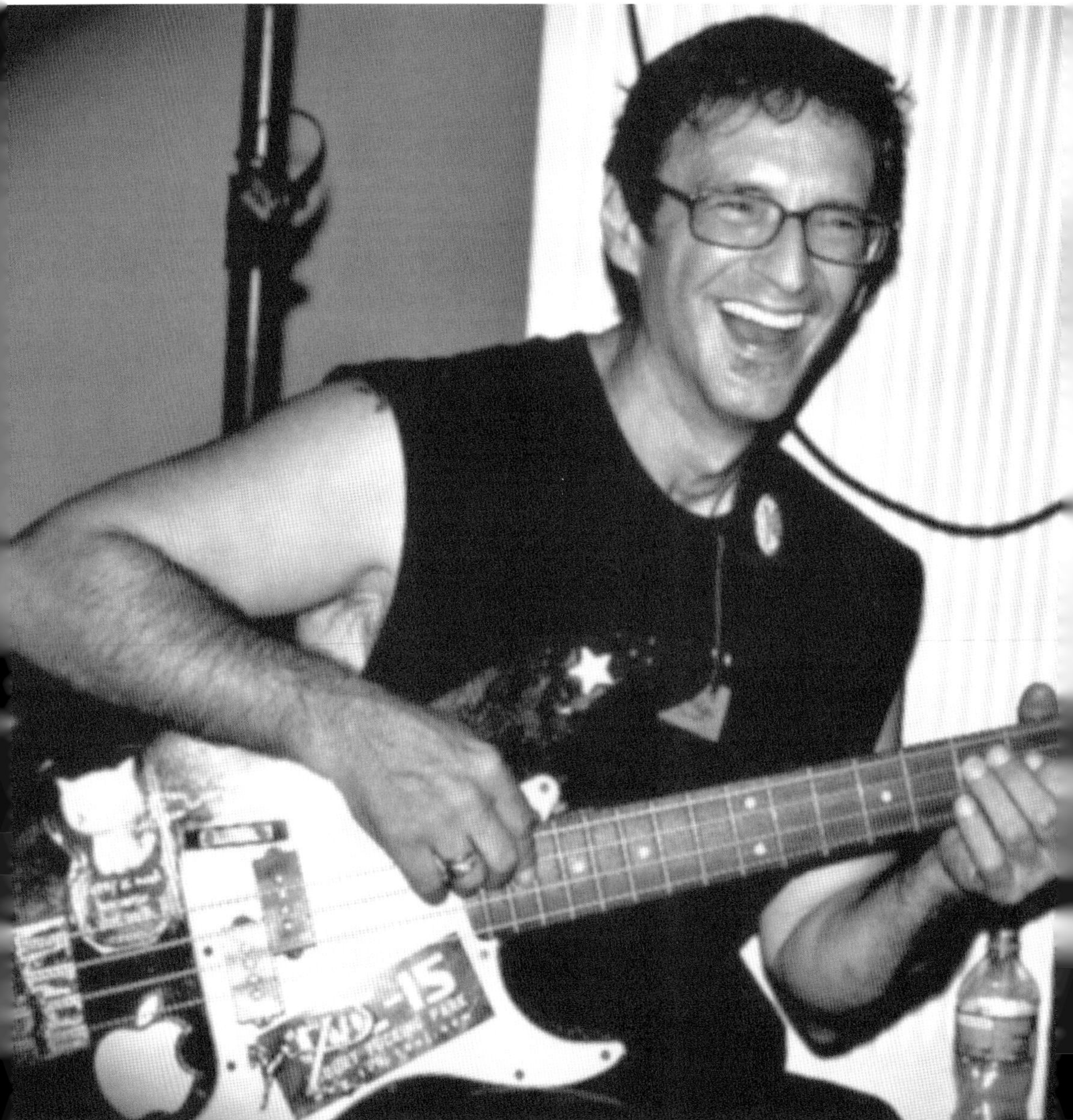

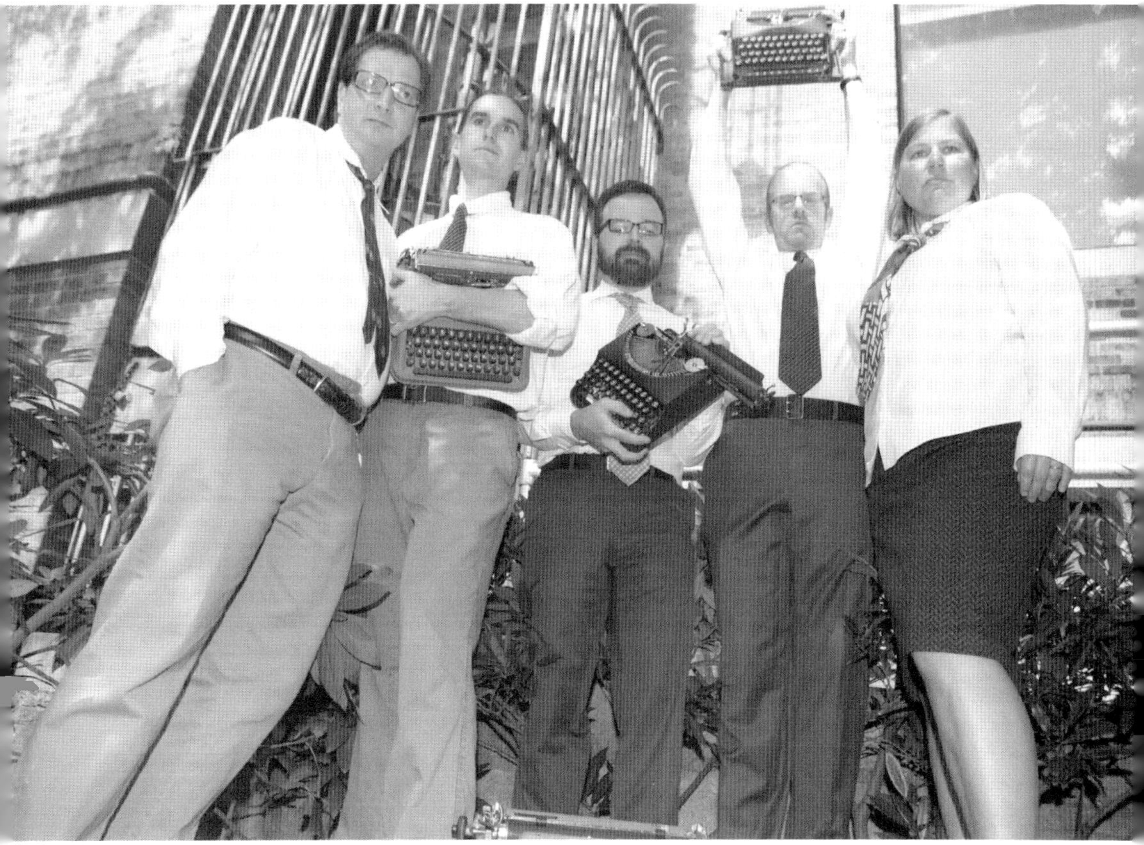

Jay O'Grady

Jay O'Grady is a lifelong East Bostonian and cofounder of the Boston Typewriter Orchestra (BTO), a quirky ensemble that makes music from syncopated typewriter manipulation combined with comedy. O'Grady and the BTO have been featured on NPR, NBC's *Weekend Today*, Fox News, New England Cable News, *Chronicle*, and *America's Got Talent* and have performed at Boston's Museum of Science, the Museum of Fine Arts, the Rhode Island School of Design, and many other venues. (Courtesy of Jay O'Grady.)

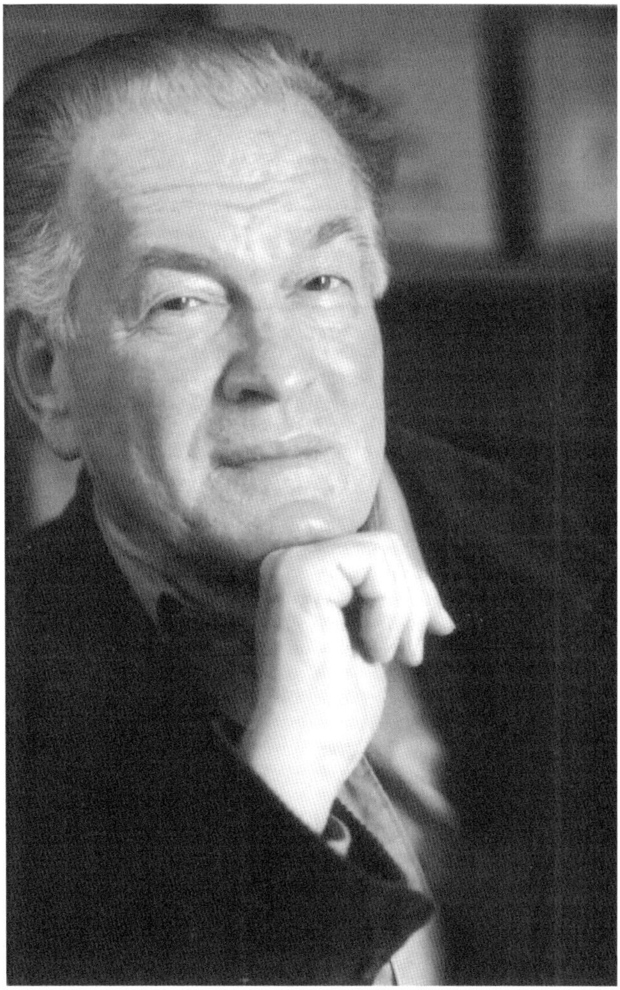

Dr. Gene Sharp

Gene Sharp is the founder of the Albert Einstein Institution (AEI), a nonprofit that advances the use of strategic nonviolent action in conflicts around the globe. Originally from Ohio, he received a doctorate from Oxford University and moved to East Boston in 1968 while on a research appointment at Harvard University. He preferred living in a neighborhood of "ordinary hardworking people" to living at Harvard and grew interested in an abandoned house on Cottage Street. "I used to pass it when I'd go back and forth to Festa's corner store. The building was in terrible shape with the windows boarded up." Mr. Festa told him the property was for sale and put him in touch with the owners, who sold it for $150. Sharp has lived there ever since, renovating it into a cozy home with a large orchid garden on the roof. A professor at U Mass Dartmouth since 1972, he has authored numerous books about democratic freedoms, including *From Dictatorship to Democracy*, which has been translated into 40 languages. Sharp has spoken around the world about peaceful social movements, dictatorships, and genocide and was nominated four times for the Nobel Peace Prize. When asked what inspired him, he replied, "The atomic bomb. The hydrogen bomb. Colonization. Institutionalized racism. I'm inspired to do this work by the brave people around the world whose names will never be known." At age 25, Sharp began writing letters to Albert Einstein, sharing his thoughts about injustice and war. He assumed Einstein would never respond, but to his surprise, Einstein replied, and the two developed a lively correspondence that lasted until Einstein's death. (Courtesy of AEI.)

CHAPTER FOUR

Organizational Innovators

Since the 1800s, East Bostonians have developed innovative nonprofit organizations to meet community needs. Most have been bottom-up initiatives with intergenerational participation of residents as board members, volunteers, and staff. Many have introduced creative new program models that were later replicated elsewhere. None of these organizations would exist without the dedicated residents who attended countless meetings and enthusiastically gave of themselves as planning committee members, board members, volunteers, and staff.

A community of diverse immigrants by the turn of the 20th century, East Boston was described in 1903 by *Good Housekeeping* as "one of the most cosmopolitan districts of the city." While middle-class families lived in sections of Eagle Hill, Jeffries Point, and Orient Heights, crowded tenement houses outnumbered the genteel mansions of earlier times. Many tenements lacked electricity and indoor showers. As part of a modern sanitation movement at the end of the 19th century, the first free public gymnasium and bathhouse in America opened at 112 Paris Street. The original wooden building was built around the 1880s and was later purchased and donated to the City of Boston in 1897 by Mrs. Daniel Ahl. Here, adults and children took exercise classes accompanied by live piano music, and hot showers were available to all. In the gym's early days, Clara Bates, wife of Gov. John Lewis Bates of East Boston, headed up the married ladies' exercise class to encourage women to get physical activity—a novel concept at that time. A new brick building was built in 1909, and the gym is still an active community center today.

Mutual-aid societies and immigrant homes were founded to help newcomers, and the Trinity Neighborhood House—one of the oldest settlement houses in Boston—was inaugurated at 406 Meridian Street in 1917. It was part of the US settlement-house movement made famous when Jane Addams founded Hull House in Chicago in 1889. East Boston had its own Addams in social worker Caroline Orr, the director of Trinity House for 40 years. Back then, settlement house directors lived on site, and Orr was fully integrated into the community. A predecessor of today's social-service agencies, Trinity House offered English classes, daycare, job training, cooking, and craft and drama lessons. Around the same time, there was a national movement to promote literacy and democratize access to books, which were previously available only to the wealthy. East Bostonians established the first municipally supported branch library in America in 1869 and opened it in the basement of the Lyman School in 1871. In 1914, a two-story main branch building was opened at 276 Meridian Street. (A small Orient Heights library had been built in 1912 with funds from the Druker family, who later donated it to the city.) Both branches served the community until 2013, when a new library on Bremen Street opened.

The history of the East Boston Social Centers dates to the 1880s, when reformers organized public health and social services to help immigrants. Combining predecessor agencies such as the Good Will House in Jeffries Point and Trinity House, the EBSC was incorporated in 1918. Early funding came from sisters Sarah and Isabel Hyams, philanthropists from a wealthy Jewish family. In 1937, in response to a scourge of tuberculosis striking East Boston children, the Hyams sisters purchased land in Westford, Massachusetts, for the establishment of three interconnected "fresh air camps," Camp Nashoba (boys), Camp Wakitatina (girls), and Camp Cielo Celeste (small children). Here, generations of East Boston youth learned to swim, hike, canoe, build campfires, and appreciate nature—activities that would otherwise be inaccessible to most. Established in the spirit of the socialist ideals popular in the 1930s and led by its first director, Max Nelson, the East Boston Camps were built collectively by the men of East Boston, who traveled to Westford on weekends via the Boston & Maine Railroad to volunteer their time building cabins, a boathouse, and a dining hall. Each spring, East Boston mothers volunteered for a fun, weeklong mothers' camp (a rare respite in the country, away from husbands and daily duties), to get the cabins ready for campers who would arrive when school was out. Some mothers stayed on during the summer to cook and clean, while fathers volunteered to repair and paint structures. The camp motto was "When All Give, All Gain," which was also the motto of the EBSC. With sites in Central Square, Orient Heights, and Jeffries Point, the centers today offer daycare, senior programs, afterschool and summer youth activities, and more.

In 1945, Salesian missionaries came to Orient Heights to serve Italian immigrants. They were housed and fed by local families while the community raised funds to build the Salesian Boys Club in 1945 and the Don Bosco Trade School in 1946, both located at Byron and Horace Streets. "People made a lot of sacrifices to get these programs going," notes Fr. John Nazzaro. Today, the Salesian Boys and Girls Club serves hundreds of youth ages 6 to 19, offering day camp in the summer and afterschool programming in sports, dance, computers, art, photography, homework help, and more.

For medical care prior to the 1970s, East Bostonians relied on local doctors who lived in the neighborhood. When someone was gravely ill, they had to cross the harbor to reach a downtown hospital, sometimes dying en route. Built in 1907, the overcrowded Relief Station at 14 Porter Street offered temporary relief for walk-in emergencies and some preventive care (such as vaccinations) but lacked advanced technologies for handling heart attacks, strokes, or other life-threatening conditions. By the 1960s, as Evelyn Morash explains, "A lot of the old family doctors who used to make house calls were dying off, and they weren't well versed in the latest medicine. When my mother had high blood pressure, the doctor put leeches on her!" In 1968, East Bostonians came together to plan the East Boston Neighborhood Health Center, one of the first neighborhood health centers in the country.

Over the years, numerous other nonprofit organizations were founded, serving the recreational, educational, cultural, social, medical, and mental-health needs of the community. Starting and running nonprofit organizations in East Boston is not an easy job, not only because the working-class population base cannot provide the kind of financial support available in more affluent communities, but also because East Boston's physical isolation has meant sometimes being forgotten by other institutions in the city. For years, East Boston was not included on the official map of Boston neighborhoods published annually in the *Yellow Pages* telephone directory. The map simply showed a landmass called Logan Airport. Many inhabitants of Greater Boston have never been to East Boston or even heard of it. When Fr. John Nazzaro once called city hall to arrange transportation services for the Boys and Girls Club, the employee on the phone told him East Boston was not part of Boston. "I had to explain to her that it was!" Nonetheless, the community has always had a special resource—the dedication and volunteerism of its residents. Manny Lopes of the health center notes, "Our isolation makes us unique. Whether it's old timers or new folks, people really care about the neighborhood and feel a sense of ownership. It's a place where people make things happen, despite the obstacles."

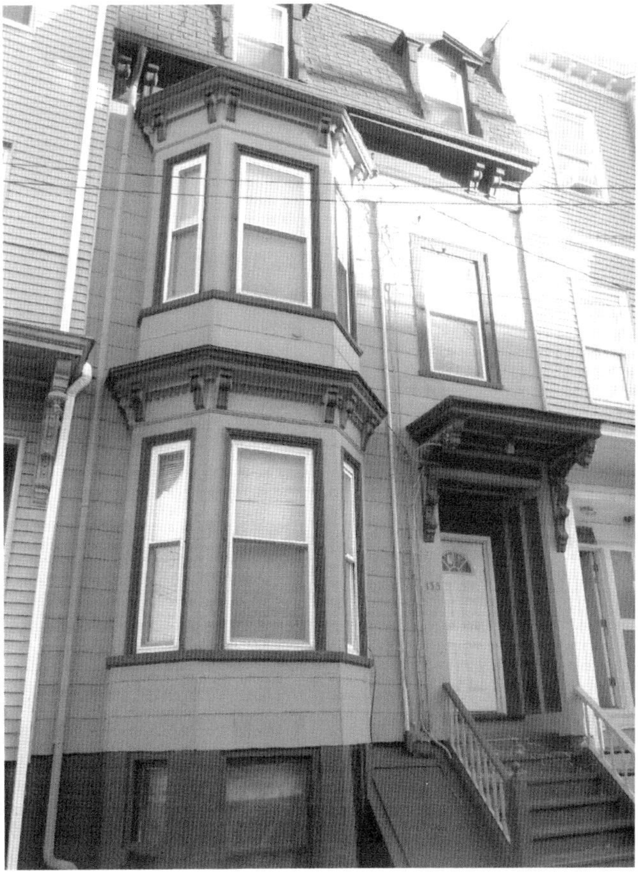

John "Jack" White

John White has the unique distinction of having grown up in a funeral home. "In those days," he notes, "the tradition was to wake people in homes. Funeral homes weren't the amphitheater-like institutions you see today, they were real homes." From the 1920s to the 1960s, White's family ran David J. Dooley Funeral Home on 135 London Street, operating on the first floor of their three-decker home (pictured), with his parents and grandparents living in the two apartments above. There were 15 other family-run funeral homes in East Boston at the time. In response to children who teased White about living with the dead, his father told him, "Son, you've got nothing to fear from the dead. It's the live ones you need to worry about!" White attended the Fitton School (now East Boston Central Catholic), where he was a distinguished student and athlete. After graduating from Cathedral High, he worked at Riverside Press, which reinforced his love of books. Feeling he should work in the family business, he did a four-year internship as an undertaker, but knew it was not his calling. He later worked his way through Boston College, earning a degree in psychology and later becoming a licensed social worker. White took a job directing the anti-poverty agency Area Planning Action Council (APAC), located on Meridian Street, where he has worked for more than 40 years. "What stood me in good stead is that I knew the turf. This work is very intense. You have people sitting across from you with some very serious problems. I wanted to use the tools I had to help them." White credits his Jesuit teachers with influencing him to help others. "They exposed me to Hegel, Immanuel Kant, Rene Descartes, Arthur Schopenhauer, great literature, liberal arts. I believe you are always better off being exposed to the arts. I was fortunate to have that exposure." Having lived and worked in East Boston for more than seven decades, White knows thousands of East Bostonians on a first-name basis and is widely respected as a friend and neighbor who helps people find solutions to their problems. (Author's collection.)

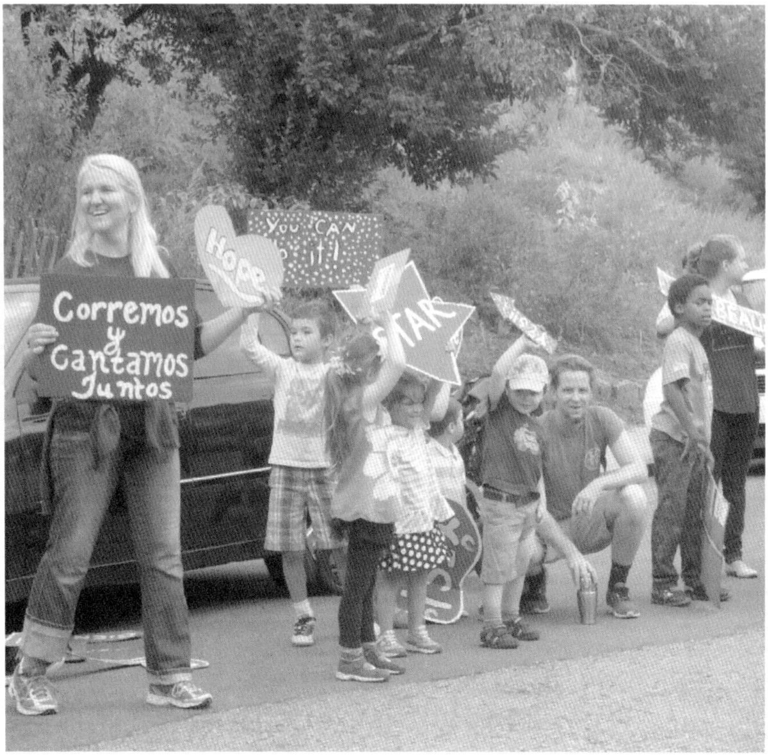

Madeleine Steczynski

The executive director of ZUMIX, Madeleine Steczynski is much more than the head of a nonprofit arts agency. She is a friend, neighbor, mentor, informal social worker, and go-to person for hundreds of kids who regularly seek her guidance. She has inspired and aided countless young people, whether helping them deal with school troubles, domestic violence, or a sick dog that needs to be taken to a veterinarian at 3:00 a.m. For this, she is widely admired by families in the neighborhood. Steczynski and ZUMIX cofounder Bob Grove, who both moved to Maverick Square in 1990, were troubled by an epidemic of crime, drug overdoses, and suicides among Boston's inner-city youth. In talking with local residents, they realized that there was a need for music and arts programming in East Boston. (In earlier times, the community had multiple music schools, but by 1990 there were none. Moreover, for years, art and music programming had been defunded in the public schools.) Steczynski and Grove quit their day jobs and began offering free youth programming from their living room, employing music and art as empowerment tools. As they outgrew the space, local residents and businesspeople joined them to form a board of directors. Novel at the time, a youth board of directors was also formed, making young people an integral part of program planning, hiring, and fundraising. Youth were asked to invent a name for the new agency, and ZUMIX was born. Working enthusiastically on collaborations with board members, local residents, businesses, and social-service agencies, Steczynski grew ZUMIX from a tiny program into one of the premier youth arts centers in the country. ZUMIX has won numerous prestigious awards, including one from President Obama, commending its community-based, youth-driven programming. Under Steczynski's leadership, a $4.6-million capital campaign was carried out to convert an abandoned historic firehouse on Sumner Street into a state-of-the-art music education and performance space, opened in 2010. Today, ZUMIX offers free and low-cost classes in instrumental music, song writing, sound recording, engineering and production, dance, and theater. It also runs a community radio station. As East Boston's musical heart, ZUMIX provides year-round concerts and other cultural events and is a second home for hundreds of youth who span diverse ages, races, religions, and social classes. (Courtesy of Ann Antonellis.)

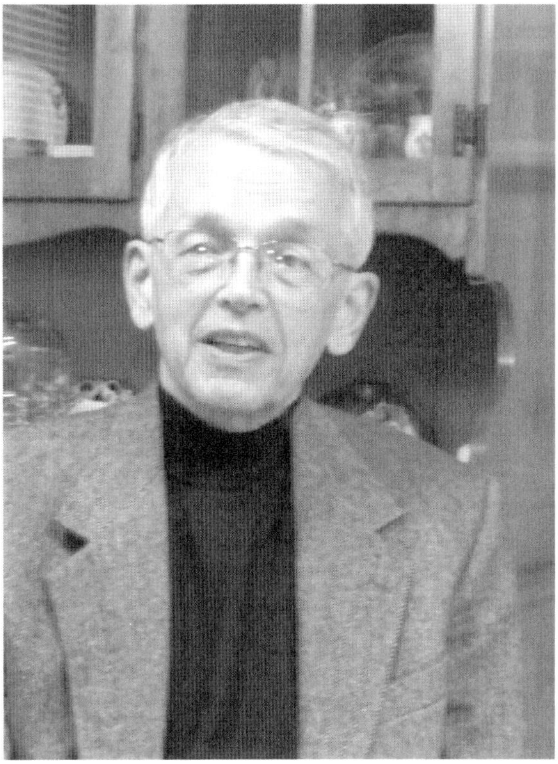

Pastor Don Nanstad
Don Nanstad grew up in Blair, Wisconsin, a picturesque farm town where almost everyone was Norwegian and Lutheran. After graduating from Yale Divinity School, he became pastor of Our Savior's Lutheran Church in Maverick Square in 1980. Built by Norwegians in 1911, the church's congregation in 1980 consisted of 20 elderly Scandinavians. When Nanstad arrived, he experienced culture shock. "I couldn't get used to the houses so close together, trash on the sidewalks, guys on the corner drinking beer. Cars were set on fire every few weeks. I saw people bust the windows of the gas station across the street and rob cases of motor oil." He feared he had made the biggest mistake of his life. Today, he says, "I wouldn't want to live anywhere else. Wisconsin seems so boring now!" East Bostonian loquacity was a refreshing contrast to Nanstad's Midwestern reserve. "The neighbors started talking to me on the street, saying quirky things, telling me their concerns. I could get half my pastoral work done just taking out the trash!" On hearing stories of theft, domestic assault, and racial violence, he organized meetings with neighbors and the community-policing program at Precinct 7. In 1980, he became director of the East Boston Ecumenical Community Council, started two years earlier by Sr. Carole Rossi and Sr. Noel Doyle. Operating out of the church's basement, EBECC helped start Harbor Me, a shelter for battered women, and temporarily housed victims of fires at a time when many East Boston houses were burning down. Since the Lutheran Immigration and Refugee Service is the largest immigrant resettlement service in the world, Nanstad's congregation voted in 1982 to sponsor refugees. EBECC resettled hundreds of Cambodian families fleeing the Khmer Rouge, as well as Vietnamese and Latino families escaping war and political turmoil. Nanstad went door-to-door soliciting donations of food, clothes, and furniture for the refugees and helped them find apartments, register for school, and get healthcare. "Many of them had PTSD from the war. I wasn't trained in mental health counseling. I didn't speak their language. North Suffolk Mental Health was very helpful." Nanstad invited immigrant groups to celebrate their traditional holidays at the church, practicing their differing faiths. He formed Cambodian, Vietnamese, and Latino youth clubs, coached them in basketball, and took them camping. Over the years, he has had other job offers, but he loves East Boston and has no plans to leave. (Author's collection.)

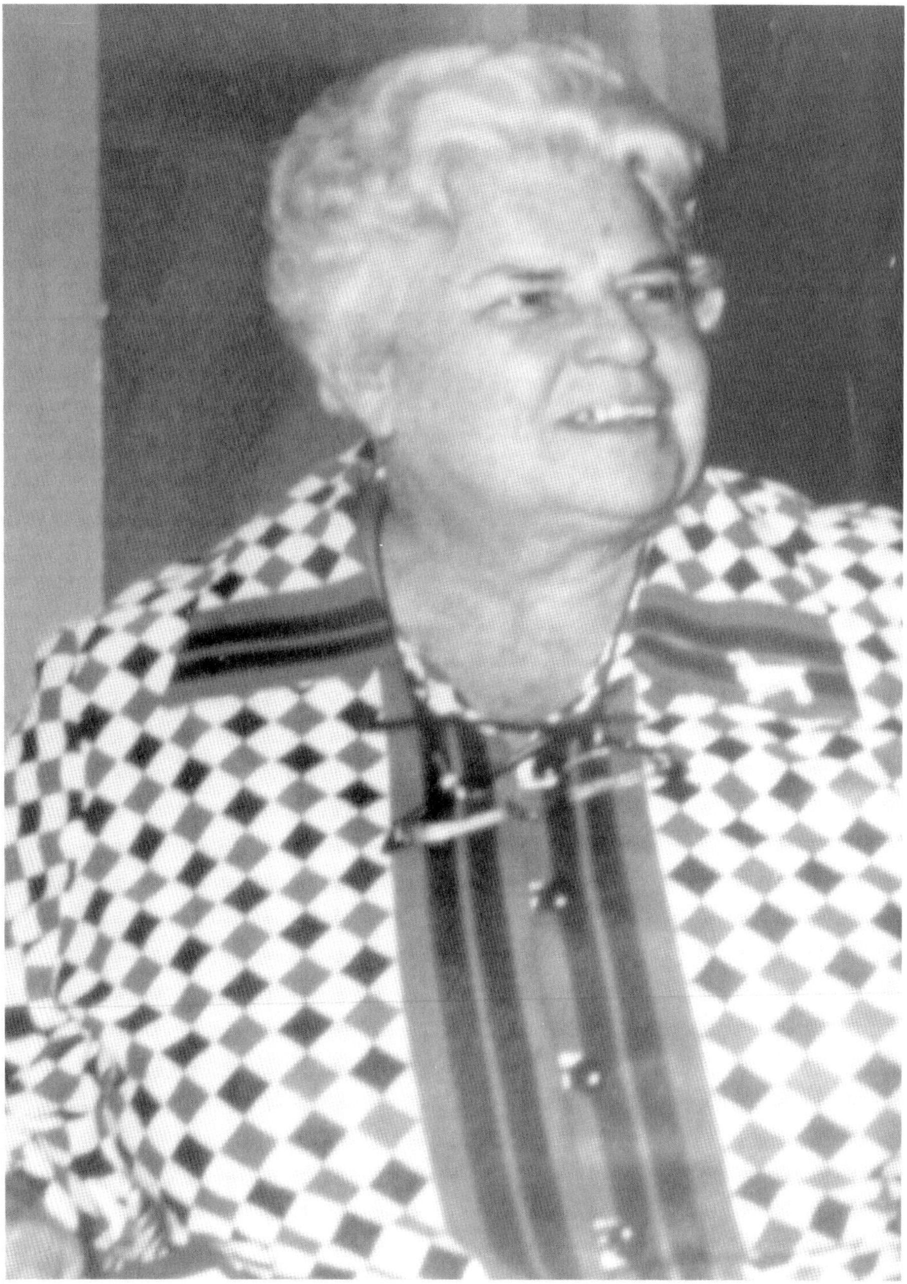

Caroline Orr (1910–1982)

A pioneering social worker, Caroline Orr directed the Trinity Neighborhood House from 1942 to 1973. She developed educational, athletic, and enrichment programs for children and teens, including Girl and Boy Scout troops and one of the first girls' camps in Boston in 1933. An ardent photographer, Orr taught generations of youth to photograph the world around them. She led hikes and outings, inspiring youth who might otherwise never see nature to appreciate it. Her enthusiasm exemplified the spirit of the US settlement house movement, of which Trinity House was one of Boston's early examples. (Courtesy of Mary Cahalane.)

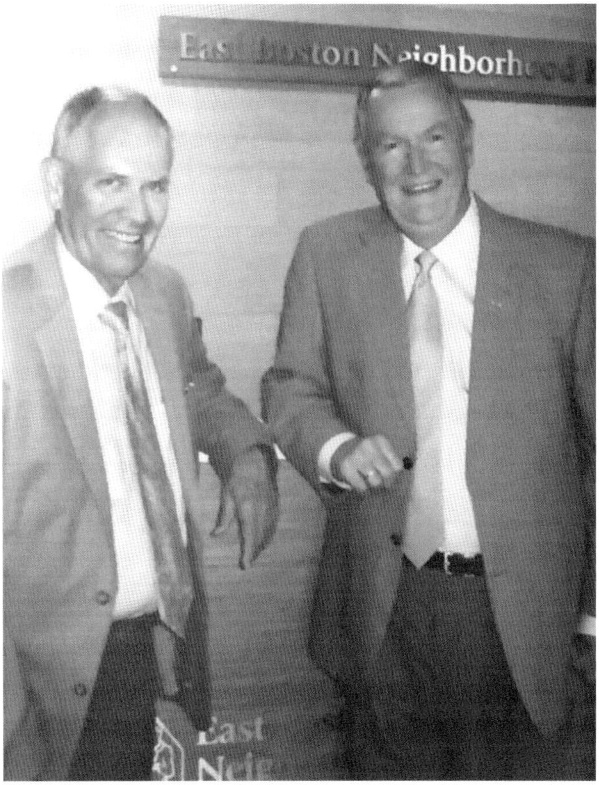

Dr. Jim Taylor and Jack Cradock

Dr. Jim Taylor (left) and Jack Cradock (right) are the dynamic duo who, for more than four decades, guided the success of the East Boston Neighborhood Health Center, one of the first community-based health centers in the country. As a young doctor in the 1970s, Taylor came to East Boston to serve the geographically isolated, underserved community and cared for thousands of East Boston patients over the years. Cradock, previously the director of the Jamaica Plain Health Center, was hired as EBNHC's director in 1977. However, the birth of the EBNHC started in 1968–1969, when local residents formed a health committee at the East Boston APAC. At the time, East Bostonians had to traverse the Sumner Tunnel in emergencies, sometimes dying or giving birth in traffic. The story of the EBNHC is one of grassroots involvement and community planning. Cradock, the health center's longtime CEO, recalls, "It was all women on the planning committee, but the medical establishment was dominated by men. They had very patronizing attitudes towards community people and especially towards women." The notion of a major health facility located in a working-class neighborhood challenged established models of healthcare at the time. But, the women were persistent and succeeded in incorporating in 1970. Cradock and Taylor worked with local residents to carry out a bricks-and-mortar campaign to construct the first building at 10 Gove Street, followed by years of grant writing to fund health services and expansion. They were pioneers in developing bottom-up health programs in response to expressed community needs. Among other things, local residents strongly advocated for bilingual health services, as they saw elderly monolingual Italians, who were fairly healthy but needed monitoring, being prematurely sent to nursing homes. The groundbreaking Elder Service Plan was developed, which sent bilingual nurses into homes and allowed seniors to maintain independence for as long as possible. The health center later built senior-citizen housing with clinics on site—a model later replicated by health-care providers across the country. EBNHC is a national leader in community-based health services, prevention, and outreach for culturally diverse urban populations. It now offers comprehensive medical care in 20 languages and is one of the largest community health centers in the nation. (Courtesy of EBNHC.)

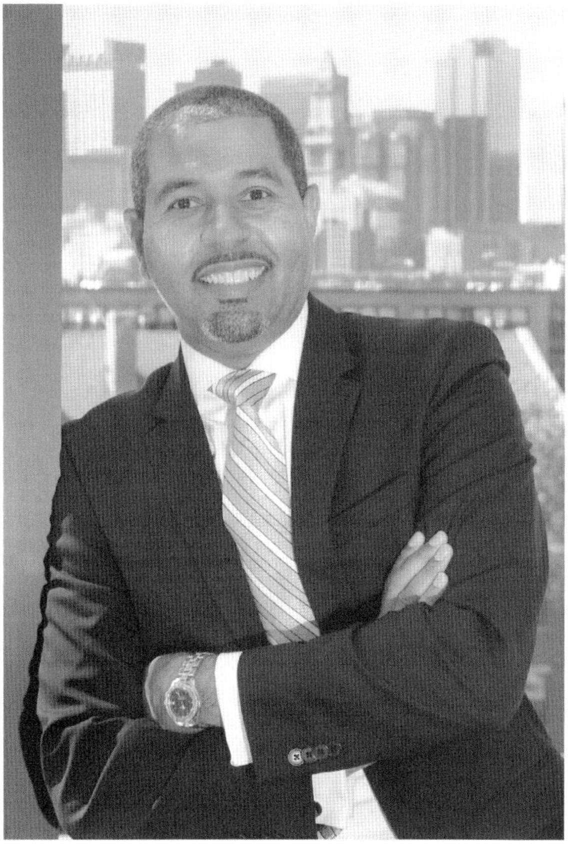

Manuel "Manny" Lopes

Of Cape Verdean descent, Manny Lopes, the new CEO of the EBNHC, grew up on Webster Street. "There was a small group of Cape Verdeans in East Boston when I was young, during really difficult racial tensions in Boston." Lopes started working early to help his family, delivering newspapers on roller skates at age 11 and cleaning squid at age 14 in a Nay Street warehouse that sold calamari to restaurants. While still in high school, he started his own DJ company. His best friends were first- and second-generation Italians. "We had a lot in common, because our families were immigrant families." Lopes had Cape Verdean relatives living in Angola, a country on the verge of war at the time. His mother wanted to bring them to the United States, but she first had to become a US citizen. As a teenager, Lopes tutored his mother for three years to prepare her for the citizenship exam. "When my mother became a citizen, it was a huge change in my life. We went from being a family of five to a family of 22 living in a one-bedroom apartment. It was a blast having so many new cousins! I was the person who helped everyone find jobs, get enrolled in school, etc. This helped me learn more about Cape Verdean culture and improve my Portuguese creole language skills." It also helped him become an expert on the needs of immigrant communities. At East Boston High, Lopes found himself in the middle of racial groupings. "The kids from Roxbury and Dorchester would say, 'You look like us but you don't talk like us.' My best friends were Italian kids. So, I was stuck in the middle. In the end, I made friends of diverse races." After graduating high school in 1987, he got a part-time job at the EBNHC recruiting patients for a blood-pressure study being conducted by Dr. Jim Taylor. Taylor saw great potential in Lopes and mentored him while Lopes worked his way through college. Over the course of 25 years, Lopes served on the EBNHC board of directors and worked his way up the ranks, holding jobs in the health center's human-resources and operations departments and becoming its new CEO in 2015. (Courtesy of Jim Hill and EBNHC.)

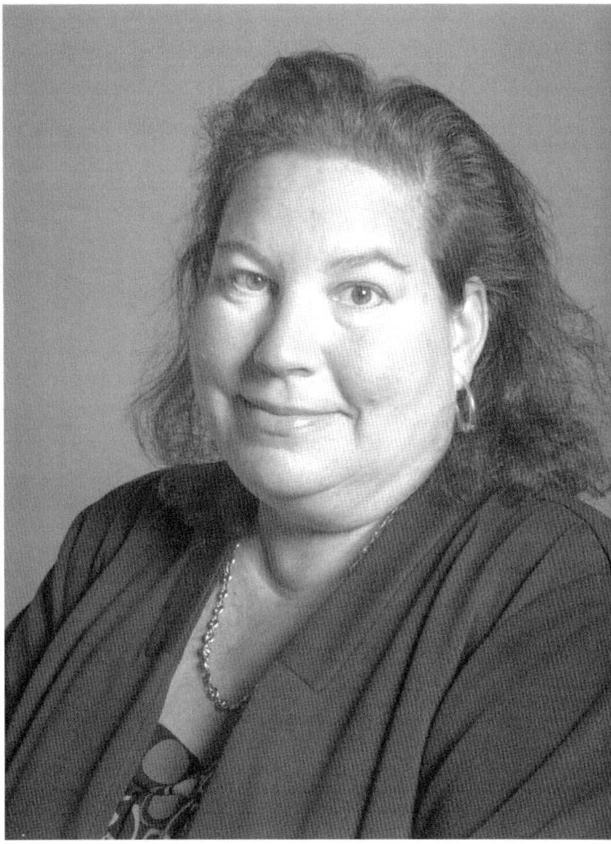

Wendy Zinn

Wendy Zinn, executive director of the YMCA of Greater Boston, moved to East Boston with her family in 1999 to start a YMCA daycare program. With over 600 children waitlisted, she opened a site at the mini mall on Bennington Street across from Shea's Beach. In 2000, City Hall solicited proposals for the reuse of a 1909 Boston-Albany engine house on Bremen Street. The handsome structure had been abandoned and rendered virtually invisible, covered in corrugated tin and surrounded by airport rental-car lots. Zinn's proposal to convert the building into a YMCA was accepted, and she embarked on a $6.5-million fundraising campaign to hire researchers, architects, and engineers. Today, the site is an architectural gem, offering daycare and afterschool programming along with a state-of-the-art fitness center. Zinn credits local residents, city councilors, and state representatives for supporting the project and helping make it happen. (Both, courtesy of Wendy Zinn.)

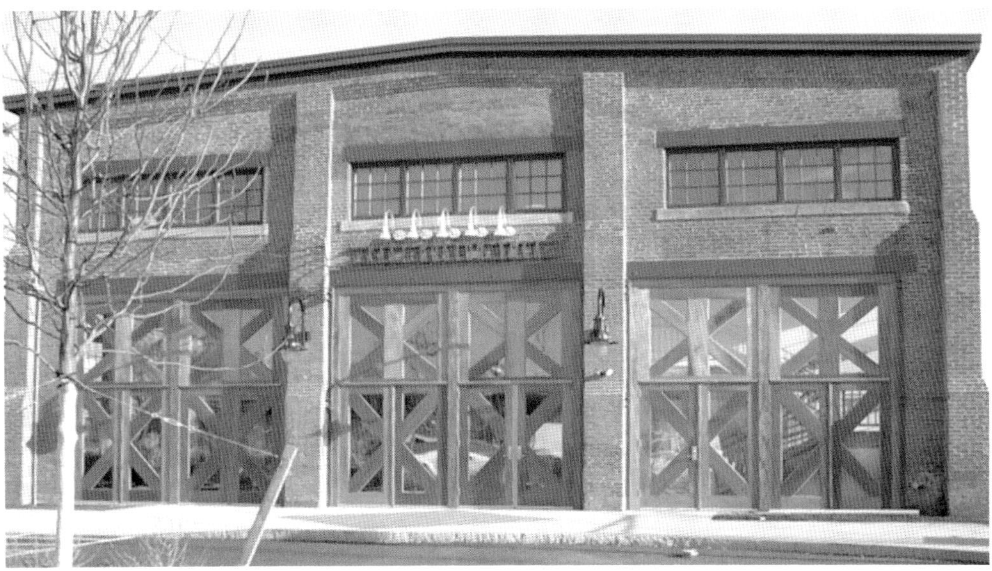

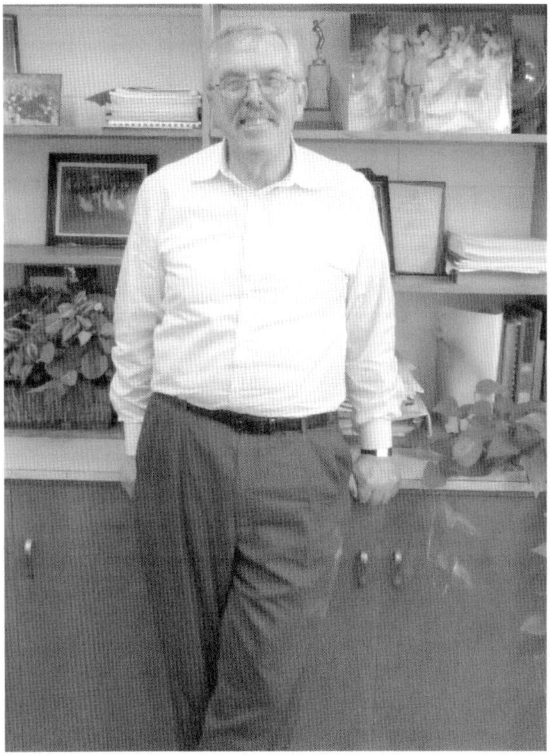

John Kelly

John Kelly, longtime director of the East Boston Social Centers, has worked in East Boston since 1970, when he was the supervisor of a youth-employment program. His father immigrated to East Boston from Scotland in 1925 and worked at the Mystic Steamship Company, living in one of East Boston's many rooming houses for maritime men before marrying. Kelly, a social worker who ran a citywide food-service program in the 1960s as part of President Johnson's War on Poverty, was hired as director of the EBSC in 1983. Incorporated in 1918, the agency faced financial difficulties by the 1980s. Kelly raised funds and redesigned daycare, senior, and youth programming. EBSC's strength, he says, is its dedicated board members. "People here are extremely active in their neighborhood. Even if they move away, they stay active." (Both, author's collection.)

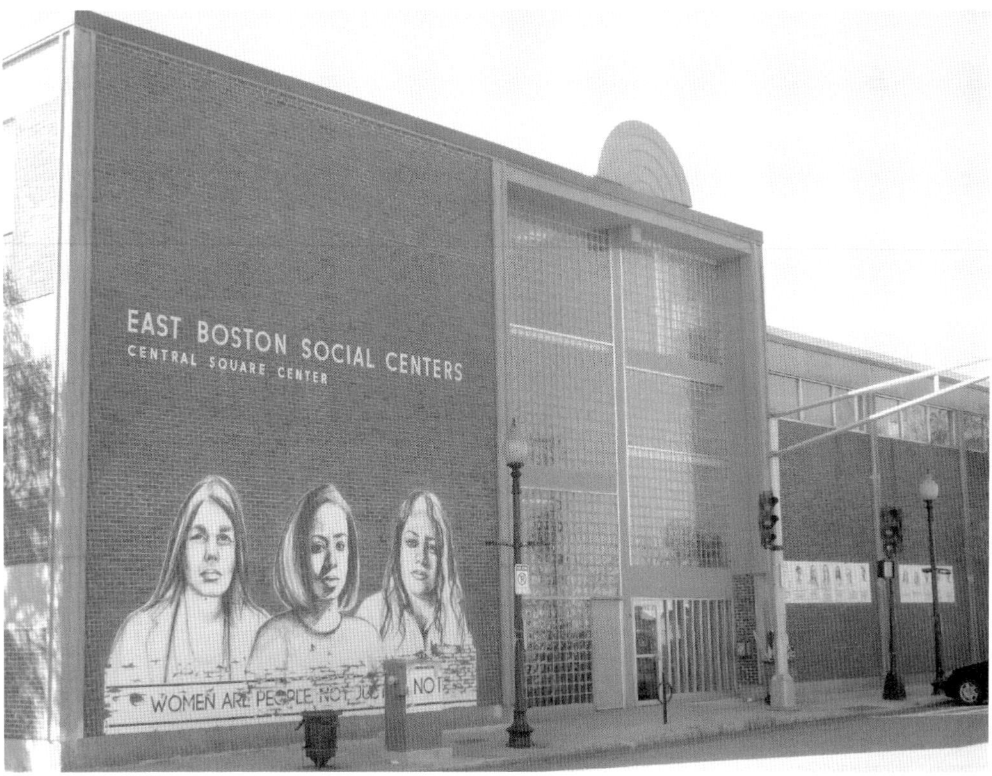

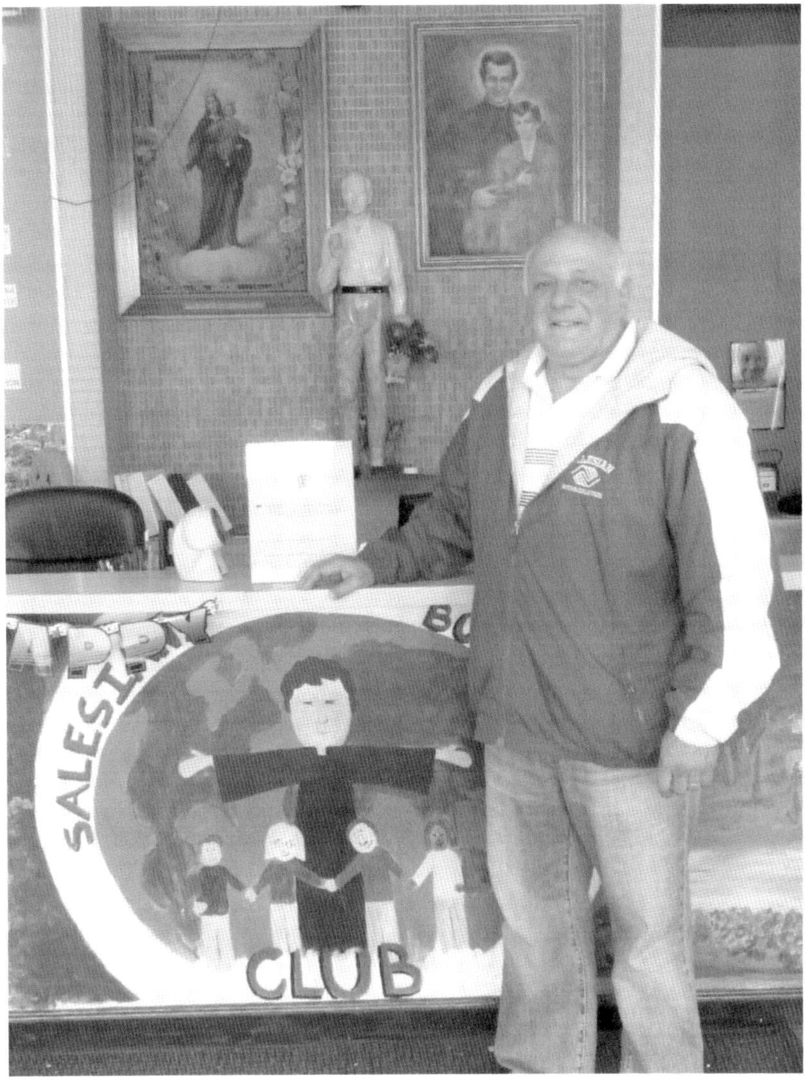

Fr. John Nazzaro
"Father John," director of the Salesian Boys and Girls Club, grew up in the 1940s–1950s on Falcon Street in a large extended family that came from Naples, Italy. He attended the Sheridan, Kennedy, and Barnes Schools, followed by Dominic Savio High School, and then worked in his family's restaurant before deciding to enter the seminary. Nazzaro notes, "The amazing thing about growing up here is that everyone is connected. Even when people move away, they still consider themselves part of East Boston. It's always part of you." After earning master's degrees in theology and education, Nazzaro was sent to teach and direct schools in Louisiana, Florida, New York, and New Jersey before being assigned to his home turf in 2006 to direct the Salesian Boys and Girls Club. He arrived at a period of uncertainty, as the club faced large debt, and Savio High School had just closed. He was able to get the club back on track financially and continued to expand services. "The kids I grew up with have grandchildren coming to the club now. There are generations of people involved. All of our staff attended the club as kids and they often have parents who attended the club as kids." Nazzaro recently came across an old wish list he made when he first became a Salesian. Although he had long forgotten about it, working at the club was on the top of his list. "It's an honor to work here. It isn't work. It's home." (Author's collection.)

Phil Giffee

Phil Giffee moved to East Boston in 1971 when hired by the Planning Office of Urban Affairs, a nonprofit affiliate of the Roman Catholic Archdiocese of Boston focused on affordable housing and neighborhood revitalization. In 1987, he founded NOAH (Neighborhood of Affordable Housing) and, with a staff of two, began offering services out of the basement of Our Savior's Lutheran Church, in collaboration with the East Boston Ecumenical Community Council. The agency built new housing where there had been vacant units or where homes had burned down. It also played a leading role in desegregating housing. Giffee notes, "There are many good people here with a sense of fairness who stood up for it. Not easy at all in the 1970s." With the guidance of an active board of local residents, NOAH evolved into a multiservice agency that builds affordable housing, offers first-time homebuyer programs, and runs a variety of environmental projects. (Author's collection.)

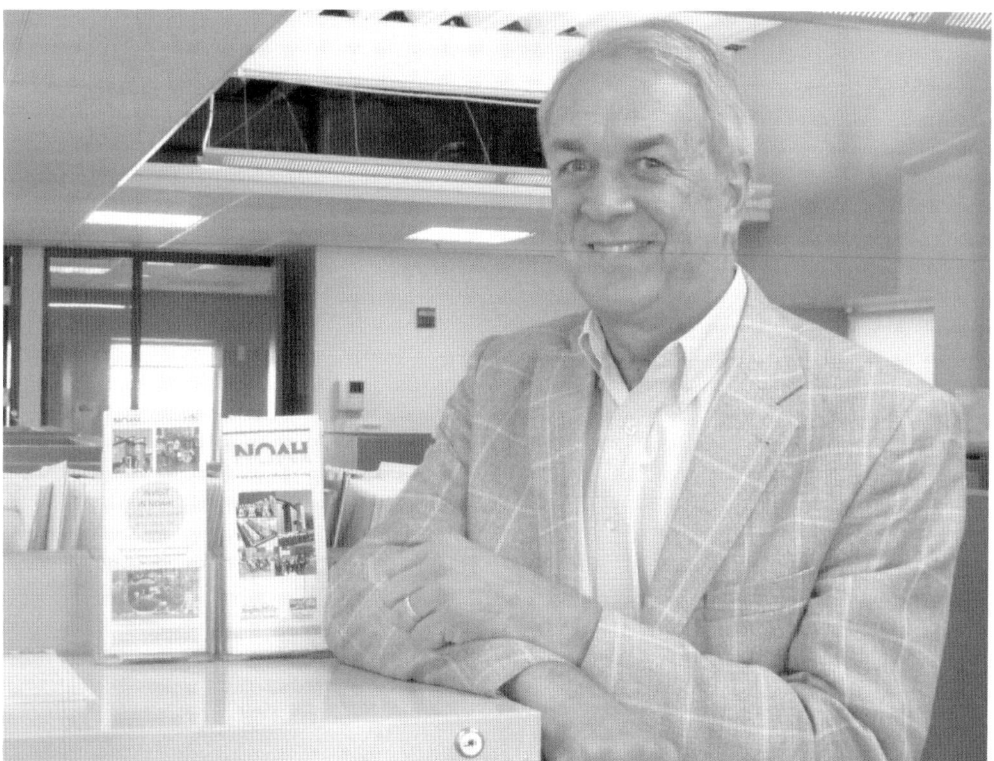

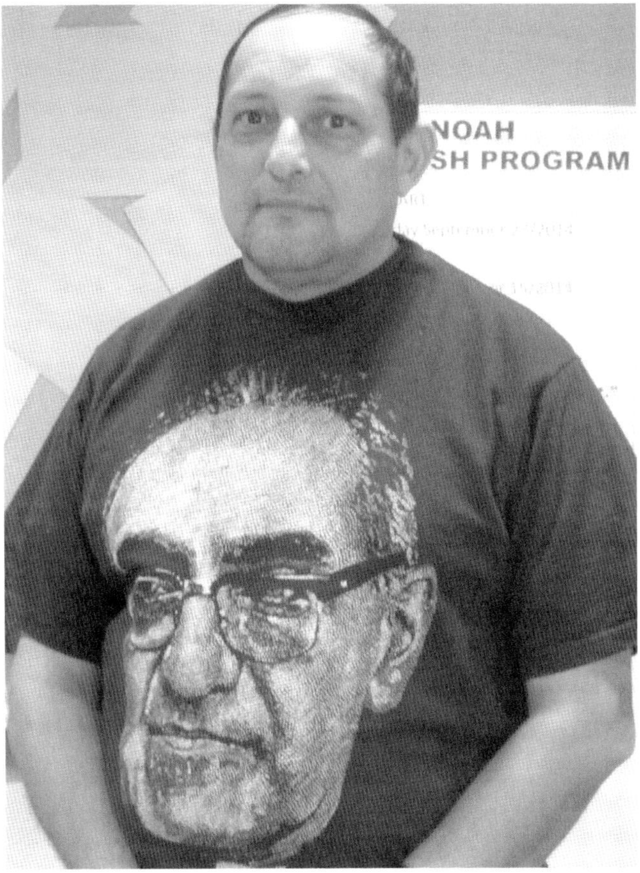

Manlio Méndez

Manlio Méndez has an interesting story of how he came to East Boston in 1990. "Since I'm Catholic, I was very active in my church in El Salvador. Our pastor, Father Mucci, was from East Boston. On his office wall, he had tons of photographs and newspaper clippings from East Boston and he always talked about how great his hometown was. Each year he would return to visit his mother, who lived at the Lyman elderly apartments. As a boy, East Boston stuck in my head as a place that must be wonderful and I knew I wanted to go there someday." Méndez's father died when he was young, and Mucci was a father figure, keeping an eye on him and encouraging him to study. Méndez became an accountant, but because of the war, he applied for a visa to the United States. When Mucci learned of this, he urged him to go to East Boston; Méndez arrived at Logan on a frigid November day when Mucci was in town visiting his mother. "It was dark at 4:30 and so cold and rainy! I took one look around and wanted to leave!" Mucci gave him a tour of East Boston, invited him to eat at his mother's apartment, and introduced him to people. "In El Salvador, everyone assumed Father Mucci must be rich, because he was the director of the nation-wide AGAPE project. He is a huge figure in El Salvador! But, when I saw his mother's simple apartment and how he slept on the couch, I realized how humble he was, and I admired him even more." Méndez got a job cleaning buildings and visited Laura Mucci regularly for the rest of her life. He became very active volunteering with his new parish, the Most Holy Redeemer, filming Mass each Sunday for broadcast on cable television, participating in the chorus, hosting a Catholic radio show, and doing church repairs such as rebuilding the kneeling benches. He met his wife at church, and they were married there. Years later, he was hired as a community organizer for NOAH. He loves his job. "I've always done community organizing with my parish, so this is a job that comes naturally to me." He and Father Mucci remain close. (Author's collection.)

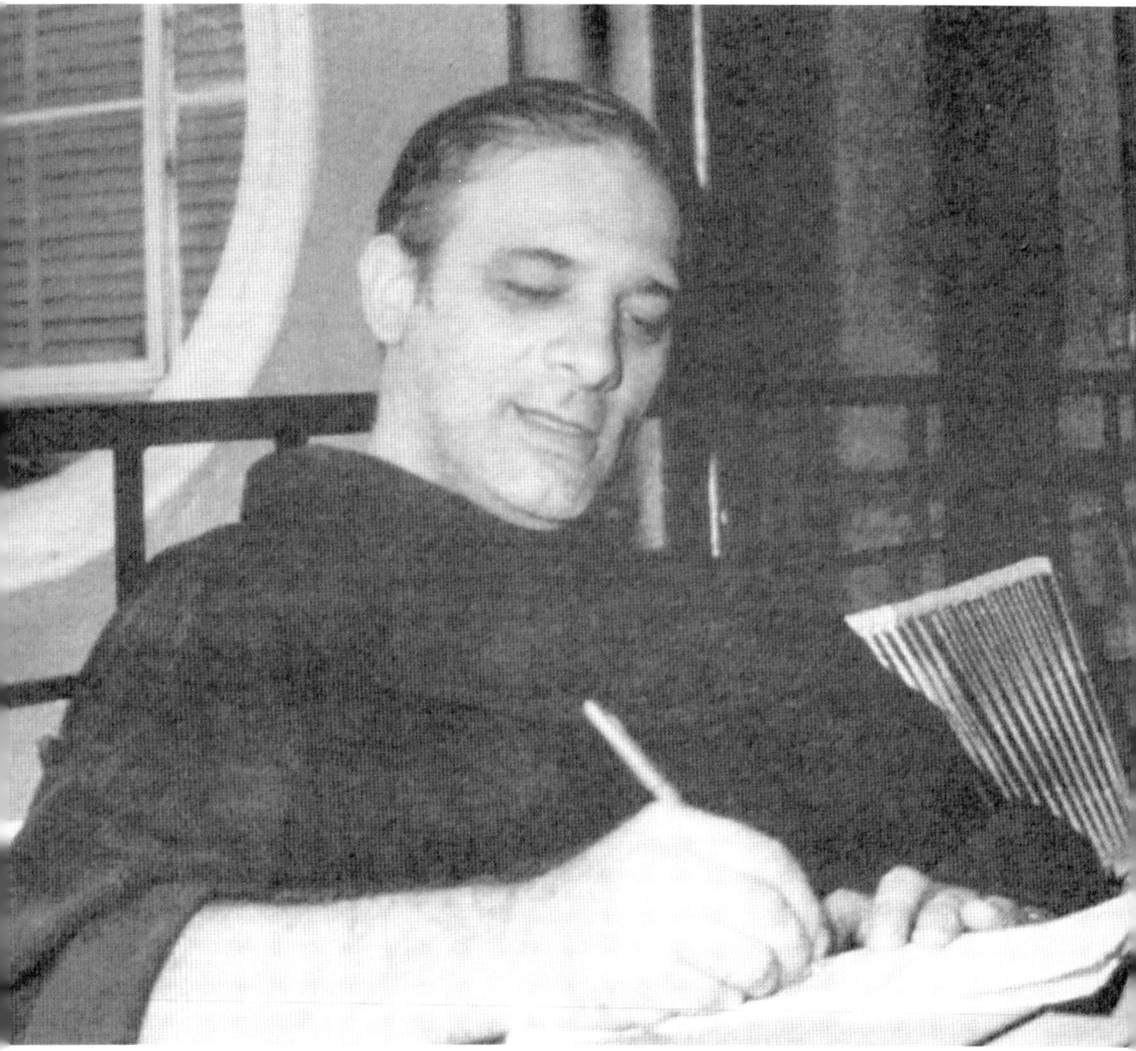

Fr. Dominic "Flavian" Mucci

Dominic Mucci grew up in East Boston and graduated from the Franciscan Seminary in Lowell, becoming ordained as a Catholic priest in 1963. In 1964, he went to work in Central America, taking the name Father Flavian. In 1967, he founded AGAPE, an association that funds community newspapers, daycare centers, schools, clinics, and job-training centers in the poorest areas of El Salvador. Mucci is famous there for his humanitarian work and has received myriad national honors and awards. (Courtesy of Manlio Méndez.)

CHAPTER FIVE

Athletic Legends

Sports have been an integral part of East Boston's history. In Colonial times, rowing, swimming, and fishing were popular in summer, and people skated, sleighed, and ice-fished on the frozen harbor in the winter. In 1843, Guy Haynes described athletic games occurring "within a large fenced piece of land on Chelsea Street." These included "running, leaping, wrestling, vaulting, bowling, football, rifle shooting, and balloon ascension." In the 1880s, boxing, baseball, rowing, and yachting were popular, with hundreds of yachts docked at the Jeffries Yacht Club. East Boston's Columbia Rowing Association produced award-winning rowers, including the 1893 City of Boston champion, Charles Stafford, and the 1904 Olympic gold medalist Frank Greer. Youth camped and fished on nearby islands, rowing back and forth. They also traveled to "the country"—unpopulated areas of Orient Heights and Revere—to pick berries, hunt birds, hike, and cut hockey sticks from trees in the woods. Horse-drawn sleigh races were held on Chelsea Street from the mid-1800s into the early 20th century.

Before the days of widespread car ownership, television, and hyper-commercialized professional sports, inner-city neighborhoods created their own entertainment. In winter, youth ice-skated at Wood Island Park or on flooded vacant lots. In summer, they jumped off the piers to swim in the oily but cool Boston Harbor, dodging underwater pier piles and jellyfish. A favorite summer pastime of East Boston children was "running in the hydrants," which happened when somebody's mother had the right kind of wrench to illegally open a fire hydrant. Like a miraculous geyser bursting forth from the desert, thousands of gallons of water would cascade in arcs across residential streets, with dozens of children running back and forth in their bathing suits and underwear, shrieking with delight under the spray. The streets of East Boston were the "plazas" of the community, with children and men playing a variety of sports while the neighborhood watched and cheered from windows and stoops.

Sal LaMattina remembers the vibrant street culture of "the Marsh," a neighborhood between Chelsea, Porter, Paris, and Gove Streets. There was once a marsh there, but when LaMattina was growing up, the Marsh referred to a playground lot near what is now the Paris Street Pool. "It was the best neighborhood in the world because there were two schools there—the Lyman and the Alighieri—plus the Paris Street Gym, so there were tons of kids playing on the streets. All the families knew each other and all the kids went to school together. After school, the streets and the lot where the Paris Street Pool is now would be packed with 40 or 50 kids playing softball and other games. On each corner, there was a different group of kids that hung out, based on age and what street you lived on." Everyone rooted for the teams of their own street or block. Bocce courts were commonly built in backyards and community victory gardens, and racquetball was one of the most popular sports. Men organized racquetball and handball clubs and played at the Paris Street Gym, the Good Will House, the Shea's Beach wall, and any other available vertical surface. Neighborhood ice-hockey teams competed at Porrazzo Rink, a place where many East Boston children learned to skate.

Kids of all ages engaged in street games such as stick ball, steps, errors, and relievio, along with bases, dodge ball, manhunt, and other competitions. Like clockwork, someone would yell, "Car!" and youth playing in the street would instinctively step aside to let a car pass, then resume their places without missing a beat. In the early-to-mid-20th century, men played competitive games in neighborhood lots. At the time, many East Boston streets were segregated according to the region or town of Italy where residents originated. Bocce, racquetball, and other games were played by teams representing towns from Naples, Calabria, Sicily, and so forth—a dynamic also seen today among East Boston's Latino soccer leagues. Joe Incagnoli Jr., whose father was the champion sandlot athlete Joe "the Shoemaker" Incagnoli of Jeffries Point, explains: "The 40s and 50s were days of ethnically-charged competition among teams from Boston's immigrant communities, and it was akin to a religious experience for the crowd when my father co-captained the East Boston Tornadoes to a win over the South Boston Chippewas or Dorchester's Saunders Post. In the sports boom that followed World War II, semi-pro teams and leagues proliferated nationwide. In Boston, these events drew crowds of up to 10,000—especially during the Sandlot championships at Fenway Park—which got heavy newspaper and radio coverage." Joe "Shoes" was one of a number of exceptional East Boston athletes who left school to work and help their families during the Great Depression, thereby losing opportunities for college or professional sports careers. Lots of young men fought in World War II and returned to blue-collar jobs on weekdays and neighborhood sandlots and gyms on nights and weekends. Many sandlot athletes were as good as the professionals of their day, playing football, basketball, baseball, racquetball, and hockey simply because they loved it. The best players were known throughout the city, and many East Boston sandlot athletes made the neighborhood proud.

Before the 1972 passage of Title IX, which prohibits gender discrimination in education programs receiving federal funding, there were comparatively few athletic opportunities for females. For centuries, sports had been considered a male realm; so when Trinity House director Caroline Orr started a summer camp for girls to teach them to hike, swim, fish, and camp, it was unprecedented. Females were taught that participating in sports was unladylike and "harmful to the uterus." This is why, when the Paris Street Gym began offering "married ladies exercise classes" around the turn of the 20th century, they recruited the governor's wife, First Lady Clara Bates, to lead the class as a way to encourage women to exercise. Joanne Pomodoro, a lifelong East Bostonian and winner of 10 world championships in racquetball, remembers the stigma of liking sports as a girl in the 1960s: "I played softball when I was 13 years old. I was so embarrassed to carry my glove to the field. I'd put it in a bag. I'd pass my friends and then get to the field and it was like magic—I loved competing! I loved the natural high of an athlete! I always wanted to be a professional in sports. I taught myself how to play tennis, going to the wall court at Shea's Beach, although in East Boston, we didn't have the kinds of sports that suburban kids had."

Dance was an athletic pursuit deemed appropriate for girls, and many East Boston youth in the 1950s and 1960s attended dances at local school gyms and church halls. Others joined the Our Lady of the Assumption Cadets, a competitive marching drum and bugle corps, color guard, and drill team. Here, boys marched in precision while playing band music, and girls were color guards who maneuvered large flags in synchronicity or drill-team members who performed choreographed marching formations taught by former military personnel. City, state, and national competitions were held for drum and bugle corps, and the Assumption Cadets won their share of awards. For many East Bostonians, sports were a hobby that brought personal growth and pride. For certain individuals, sports brought them professional careers, fame, and fortune.

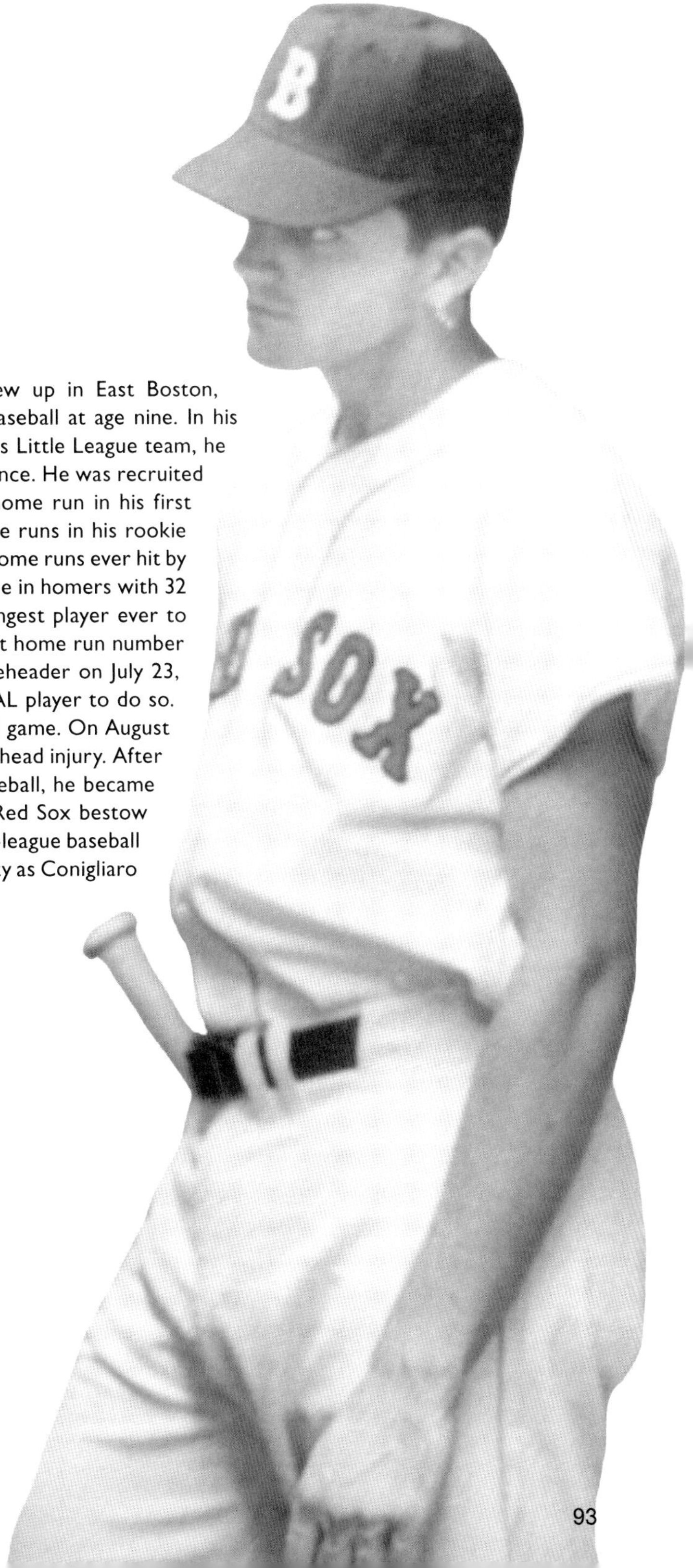

Anthony Conigliaro (1945–1990)

Red Sox legend Tony Conigliaro grew up in East Boston, where he first played Little League baseball at age nine. In his very first at-bat for the Orient Heights Little League team, he hit a home run over the center-field fence. He was recruited by the Red Sox at age 19 and hit a home run in his first at-bat at Fenway Park. He hit 24 home runs in his rookie season, setting a record for the most home runs ever hit by a teenager. He led the American League in homers with 32 the following year, becoming the youngest player ever to win the home-run crown. When he hit home run number 100, during the first game of a doubleheader on July 23, 1967, he was only 22—the youngest AL player to do so. He hit number 101 in the day's second game. On August 18, 1967, his career was cut short by a head injury. After trying unsuccessfully to return to baseball, he became a sports broadcaster. Each year, the Red Sox bestow the Tony Conigliaro Award to a major-league baseball player who bravely overcomes adversity as Conigliaro did. (Courtesy of BPL.)

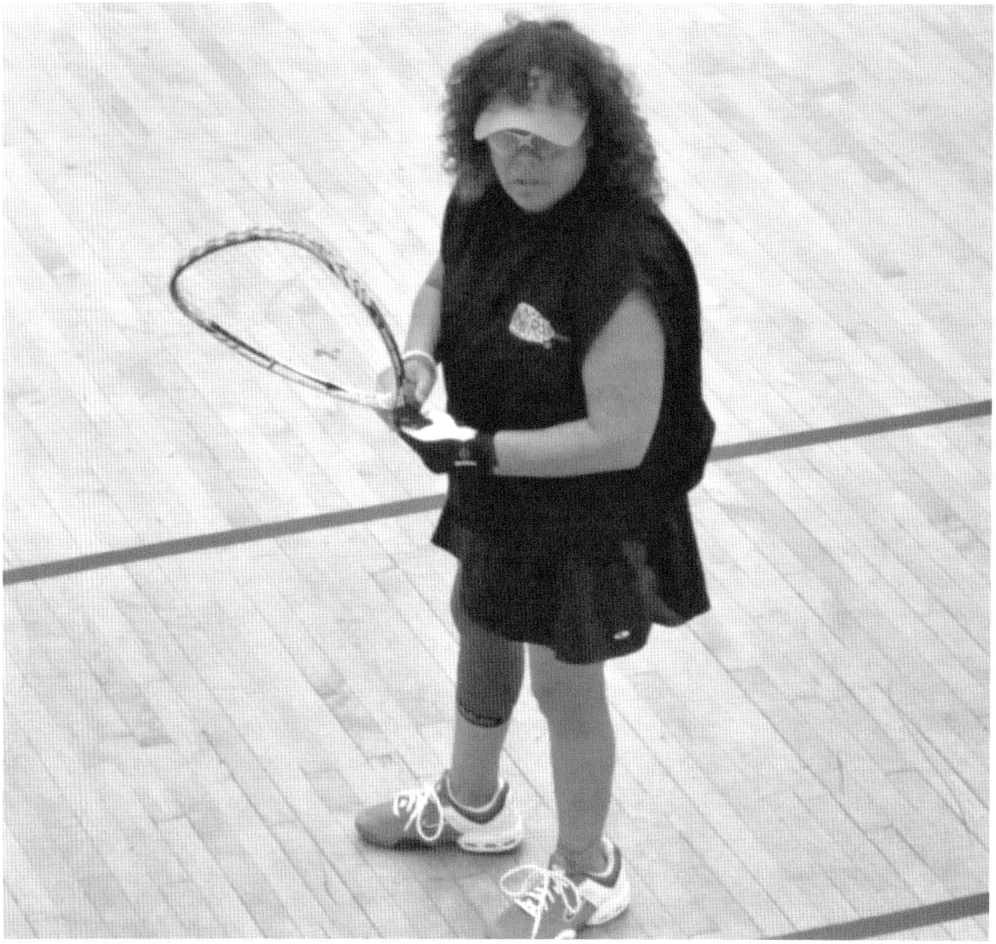

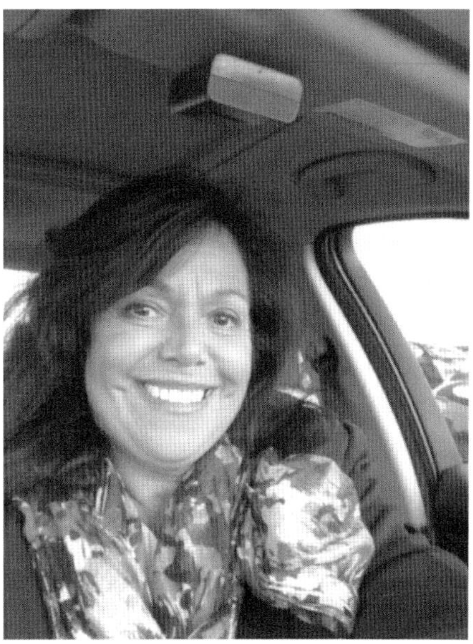

Joanne Pomodoro
With family roots in East Boston since 1912, senior racquetball world champion Joanne Pomodoro grew up in the Bennington Street house where she now lives. As a teenager, she played softball, taught herself tennis, and learned fencing from her father. At the age of 34, she began to play racquetball, going from a novice to an open tournament player in three years. She won her first world championship in 1995 and has won 10 world titles. (Both, courtesy of Joanne Pomodoro.)

Joe "the Shoemaker" Incagnoli (1918–2000)

Tired of being bullied as a kid, Joseph Incagnoli Sr. began to work out and play sports at the Paris Street Gym. He first came to the public's attention playing with the 1938 undefeated Texas Club baseball team and honed his sporting skills at White Stadium until the outbreak of World War II. After two tours of military duty in Europe, he resumed his sports career in East Boston. With trophies from over 50 championship teams in baseball, softball, bocce, and football, he received the 1954 Milano Trophy for Best Sandlot Athlete in Boston. He was cocaptain of the East Boston Tornadoes, leading them to numerous championships in Fenway Park. Named "the One Man Tornado" by the *Boston Post* in 1952, Incagnoli practically lived at the Paris Street Gym and in 1966—at age 48—was the Class A Doubles champion in handball. (Courtesy of Joe Incagnoli Jr.)

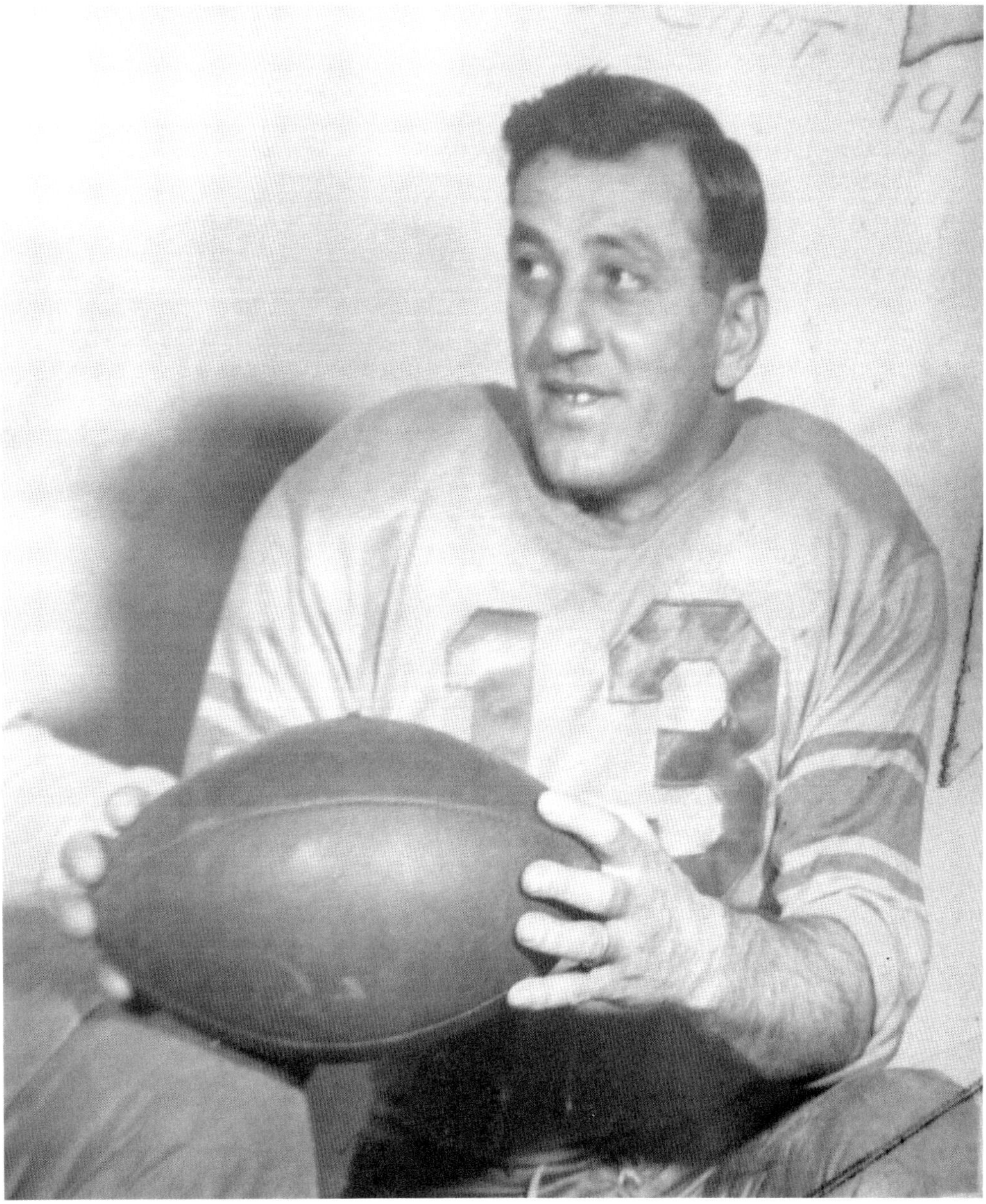

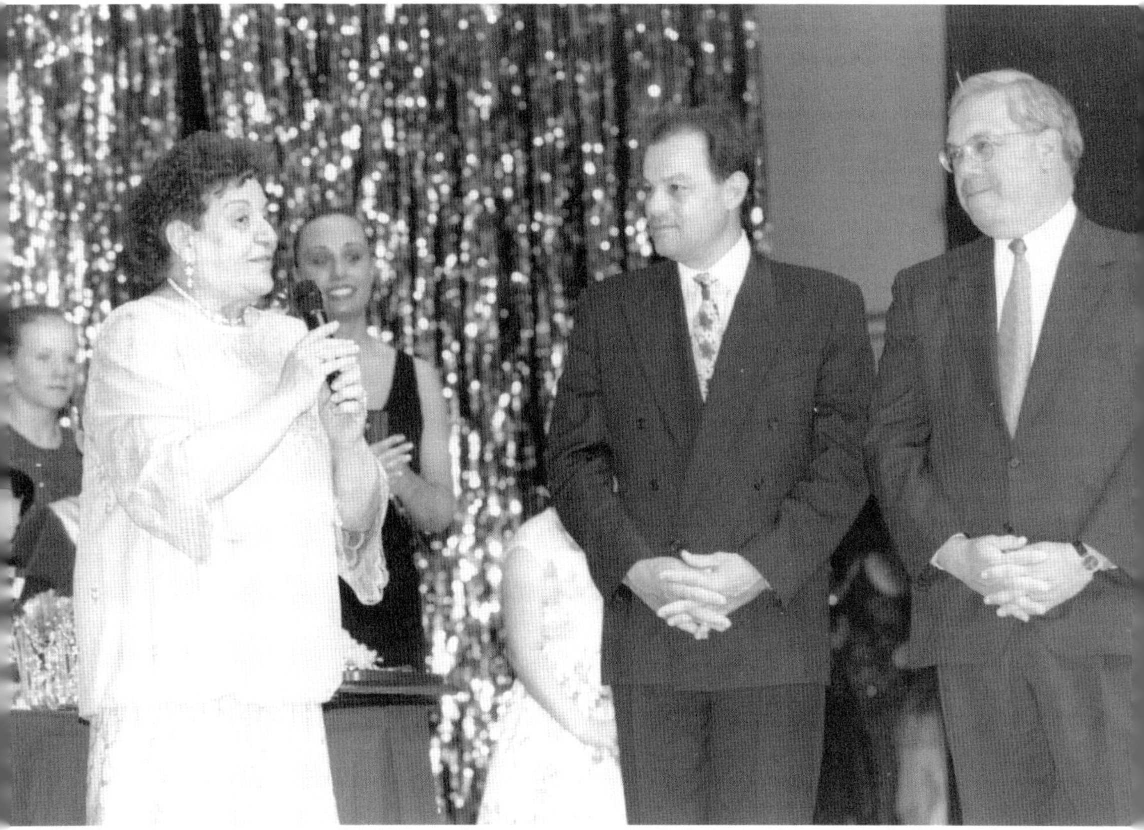

Eleanor Rubino

After graduating from East Boston High School, Eleanor Rubino studied at the School of American Ballet in New York. In 1947, she opened the Rubino Academy of Performing Arts in East Boston, where she lived and taught dance for over 60 years. In 1997, she was inducted into the Massachusetts Dansport Hall of Fame. She is former president of the Dance Teachers' Club of Boston and former performing arts director for the National Council of Dance. At age 86, she still teaches ballet part-time at her daughter Paula Terenzi's dance complex in Malden. (Courtesy of Paula Terenzi.)

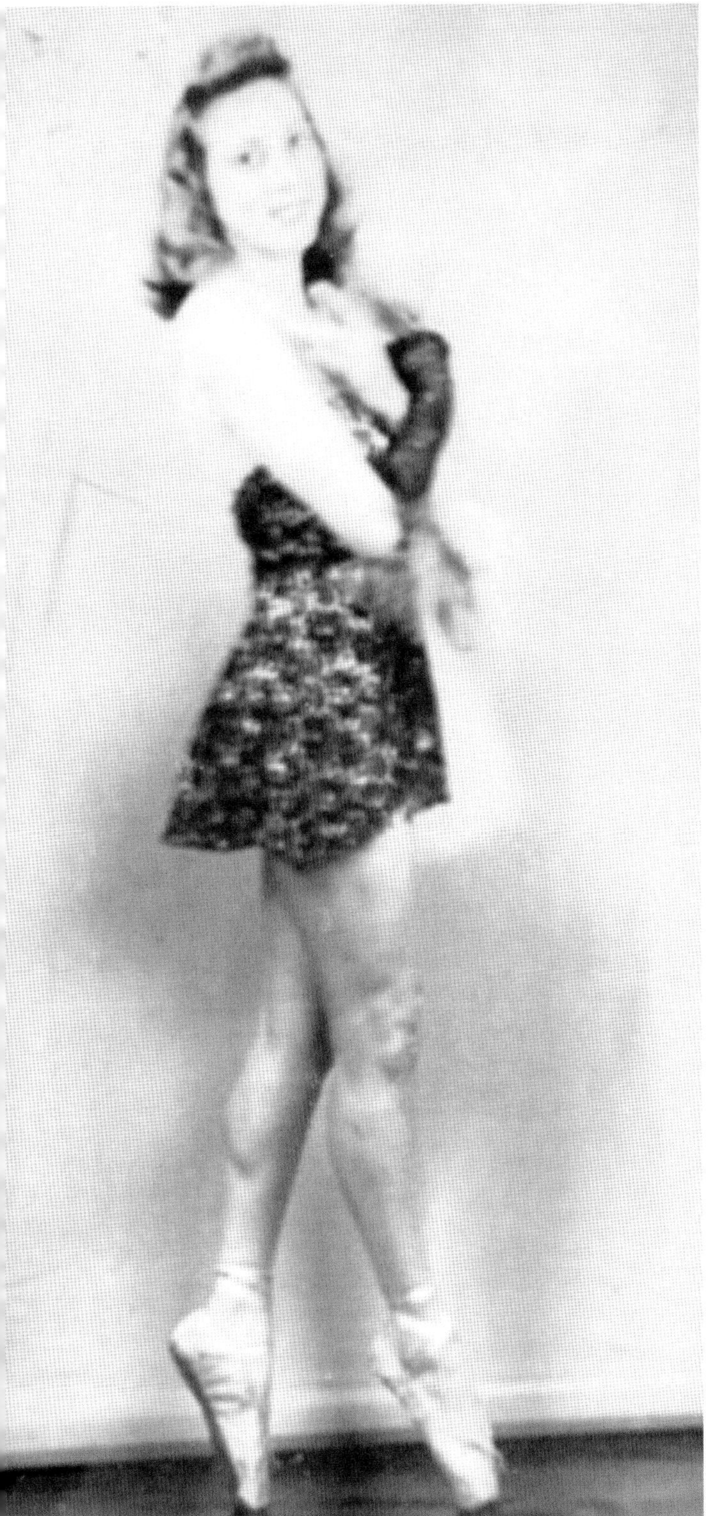

Lillian Arden Chiampa Laurano (1918–2001)
Elidia Chiampa grew up on Chelsea Street and studied dance in Boston and New York, adopting the stage name "Lillian Arden." In 1937, she opened the Lillian Arden Chiampa Dance School in East Boston, which she directed for more than 60 years. She taught generations of children and was president of the Dance Teacher's Club of Boston. Her school's spring recitals, held at John Hancock Hall, were legendary, with hundreds of parents lined up at dawn each year to get tickets. (Courtesy of Michael Laurano.)

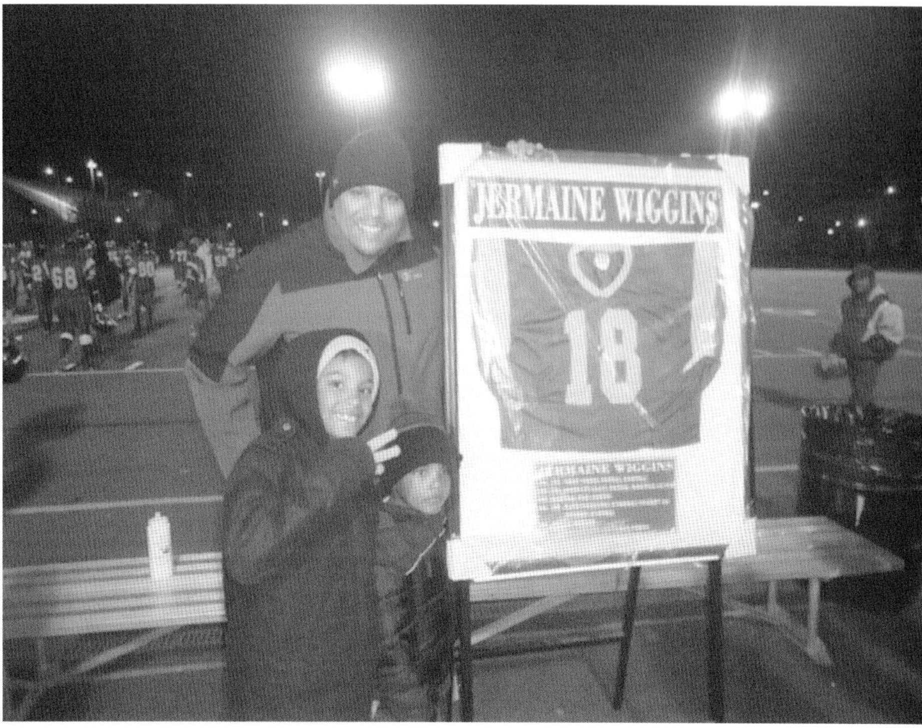

Jermaine Wiggins

Jermaine Wiggins grew up on Saratoga, Brooks, and Marion Streets playing street football. "We'd play two on two and get on the sidewalk when cars passed." He got his sports foundation at the Salesian Boys and Girls Club and played football at East Boston High, graduating in 1993. While at the University of Georgia, he was signed by the New York Jets and joined the New England Patriots in 2000, where he earned a Super Bowl ring in Super Bowl XXXVI. He also played with the Indianapolis Colts, Carolina Panthers, Minnesota Vikings, Jacksonville Jaguars, and Florida Tuskers. He is now a sports analyst on NESN and hosts a Boston radio show. "East Boston made me the man I am," he says. "Growing up in a blue collar, hard-working community taught me that when life knocks you down, you have to get back up and keep going." (Courtesy of John Lynds.)

Frank Greer (1879–1943)

Born and raised in East Boston, Frank Greer was a member of the East Boston Amateur Athletic Boat Club. On July 30, 1904, at the age of 25, he won the Olympic gold medal in rowing. He went on to win many more rowing competitions and later became sheriff of the Charles Street Jail in Boston. (Courtesy of Chris Flynn.)

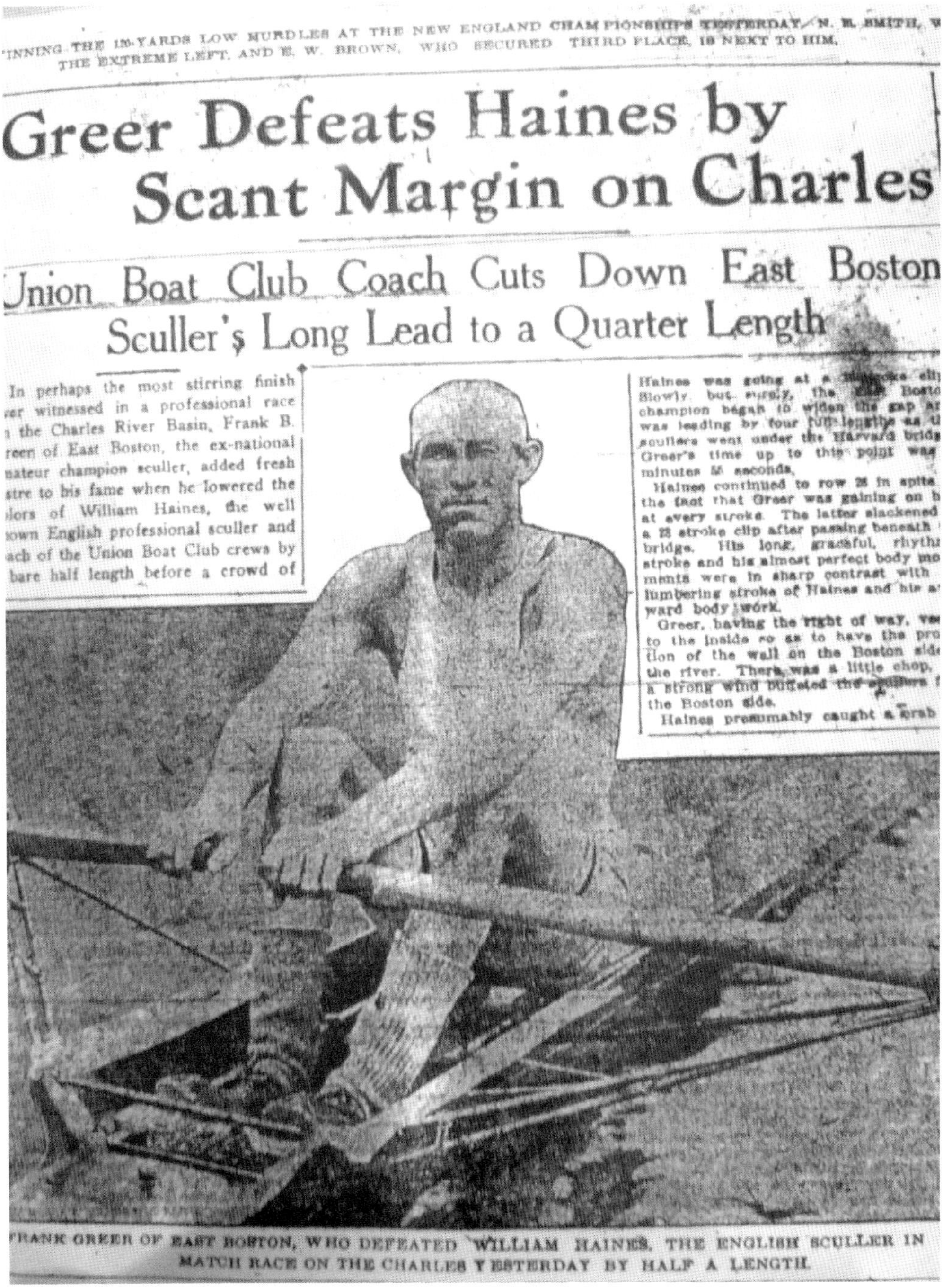

'INNING THE 120-YARDS LOW HURDLES AT THE NEW ENGLAND CHAMPIONSHIPS YESTERDAY. N. R. SMITH, W THE EXTREME LEFT, AND E. W. BROWN, WHO SECURED THIRD PLACE, IS NEXT TO HIM.

Greer Defeats Haines by Scant Margin on Charles

Union Boat Club Coach Cuts Down East Boston Sculler's Long Lead to a Quarter Length

In perhaps the most stirring finish ver witnessed in a professional race n the Charles River Basin, Frank B. reen of East Boston, the ex-national nateur champion sculler, added fresh stre to his fame when he lowered the olors of William Haines, the well nown English professional sculler and ach of the Union Boat Club crews by bare half length before a crowd of

Haines was going at a [illegible] stroke cli Slowly but surely, the East Bosto champion began to widen the gap an was leading by four full lengths as th scullers went under the Harvard bridg Greer's time up to this point was minutes 55 seconds.

Haines continued to row 28 in spite the fact that Greer was gaining on h at every stroke. The latter slackened a 28 stroke clip after passing beneath bridge. His long, graceful, rhythm stroke and his almost perfect body mo ments were in sharp contrast with lumbering stroke of Haines and his a ward body work.

Greer, having the right of way, ve to the inside so as to have the pro tion of the wall on the Boston side the river. There was a little chop, a strong wind buffeted the scullers f the Boston side.

Haines presumably caught a crab

FRANK GREER OF EAST BOSTON, WHO DEFEATED WILLIAM HAINES, THE ENGLISH SCULLER IN MATCH RACE ON THE CHARLES YESTERDAY BY HALF A LENGTH

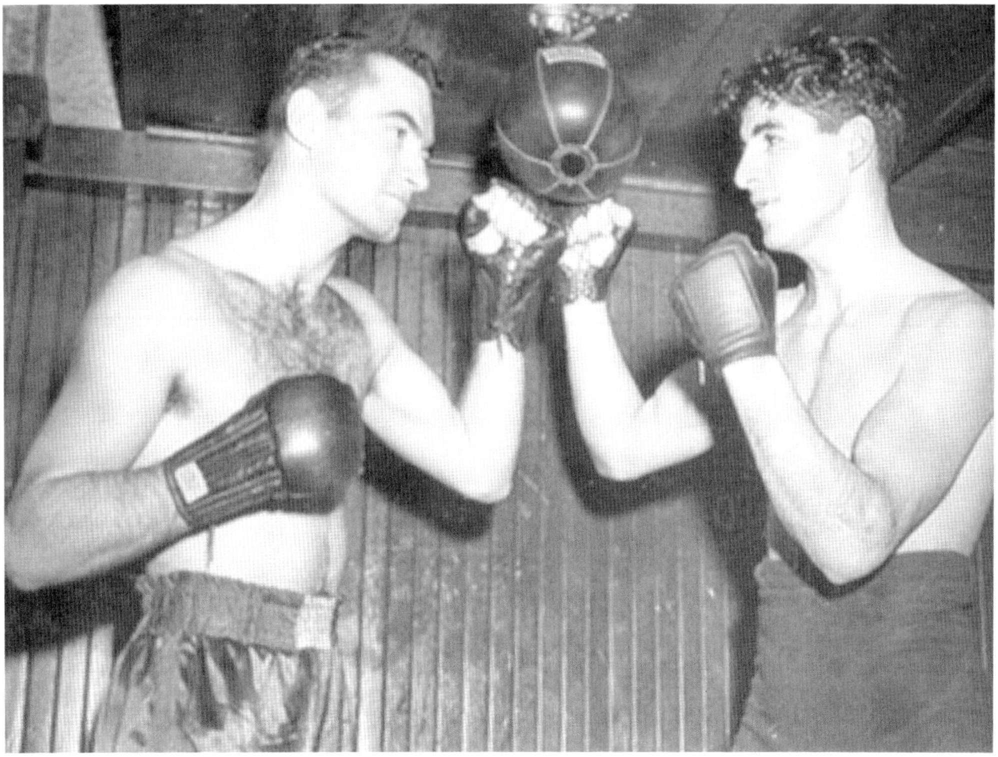

Andrew "Iggy" Vaccari (1930–2014)

Raised in East Boston, Iggy Vaccari (left) became the New England lightweight boxing champion in 1950. A well-known professional boxer, he received a master's degree in social work from Boston University and was a teacher in South Boston for many years. (Courtesy of John Mastrangelo.)

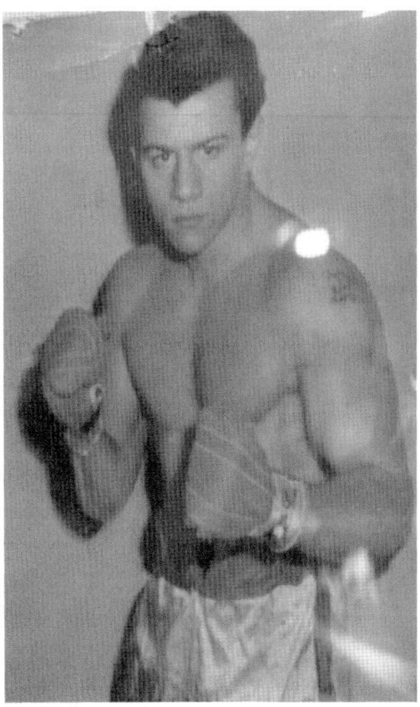

John Mastrangelo

Former professional boxer John Mastrangelo was born at 136 Bennington Street. After graduating from the Barnes School, he worked in construction until his brother-in-law Iggy Vaccari encouraged him to box. Mastrangelo won the Golden Gloves New England Amateur Championship and turned pro in the welterweight class while still a teenager. From age 16 to 20, he sparred with world champions like Tony Demarco and Paul Pender, but his career was cut short by illness. Later, he opened Kelly's Pub, which specializes in Italian food despite its Irish name. (It is named after William Kelly Square—the official name of Central Square—the pub's first location.) While Kelly's is now run by his son, Mastrangelo is always there helping out and greeting customers. (Courtesy of John Mastrangelo.)

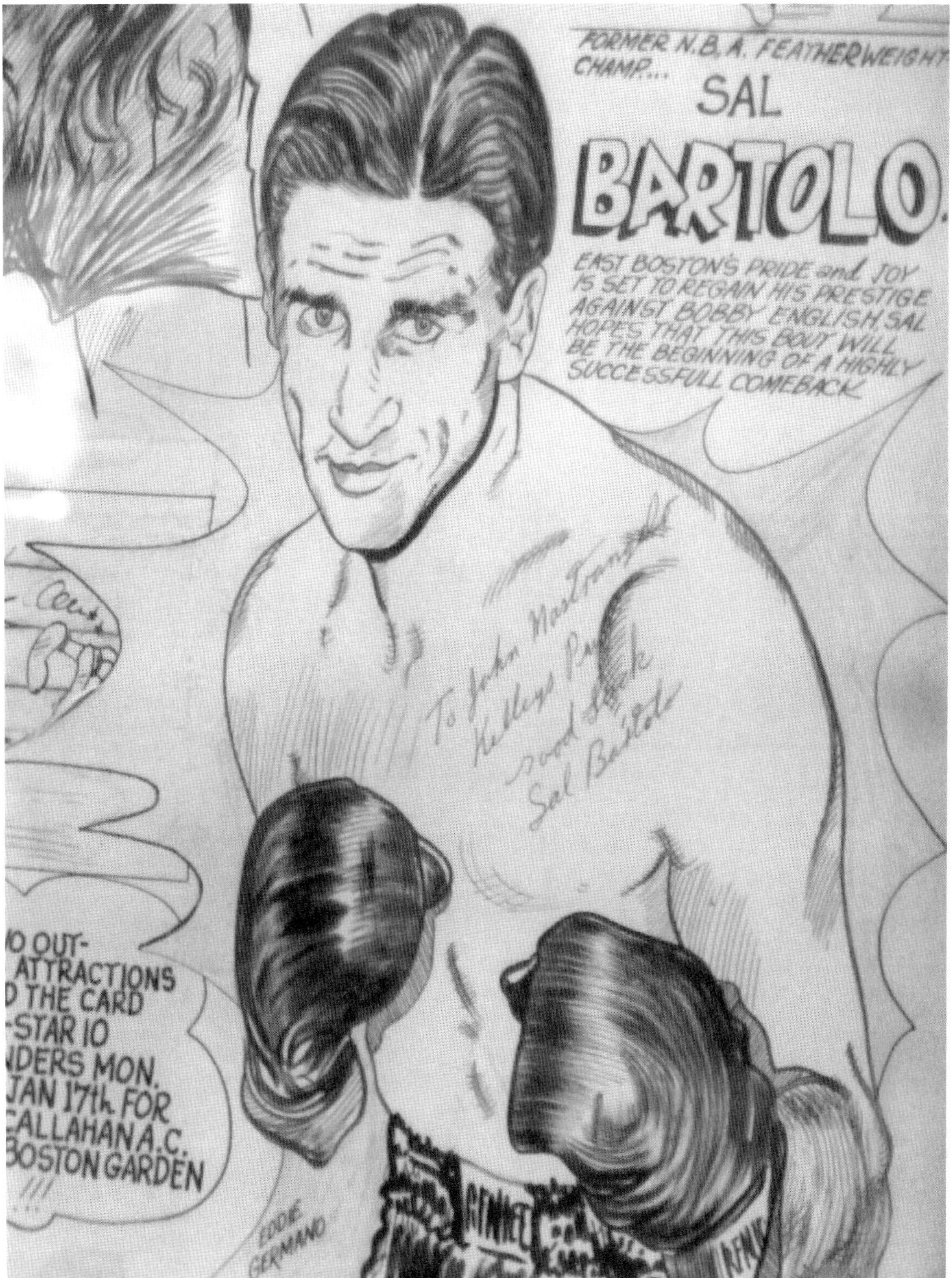

Sal Bartolo (1917–2002)

Salvatore Interbartolo, or "Sal Bartolo," was known as "the Pride of East Boston" when he became the National Boxing Association Featherweight Champion from 1944 to 1946. He had a stellar amateur career, winning the New York Golden Gloves Award in the bantamweight division in 1937. (Courtesy of John Mastrangelo.)

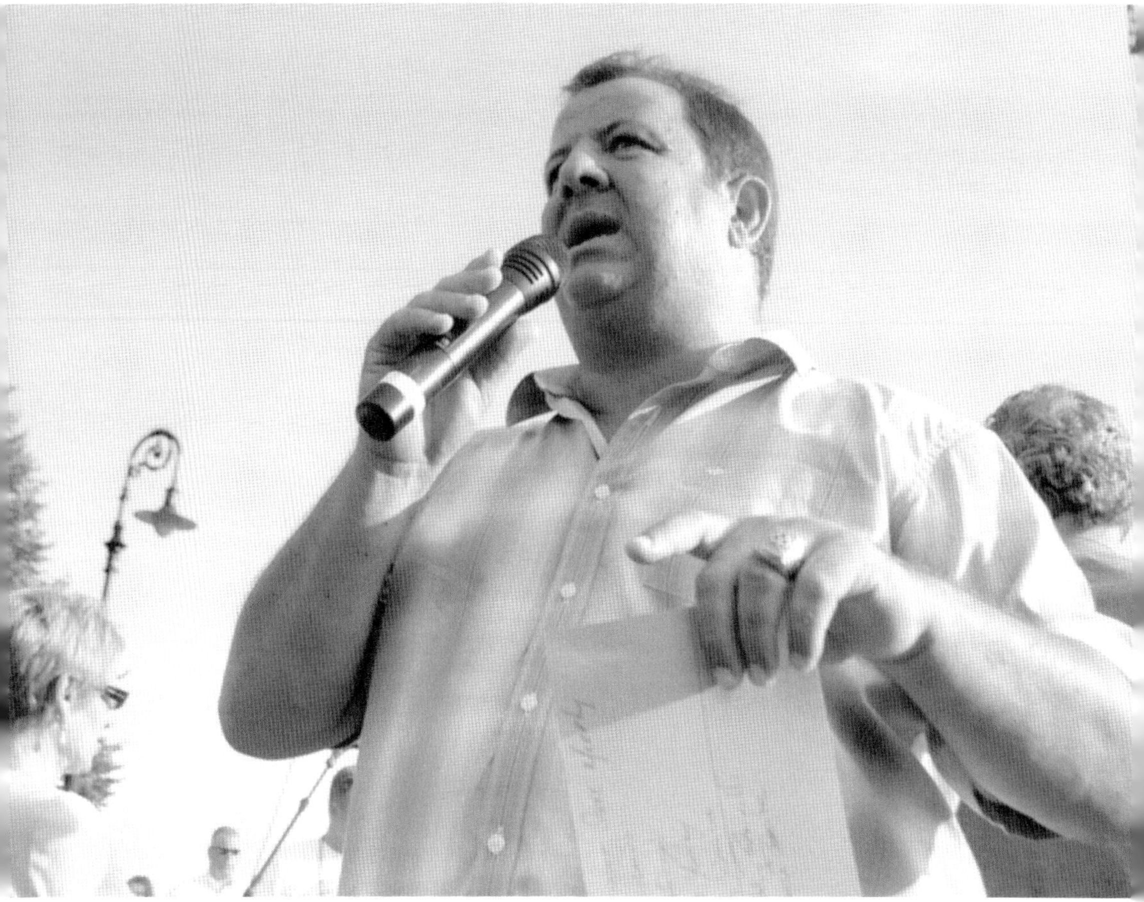

Edward Palladino

Eddie Palladino is "the Voice of the Boston Celtics." A native of East Boston and lifelong Celtics fan, Palladino has served as arena voice for the Celtics since 2003. He attended Dominic Savio High School and Emerson College, earning a bachelor's degree in communications. (Courtesy of John Lynds.)

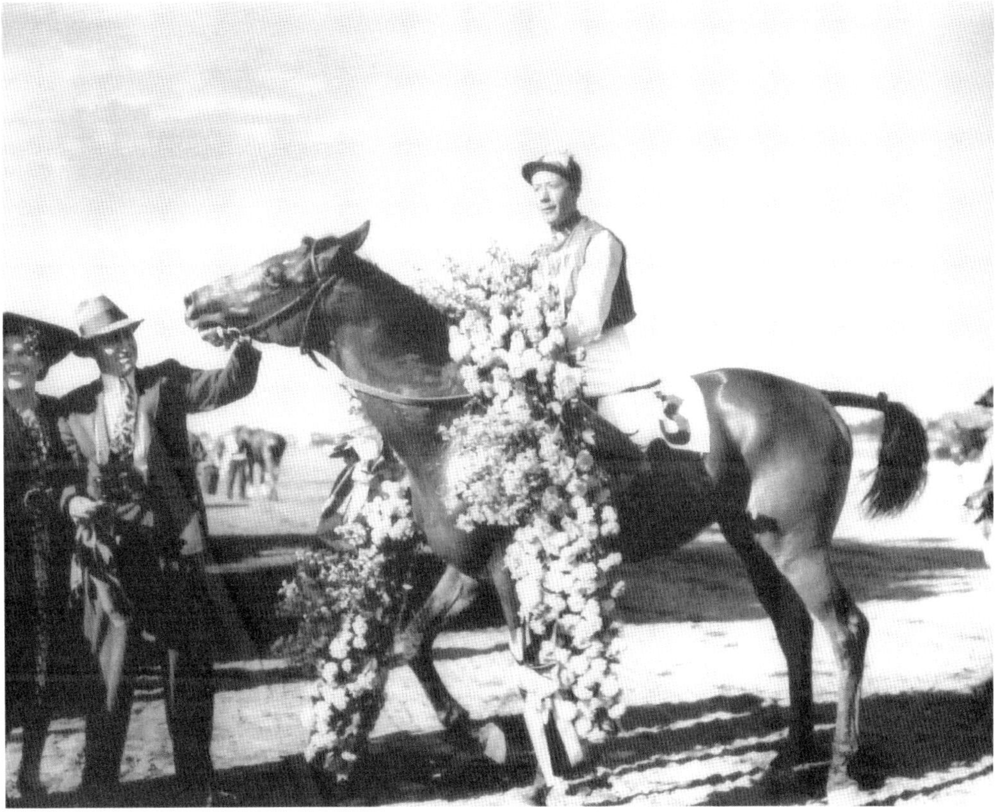

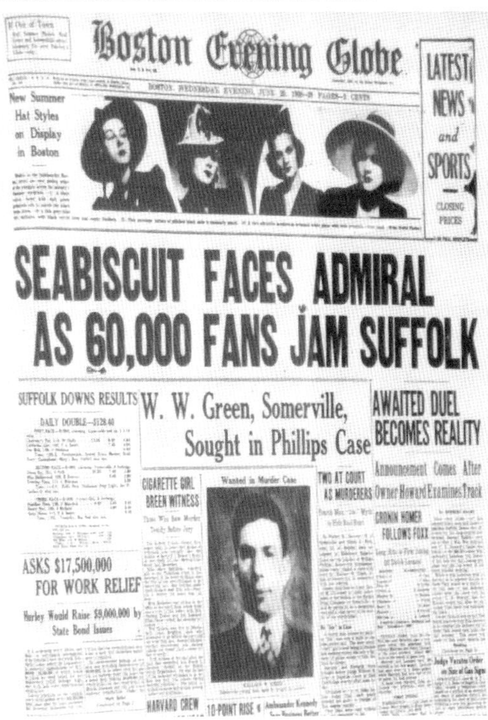

Boston Evening Globe

New Summer Hat Styles on Display in Boston

LATEST NEWS and SPORTS

CLOSING PRICES

SEABISCUIT FACES ADMIRAL AS 60,000 FANS JAM SUFFOLK

SUFFOLK DOWNS RESULTS

DAILY DOUBLE—$128.40

W. W. Green, Somerville, Sought in Phillips Case

AWAITED DUEL BECOMES REALITY

Announcement Comes After Owner Howard Examines Track

CIGARETTE GIRL GREEN WITNESS

Wanted in Murder Case

TWO AT COURT AS MURDERERS

CRONIN HOMER FOLLOWS FOXX

ASKS $17,500,000 FOR WORK RELIEF

Hurley Would Raise $9,000,000 by State Bond Issues

HARVARD CREW

10-POINT RISE

Ambassador Kennedy

Judge Vacates Order

Seabiscuit (1933–1947)

Legendary racehorse Seabiscuit was discovered at East Boston's Suffolk Downs Racetrack and later won the MassCap race there that made him internationally famous. Winning America's heart as the ultimate underdog, Seabiscuit was the biggest celebrity in the United States at the height of his career, receiving more news coverage in 1938 than movie stars, athletes, or President Roosevelt. Historic Suffolk Downs first opened in July 1935 and was one of the country's most modern and beautiful racetracks at the time. (Both, courtesy of Suffolk Downs.)

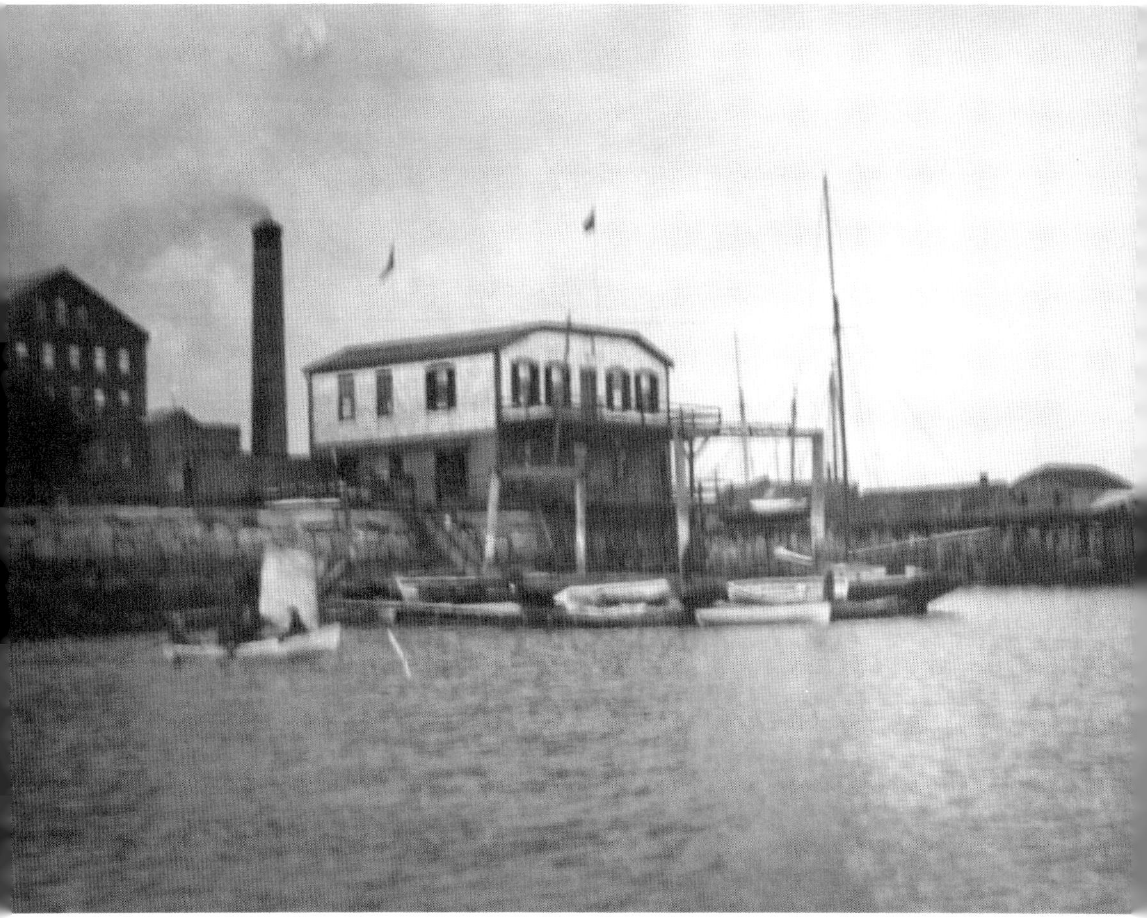

Jeffries Yacht Club

Founded in 1872 and chartered in 1876, the Jeffries Yacht Club is the oldest chartered yacht club on the East Coast. Named after John Jeffries, a founding member, it was a Boston Brahmin institution and playground for the wealthy, housing dozens of grandiose yachts. Until the mid-20th century, the club excluded Irish and other immigrant populations from membership. Today, Irish, Italians, and other ethnic groups are allowed to join, and the club is thriving, although membership still requires an invitation from existing members. (Courtesy of Jeffries Yacht Club.)

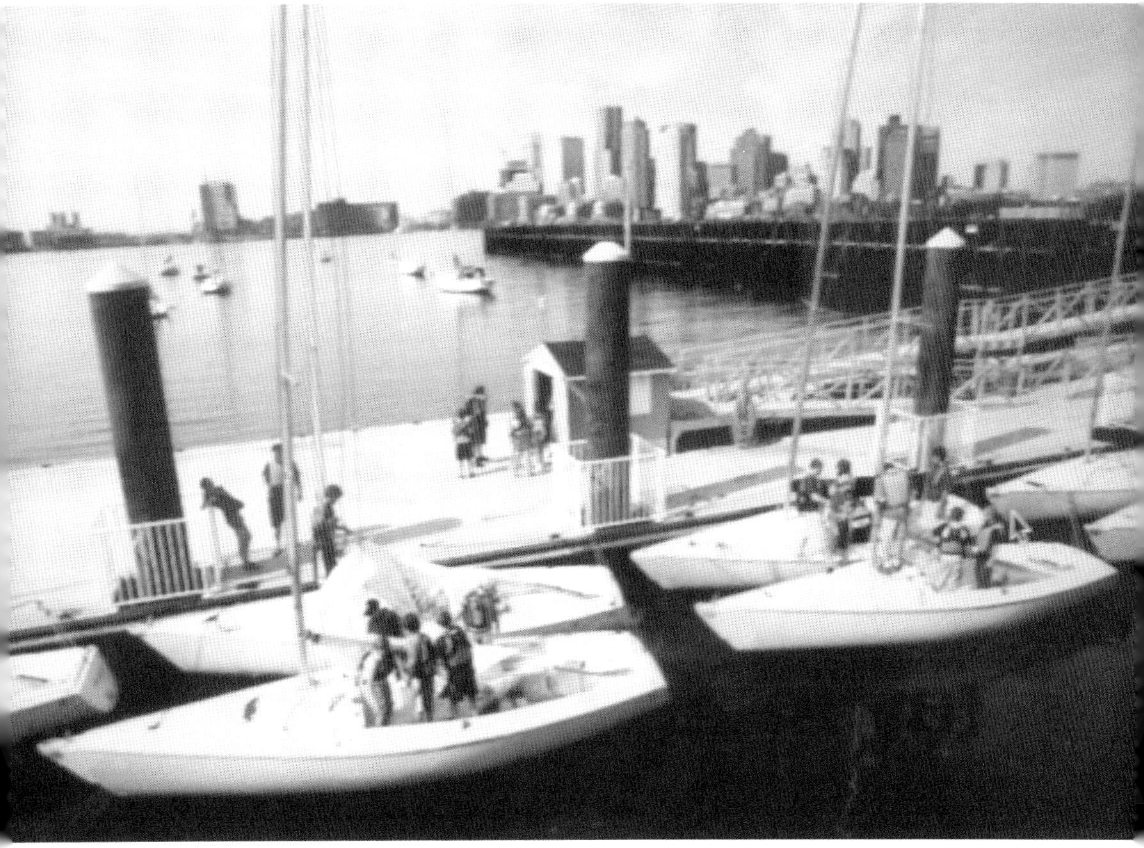

Piers Park Sailing Center

The nonprofit Piers Park Sailing Center was established in 1998, initially funded by Massport as part of airport mitigation for the community. It is the most affordable sailing center in Boston and, while serving all ages, specializes in youth sailing programs with outreach to underserved youth. Most of the Piers Park youth instructors are East Boston youth who have become talented sailors. The center is nationally recognized as the best program for disabled sailors in the country and was the training ground for Maureen McKinnon-Tucker, the gold medalist in sailing at the 2008 Beijing Paralympic Games. (Courtesy of Piers Park Sailing Center.)

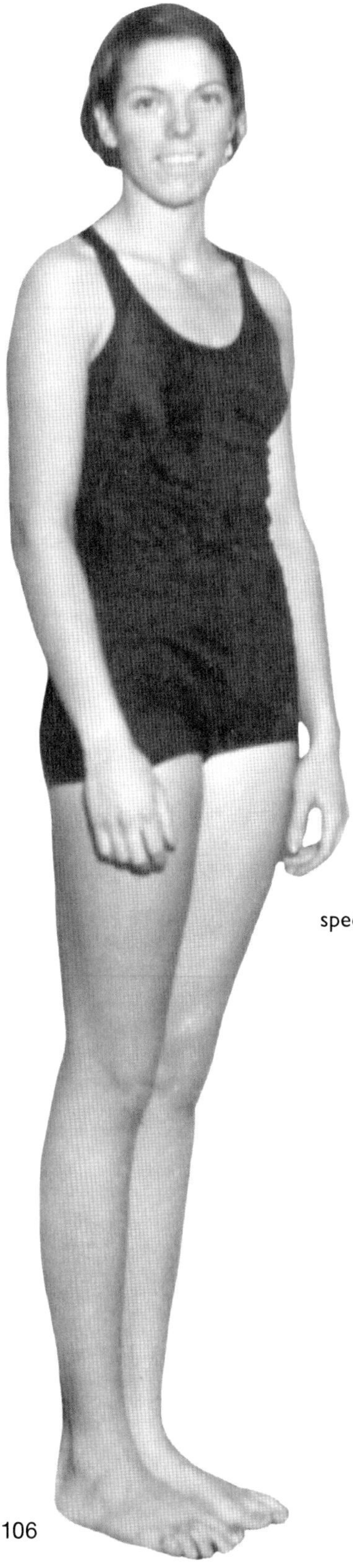

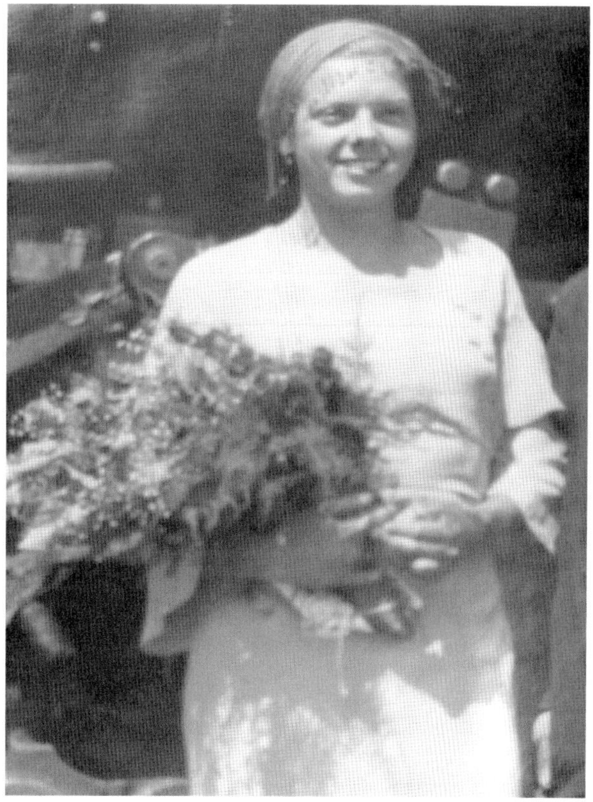

Helen Johns (1914–2014)

Born in East Boston, Helen Johns won a gold medal in swimming in the 1932 Summer Olympics, setting a new world record at the age of 17. She later became a swim coach and special-education teacher. (Both, courtesy of BPL.)

CHAPTER SIX

Taking Care of Business

East Boston can trace its business history back to the 1630s. Its first permanent resident, Samuel Maverick, owned large tracts of land throughout New England and was a wealthy trader. In contrast to the somber and self-denying Puritans, his home was filled with exotic teas, rich tobaccos, fine porcelain, stylish furniture, and other luxuries acquired through trading in ports along the East Coast. Although disliked by the Puritans, Maverick was widely respected for his business savvy and key role in making Colonial Boston financially successful. In the 1760s, another long-term Noddle's Island resident, Henry Howell Williams, developed a lucrative hay-production business by acquiring a state-of-the-art screw press for compacting the islands' salt-marsh grasses into bales of hay. It was the only such technology in America at the time, giving him a near monopoly on the export of hay to the North and South. In 1834, John Brown opened East Boston's first large-scale manufacturing business—the Boston Sugar Refinery—employing more than 100 workers. This attracted new industries to the area, leading to the development of new technologies in the community, including one of the first suspension railway systems ever built and some of the earliest steam-powered trains in the nation (the Eastern Railroad Company). East Boston's clipper-ship industry generated countless maritime-related jobs and made Boston a major international shipping port. As clipper ship production drew to a close and steamships flourished in the late 1800s and early 1900s, East Boston's wharves were transformed into railroad docks with freight haulers, coal yards, machine shops, and ship-repair facilities. Factories that produced sugar, pottery, linseed oil, glue, lamps, garments, shoes, and candy, along with a cotton mill, fish-processing plants, and other industries, were sources of local jobs for the growing immigrant population.

Many of East Boston's new immigrant families started successful businesses of their own. Patrick and Joseph Kennedy parlayed the wealth they earned in East Boston into political power and more lucrative economic ventures. Other immigrants of the early 20th century established businesses that are still thriving today, including Santarpio's, Boston's oldest pizzeria, established in 1903, and Jeveli's, Boston's oldest Italian restaurant, opened in 1924. Betty Ann's Food Shop, said to be Boston's oldest continually operating bakery, was established in 1933, although the location was a bakery as far back as 1899. Since the early 1990s, new predominantly Latino immigrants have opened diverse businesses, including restaurants, food markets, bakeries, real-estate offices, clothing stores, gift shops, Spanish bookstores, and cultural enterprises such as the Veronica Robles Cultural Center, founded by Veronica Robles of Mexico, and the New England Gallery Of Latin American Art, founded by Franz Israel of Peru.

East Boston has always been the site of many mom-and-pop businesses run by generations of the same family, with owners often living upstairs or next door to their stores. In the mid-1800s and early 1900s, Central and Maverick Squares were East Boston's major commercial districts, filled with retail shops and wholesale distributors. Porter Street looked much like Boston's Haymarket does today, lined with pushcarts, tents, and stands selling fresh fruits, vegetables, fish, meat, and poultry. With its tall, graceful trees and trolleys running up and down from Maverick Square to Chelsea, Meridian Street was the grandest thoroughfare in town, sporting the neighborhood's most prominent banks, enticing stores, opulent meeting halls, stylish theaters, and elegant homes. When residential development burgeoned in Orient Heights around the turn of the 20th century, businesses extended to Bennington Street, Day Square, and Orient Heights. Today, all of these areas remain busy commercial districts. Since 1995, the East Boston Main Streets initiative, a public-private partnership, has helped small businesses to historically restore their façades and signage, while the city has reintroduced vintage street lights and flower planters in commercial zones. A number of innovative businesspeople living in the neighborhood have invested their money to restore historic buildings. Among them are artists Melissa and John Tyler, who renovated the long-abandoned 1936 Welfare Building, converting it into loft space and a business incubator with a café and small shops on the first floor. The East Boston Community Development Corporation, under the longtime direction of Albert Caldarelli Sr., has repurposed numerous historic buildings in the community, including the conversion of an old brassiere factory (156 Porter) and gumball factory (150 Orleans) into housing and the restoration of a 1924 firehouse (260 Sumner) into a new home for the community arts center ZUMIX.

East Boston's business districts have changed over time, reflecting demographic and economic trends. This phenomenon is exemplified by the historical metamorphoses of Maverick Square, a once tranquil shore resort in the mid-1800s that grew to be a bustling commercial district in the early and mid-1900s. After deteriorating into a run-down crime vicinity in the 1970s and 1980s, it was restored to an attractive and thriving area in the 2000s. A large decline in East Boston's industrial jobs, combined with the growing allure of the suburbs—with single-family homes, spacious yards, and quality school systems—caused a major exodus of longtime East Boston residents between the 1960s and 1980s. This, in turn, affected local retail shops, many of which went out of business. With numerous vacant homes and storefronts, the neighborhood's tax base decreased and city services declined. City councilor Sal LaMattina recalls what it was like growing up at that time: "A lot of people moved out in 1974–1978, when federally mandated busing started in the schools. There were tons of abandoned buildings and vacant lots. The parks were terrible. The railroad tracks on Bremen Street were filled with garbage." Still, many longtime residents and businesses refused to give up on East Boston. They chose to stay and worked hard to improve the community they loved. In 1989, at a time of prevalent negativity about East Boston, LaMattina founded an annual event called Eastie Pride Day to celebrate the community's positive aspects. He explains, "Eastie Pride Day brought together local bands, dance troupes and other local performers. It was organized by local volunteers and supported with donations from local businesses and community organizations." Despite East Boston's problems, there was much for residents and businesses to be proud of, including the close-knit nature of the community. Realtor Tony Giacalone notes, "If you get a flat tire in East Boston, you'll have 17 people offering to help fix it."

Today, the East Boston Neighborhood Health Center is the community's largest employer, followed by Massport, but small businesses still abound. Their owners describe East Boston as a small town or village where many customers are known on a first-name basis. The compact, pedestrian-friendly nature of the neighborhood's shopping districts keeps the commercial areas bustling. Michael Laurano, whose family ran small businesses in East Boston from 1904 to 2011, describes the special rapport between East Boston proprietors and their customers: "It isn't just a business relationship. We knew and cared about the families. I had clients whose grandparents were customers of my grandfather." While this dynamic is rare in today's era of big-box stores and chain restaurants, it still exists among many East Boston businesses.

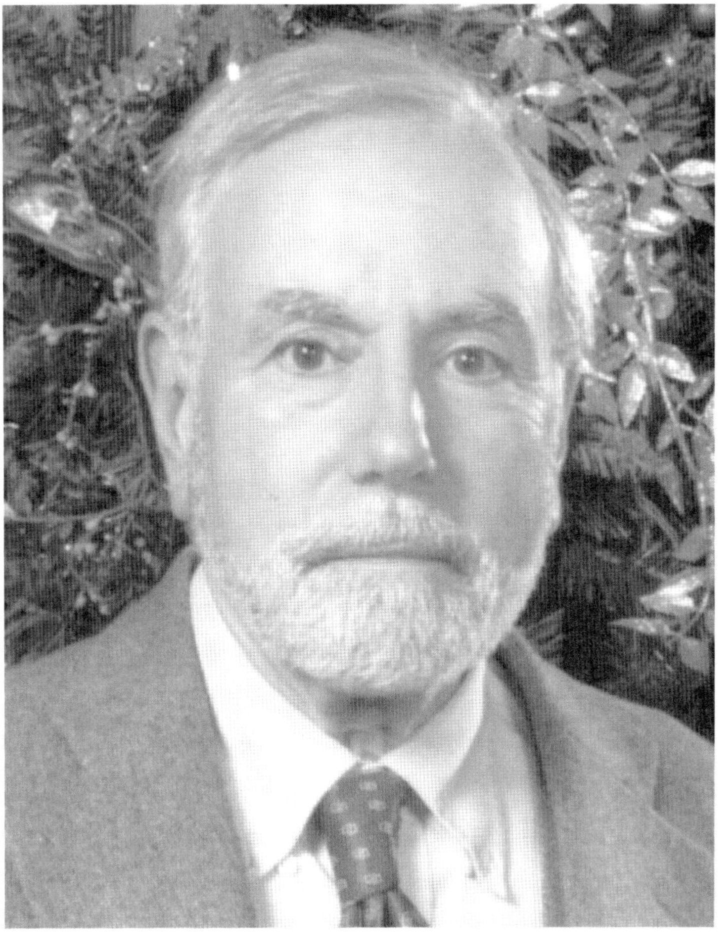

Michael Laurano III

The family of Michael Laurano III, of Laurano Insurance, came from Italy to the North End in the late 1880s, relocating to East Boston in 1902. They moved to 20–23 Chelsea Street when the block was known as Doctor's Row, and horse-sleigh races were held on the street in the winter. From 1907 until the 1920s, Laurano's great-grandfather Gaetano Laurano ran a meat shop in the lower level of the family home. In 1914, his grandfather Michael Laurano was appointed to the Boston Fire Department as one of only four Italians on the city's force of 4,000 firefighters. Seeing firsthand the devastation caused by fires and other catastrophic events, he opened an insurance agency in East Boston in 1922, which was later run by his son and grandson. Michael Laurano III remembers playing in the office as a boy: "Other kids played doctor, I played notary public. I always knew I would go into the same line of work as my father and grandfather. I started having clients before I graduated from college." Laurano's maternal grandfather, Rocco Ciampa (who Anglicized his name to Chiampa), had a barbershop at 3 Meridian Street from 1904 until the 1940s. Laurano's mother, Elidia Chiampa, founded the Lillian Arden Chiampa School of Dance in East Boston. In 1968, together with Victor Casaburi, Laurano formed the East Boston Historical Society. Despite collecting an impressive array of historical photographs, documents, and oral histories, there was sadly little interest at the time. "There weren't enough people to help do the work. The old people had neither the ability nor the interest in those pursuits. They didn't care about immigration history. The young people weren't very educated and those who were moved away." The historical society closed shop, but Laurano is still a wealth of information about historic East Boston. (Courtesy of Michael Laurano.)

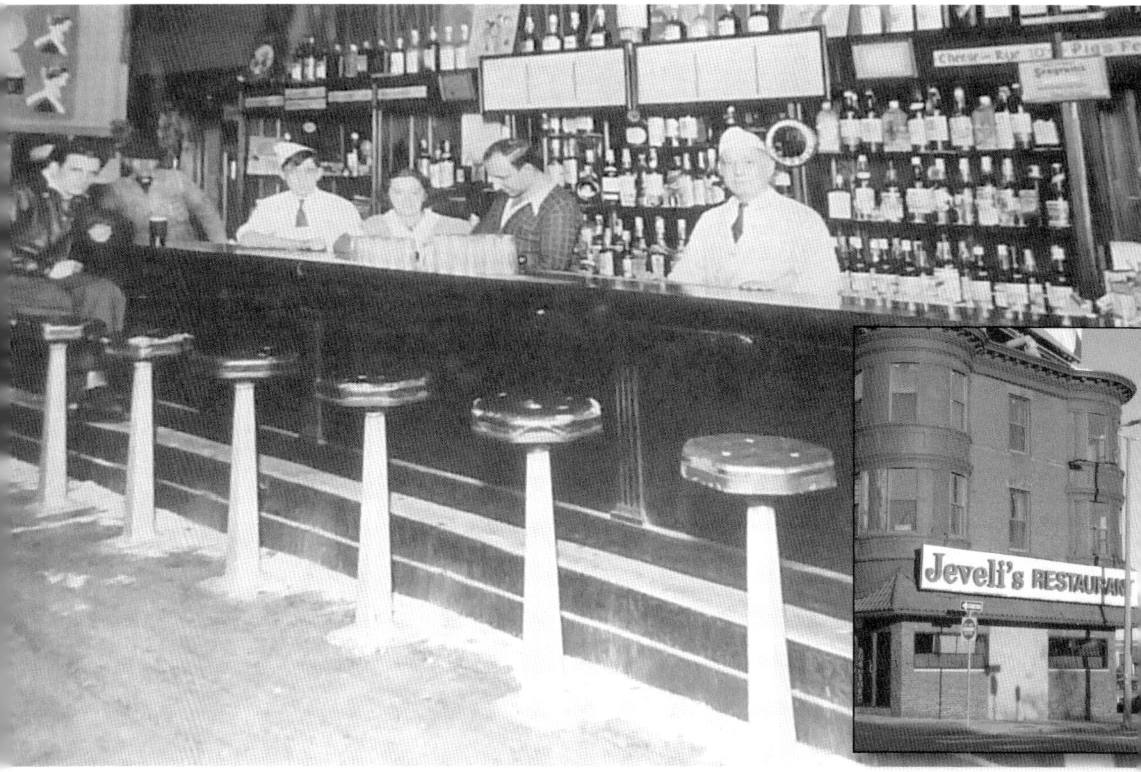

Jeveli's Restaurant

In 1899, Pasquale Ievoli left Italy for America. Through a clerical error at Ellis Island, his name became Jeveli. He joined the Navy and fought in the Spanish-American War, later founding Jeveli's Restaurant in Day Square in 1924. Boston's oldest Italian restaurant, Jeveli's is now run by Pasquale's grandson Eric Jeveli. In addition to its diehard regulars, Jeveli's is a popular place for tourists and politicians. In 1997, President Clinton ate there with 70 of his staff. (Courtesy of Thomas Philbin and Eric Jeveli.)

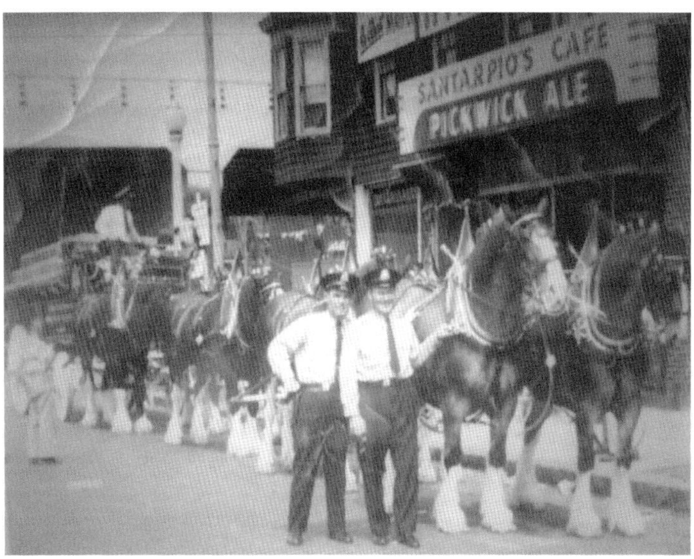

Santarpio's

Established in 1903 by Frank Santarpio and run by the same family for four generations, Santarpio's, at 111 Chelsea Street, is the oldest pizzeria in Boston and one of the first landmarks people see when they fly into the city. It has been inducted into the Boston Hall of Fame and has won *Boston Magazine*'s Best of Boston award multiple times. (Courtesy of Thomas Philbin.)

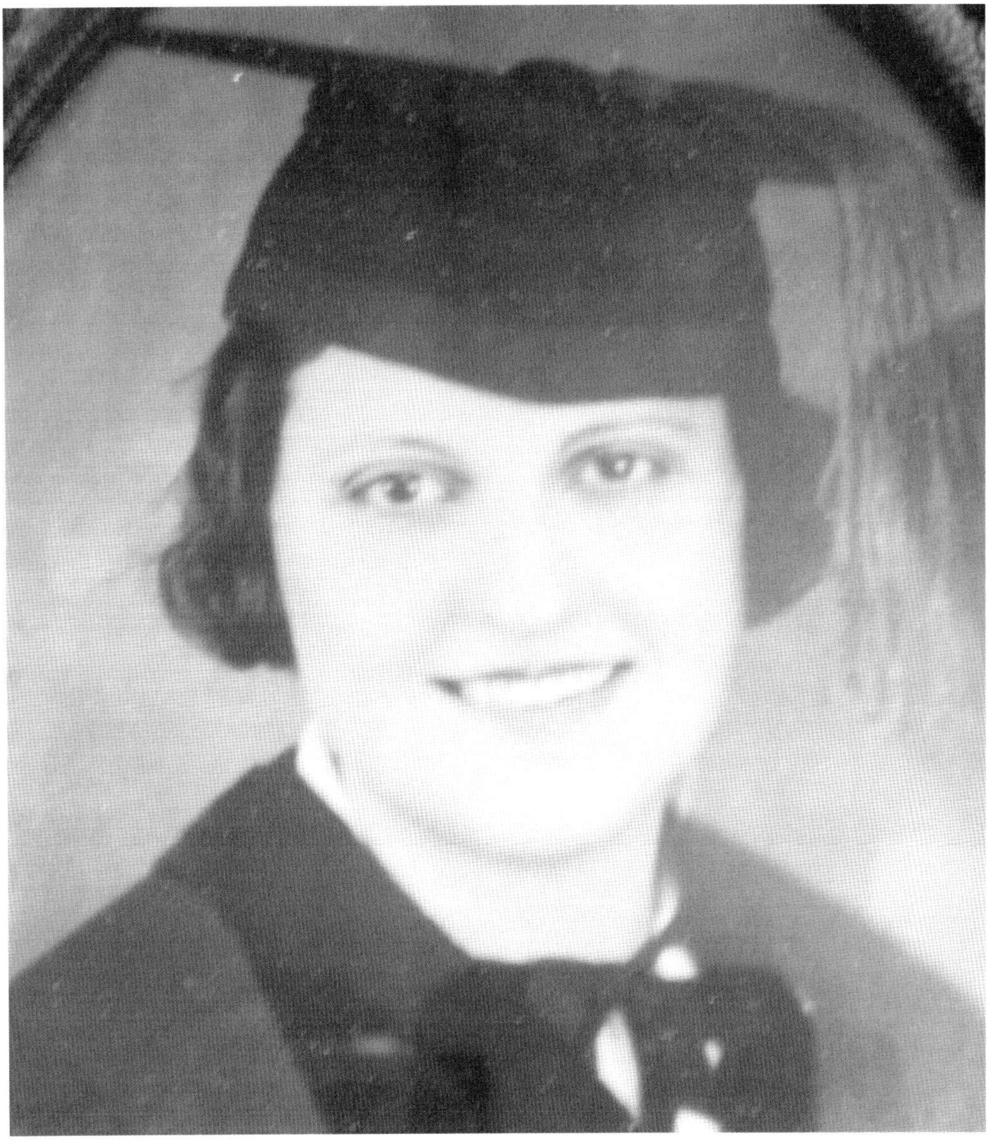

Dr. Marion Sabia (1909–1992)
Marion (Corleto) Sabia, whose parents were immigrants from Potenza, Italy, was born and grew up in East Boston, graduating from East Boston High School in 1927. One of only two women in a class of more than 100, she graduated from Tufts Medical School in 1933, becoming East Boston's first female physician. As a general practitioner and obstetrician who delivered thousands of East Boston babies, she had her office at 241 Maverick Street, living upstairs with her husband and two children. Her daughter Theodora Fiandaca notes, "My mother was a working woman long before it was in style. She worked with the full support of my father. He even paid for her medical school. Mom was a serious doctor who did surgeries like tonsillectomies, but she was also a fantastic cook and homemaker." (Courtesy of Theodora Fiandaca.)

Bill Scantlebury (1949–2015) and Family

The Scantlebury family, whose ancestors came to East Boston from Cornwall, England, ran the popular bakery Betty Ann's Food Shop since 1931. Famed for its jelly donuts, hot cross buns, Boston baked beans, and other old-time specialties, Betty Ann's did not advertise but had many loyal clients. Said to be the oldest continually operating bakery in Boston (it was Cotty's Bakery before the Scantleburys acquired it), its coal-fired brick oven had been used for all the baking since the three-story building at 565 Bennington Street was built in 1899. The bakery closed for a year in 2013 when owner and baker Bill Scantlebury got a life-threatening illness that resulted in a leg amputation. After relearning to walk with his prosthetic leg, he reopened in May 2014. Unexpectedly, Scantlebury passed away in March 2015, leaving behind hundreds of heartbroken customers, friends, and family. (Right, courtesy of John Lynds; below, author's collection.)

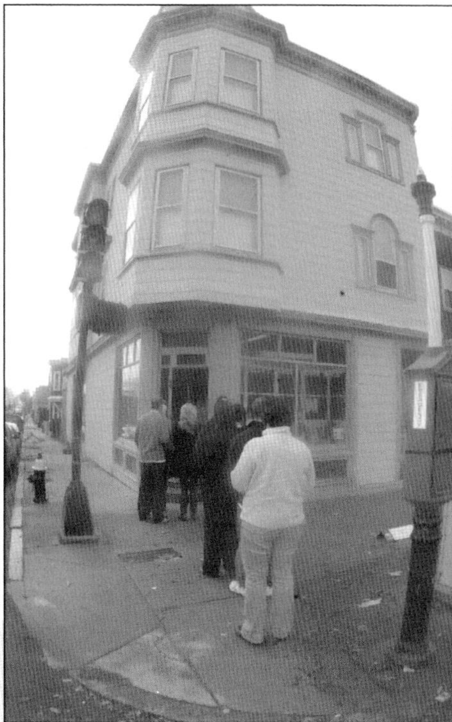

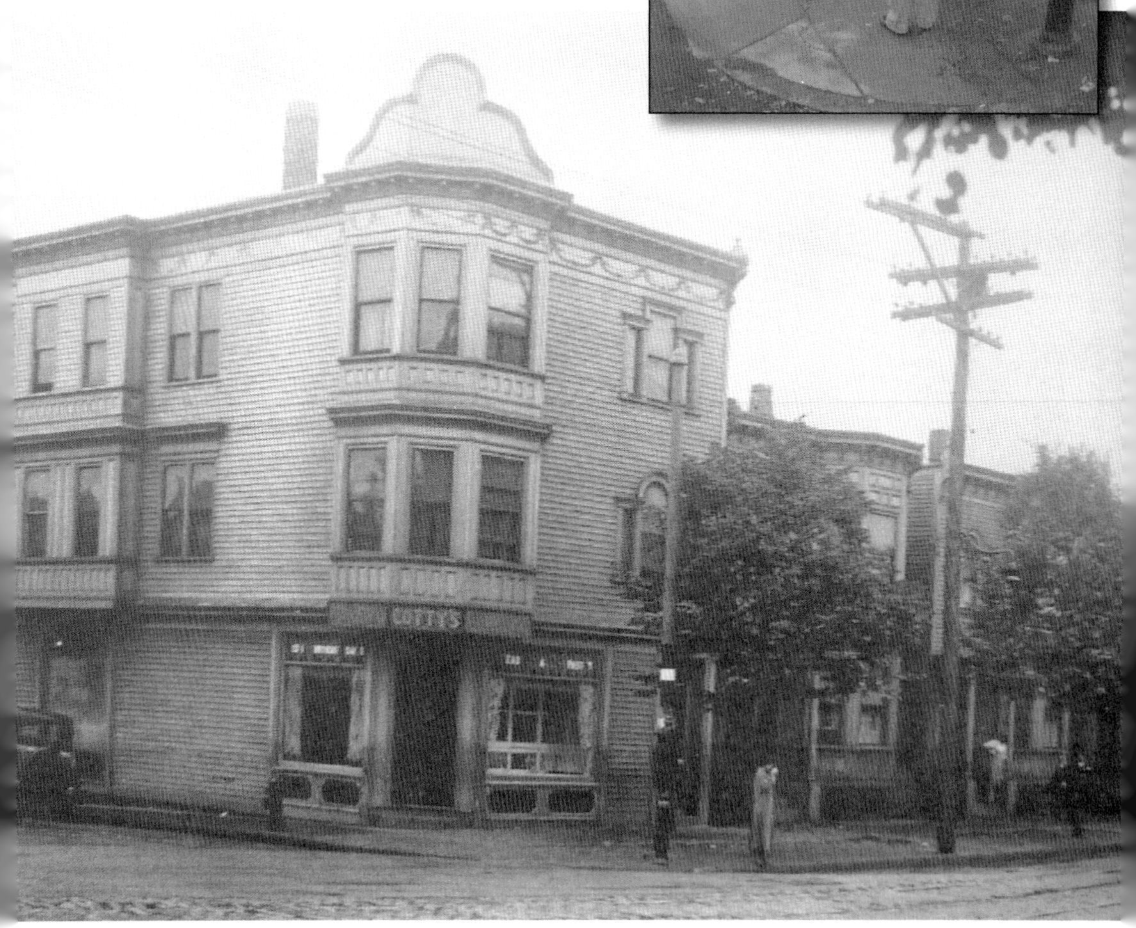

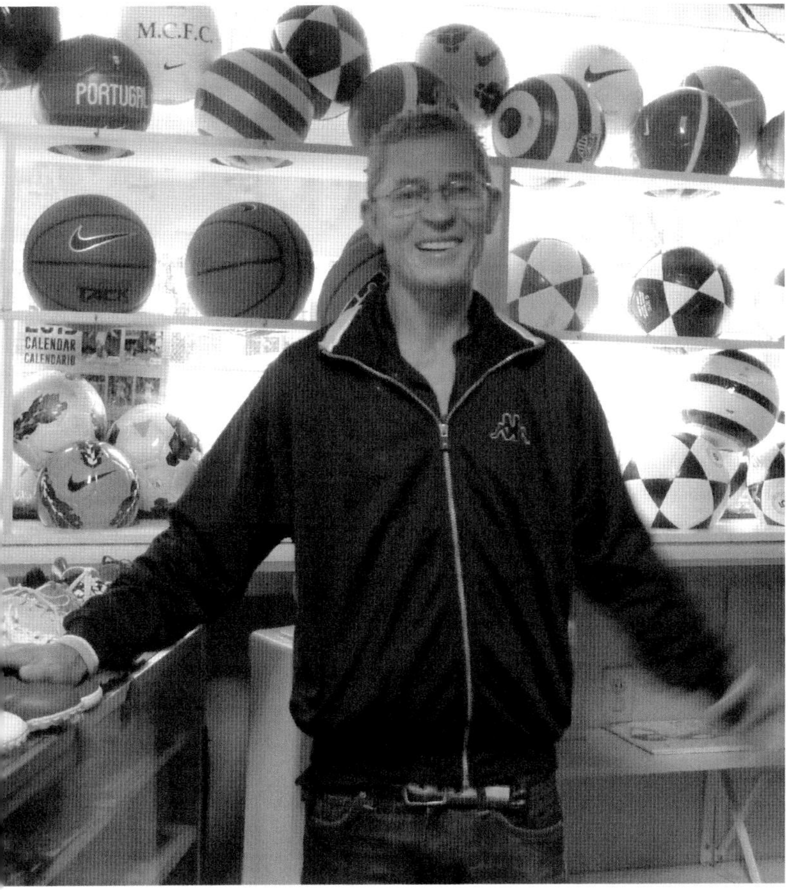

Eneias Cordeiro
Originally from São Paulo, Brazil, Eneias Cordeiro opened the Brazilian Soccer House at 110 Meridian Street in 1986 and lives upstairs from his shop. "I used to work at a soccer store in Brazil, and when I came to East Boston, I saw a need. At first, my clients were Latinos but now they're of every race and ethnicity. Soccer has grown a lot in East Boston and there are now many adult and children's teams." (Author's collection.)

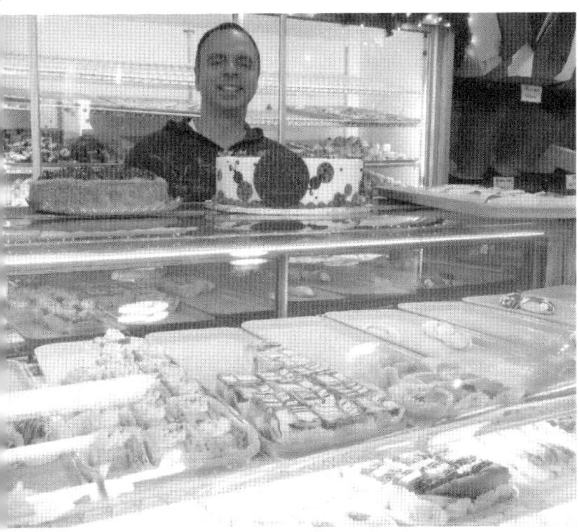

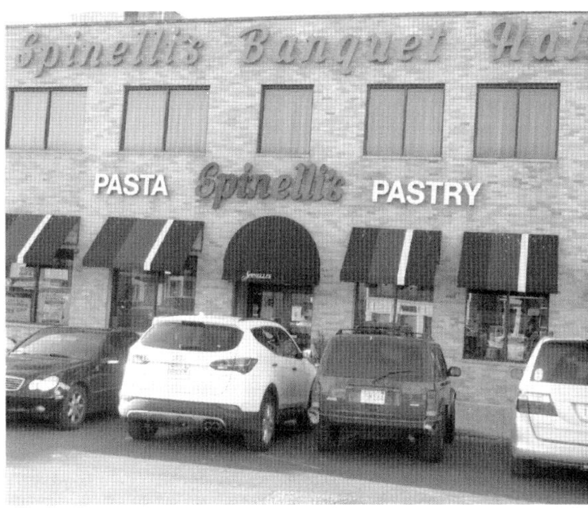

Spinelli's
Spinelli's bakery, specializing in traditional Italian pastries, cakes, homemade pastas, and breads, was first opened in 1965 by the Spinelli family. In 1983, it was purchased by the Roberto family, who added hot foods and expanded into catering. They opened a function hall upstairs and a second location in Lynnfield. Spinelli's in Day Square is the largest Italian bakery in East Boston. (Both, author's collection.)

Leo and May Lew

Any longtime East Bostonian knows about the slush sold from a doorway next to the alley of the light-green house at 55 Bennington Street—universally referred to as "the slush place." Slush, an Italian ice dessert, has been sold in this spot since at least 1945. The spot was originally a bakery where the owner, an immigrant from Italy, sold slush along with baked goods. In those days, almost every corner store in East Boston sold slush, but this slush was special. It was silky smooth, sweet, and tart, made from an old family recipe using nothing but real lemons, ice, and sugar. In the summer, a line of customers several deep always stretched down the block and cars double-parked, as people patiently waited for the next batch to be ready and scooped into small pleated paper cups. When the baker retired, he gave the slush recipe to his friend Dominic Lanzilli, who lived upstairs. Downstairs from Lanzilli's apartment was a fish pet supply shop called Golden Fins, run as a part-time hobby by Chinese-Americans Leo and May Lew. Lanzilli asked the Lews if they wanted to go into the slush business with him. "I didn't know anything about slush, but figured we could give it a try," says Lew. He was a math and science teacher, and he and his wife later worked as administrators for the Boston Public Schools. Selling slush was a good summer job, so they partnered with Lanzilli in 1980. With great respect for tradition, they never changed the recipe, even after Lanzilli passed away and competitors abounded with blue, pink, and other neon-colored artificially flavored slush products. This summer-only spot has been rated on numerous websites as the best and most authentic slush in Boston. The Lews have preserved a cherished Italian tradition in East Boston for 25 years. (Author's collection.)

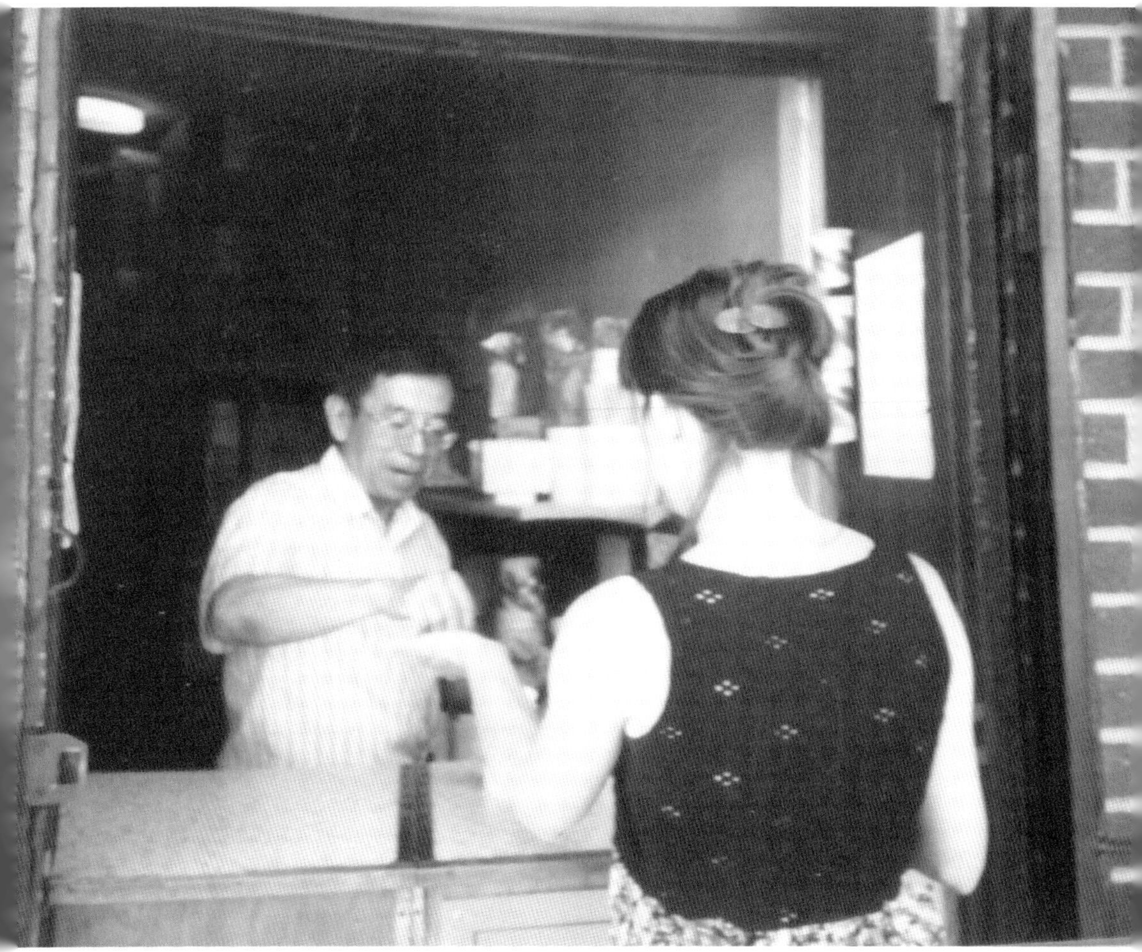

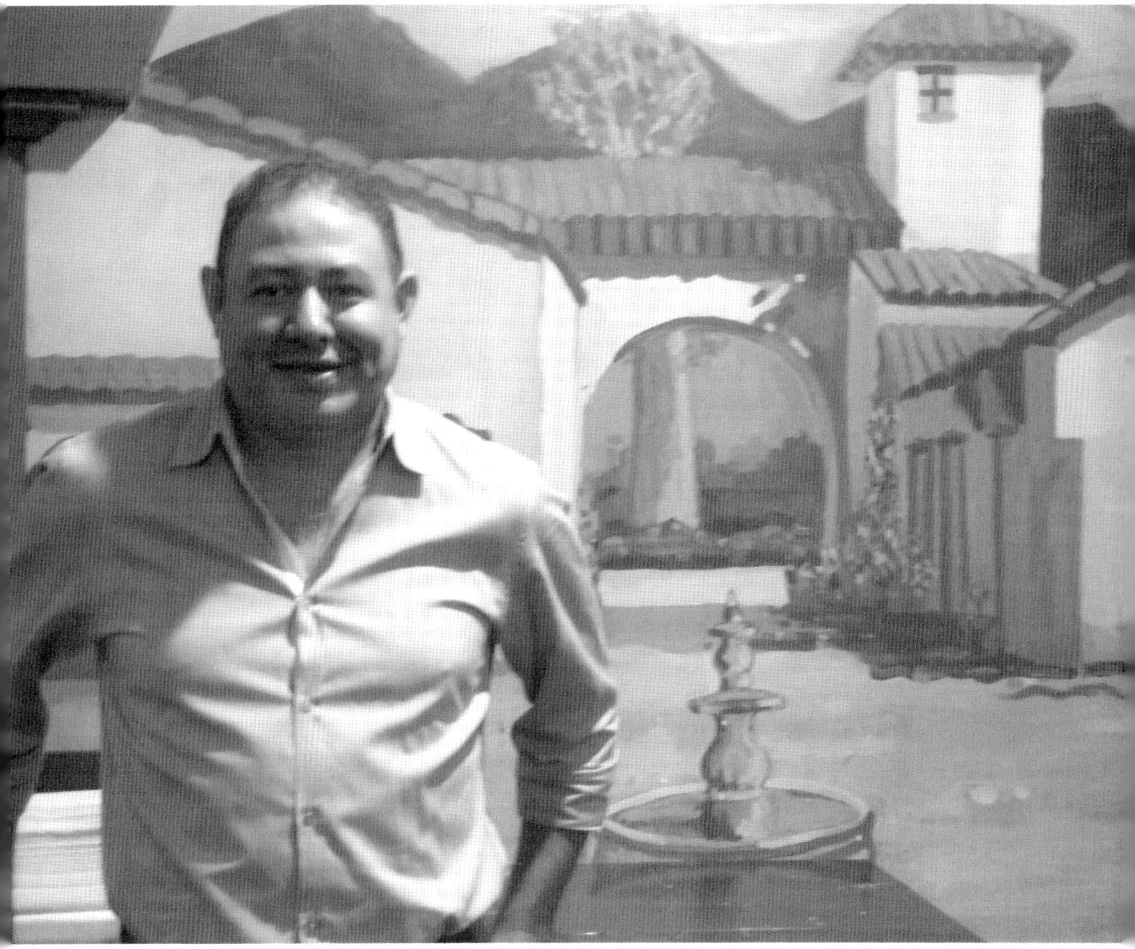

José Callejas

José Callejas came to the United States in 1981 from Usulután, El Salvador, opening East Boston's first taco shop, Taqueria Cancún, in 1993. For decades, the tiny shop at 39 Maverick Square had been Nemo's Hotdogs. Callejas explains, "When I first came to East Boston, all I could afford to eat was hotdogs, so I ate at Nemo's every day. I got to know him and when he was retiring, he asked if I wanted to buy the place. Friends lent me money and I did." Callejas later sold the taquería and now runs La Hacienda Restaurant at 150 Meridian Street. (Author's collection.)

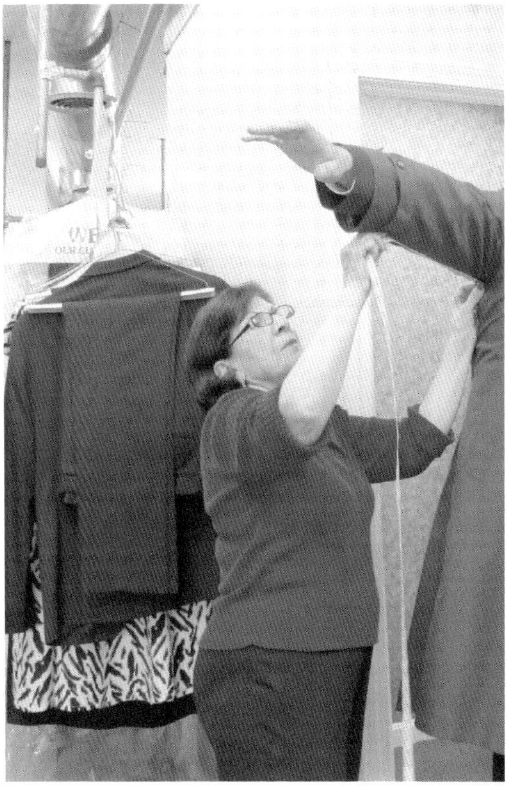

Josephine and Joe Millacapilli

Since 1994, Josephine and Joe Millacapilli, immigrants from Sicily, have run Charlie's Cleaners and Tailoring, located at 1094 Saratoga Street. They were early adopters of organic green dry cleaning and provide custom tailoring on site. They first began their business in Winthrop and then bought their current building, where they live in an apartment adjoining their shop. (Courtesy of Ariel Glanz.)

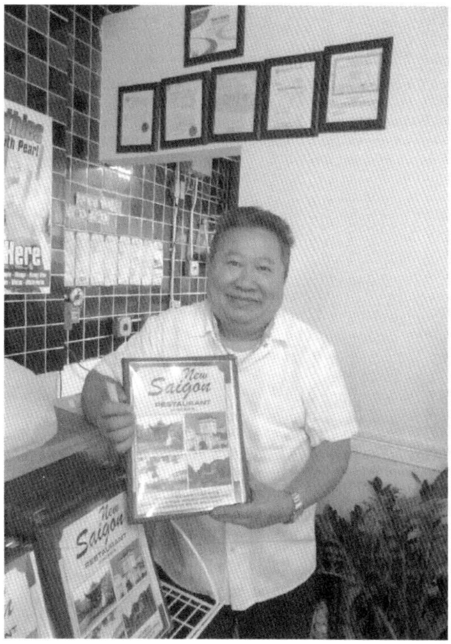

Hoa Van Cao

Hoa Van Cao, owner of New Saigon Restaurant, came to East Boston from Saigon, Vietnam, in 1981. "We were boat people—refugees in Thailand and the Philippines. We got sponsored to come to East Boston. We had no choice. But it was a very good choice!" After working in food service at the airport and the Marriott Hotel, he ran Sunrise Pizza on London Street and the Meridian Coffee Shop before opening Saigon Restaurant in its first location at 305 Meridian Street (corner of Lexington). In 2013, when the building's owners wanted to open a restaurant there, Cao relocated to 985 Bennington Street. (Author's collection.)

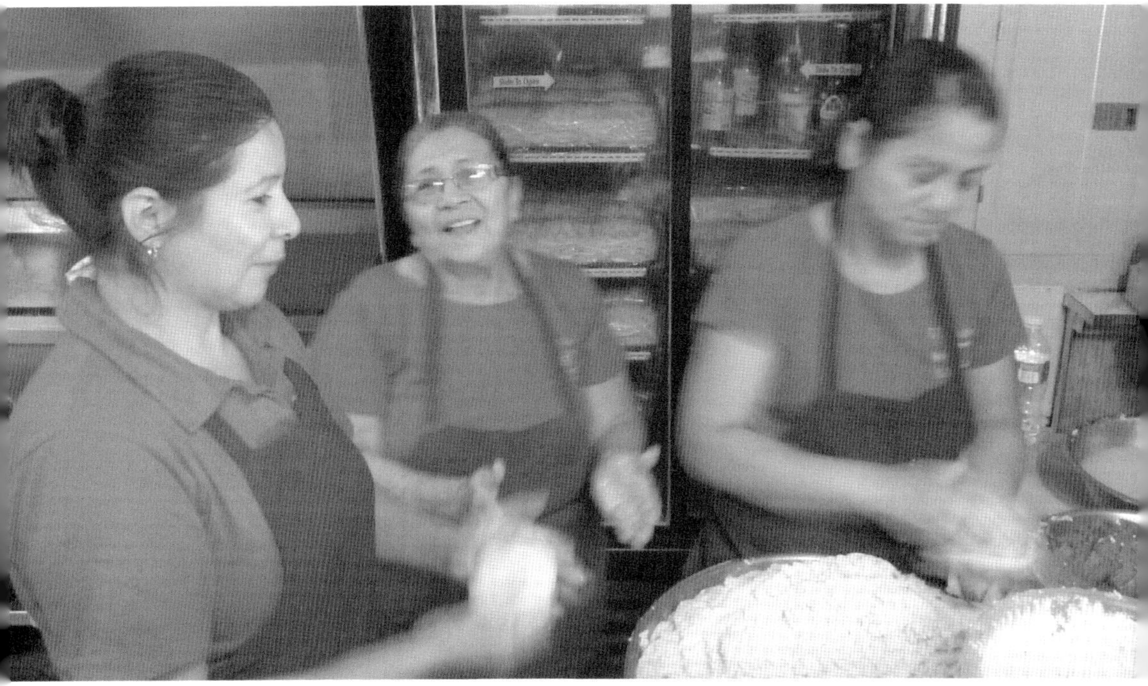

Sandra Barrera and Carlos Lopez
In 1987, Sandra Barrera and Carlos Lopez came to East Boston from La Unión and Soyapango, El Salvador, and their family has run Topacio (Topaz) Restaurant since 1994. Their daughter Karen now works there while attending college. "When we first arrived, there weren't many Salvadorans. But, the community has grown a lot," says Barrera. Specializing in *pupusas* and other traditional Salvadoran dishes, Topacio attracts customers from throughout Boston who travel to 120 Meridian Street for a taste of El Salvador. (Author's collection.)

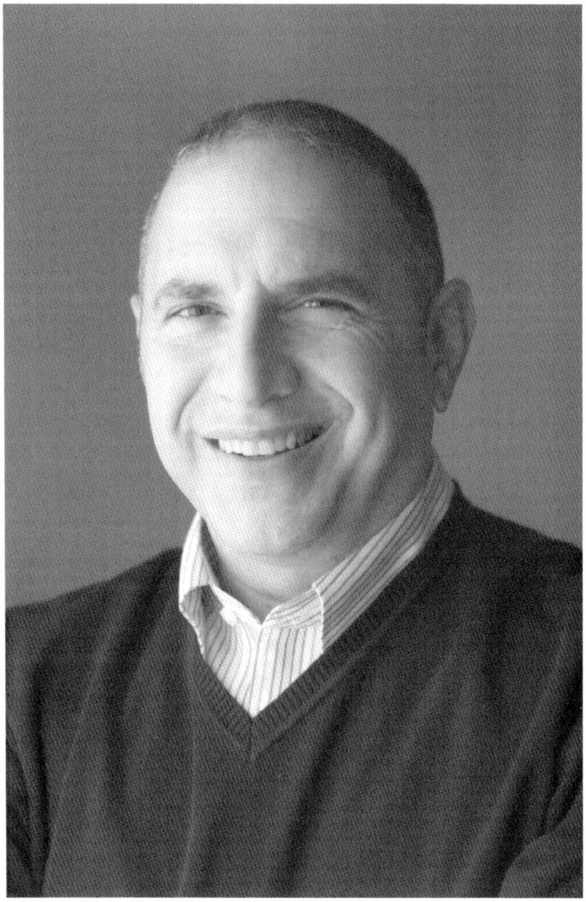

Anthony "Tony" Giacalone Jr.

Although he grew up in Melrose, Tony Giacalone, owner of Tony's Realty in Maverick Square, has family roots in East Boston. After graduating from Harvard University in 1987 with a degree in economics, he went straight to East Boston, which had just experienced a 100-percent property appreciation. "I wanted to become the next Donald Trump. I was obsessed with discovering the next big 'undiscovered' Boston neighborhood. That didn't happen. What I found, instead, was an amazingly vibrant immigrant community that needed me." In East Boston, he reconnected with his Italian heritage. "I loved all the old Italian people, the Italian shops and foods." Because he spoke Italian and had studied Spanish in college, he was able to link Italian homeowners—who tended to be suspicious of newcomers—with Latinos and other new immigrants looking to rent apartments. "The new immigrants were hard working and honest people and they needed someone who could help the Italians trust them." Giacalone bought a building at 37 Maverick Square, which had been an illegal rooming house occupied by drug addicts, and opened Tony's Realty, living upstairs from his office. Keeping pace with the community's changing demographics, his shop was the first quadrilingual realty in East Boston, serving customers in English, Italian, Spanish, and Portuguese. For more than 25 years, the office has been a hub of activity in Maverick Square, resembling a convivial version of the United Nations, where East Bostonians from Italy, Latin America, Morocco, Algeria, Vietnam, India, and elsewhere stop by to conduct real-estate business, get advice, seek job tips, share news, or just socialize. Many longtime customers savor memories of Tony's annual Christmas parties, where his mother used to cook huge pots of pasta and meatballs, and everyone who knew Tony was invited to a feast on folding tables in the office. More than just a businessman, Giacalone is a good neighbor. (Courtesy of Anthony Giacalone.)

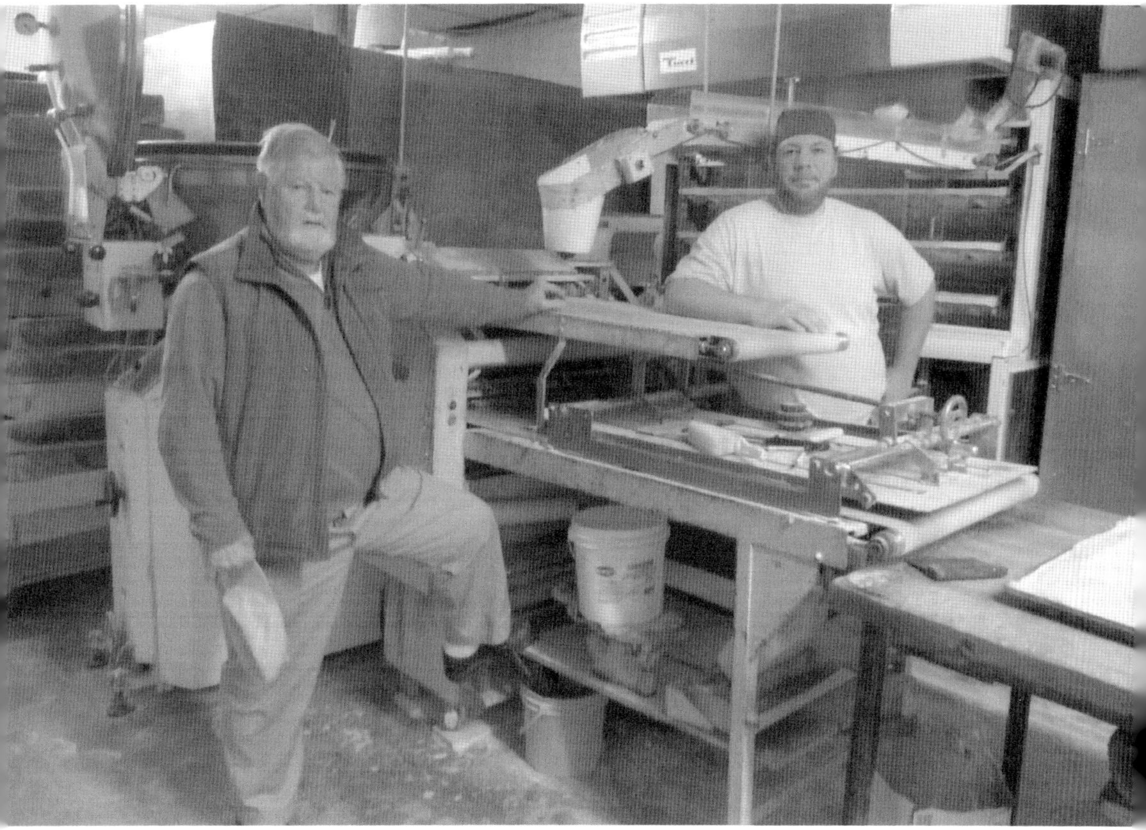

The Gnerri Family

In the late 1970s, Amedeo and Rita Gnerri, from Avellino, Italy, opened a bakery on 330 Sumner Street, naming it A&L after their sons, Antonio and Louis. The family had run a bakery for generations in Italy, and Amedeo personally traveled to Genova to buy specialized bakery machinery. While East Boston sleeps, their son Tony, who now runs the business, bakes all night. Rita works at the front counter, serving Italian breads and cookies to a loyal following of customers. (Both, author's collection.)

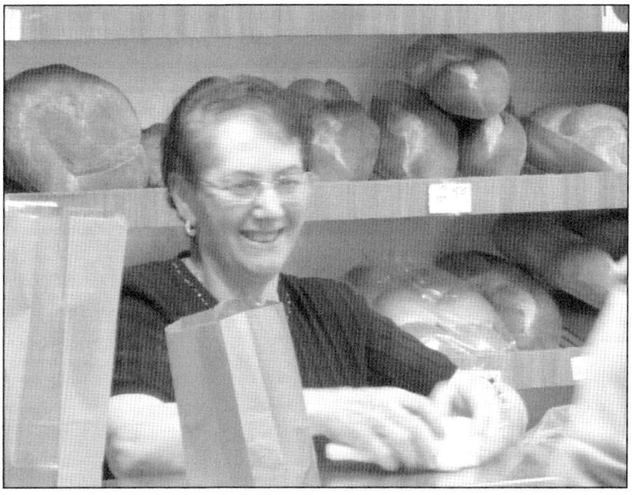

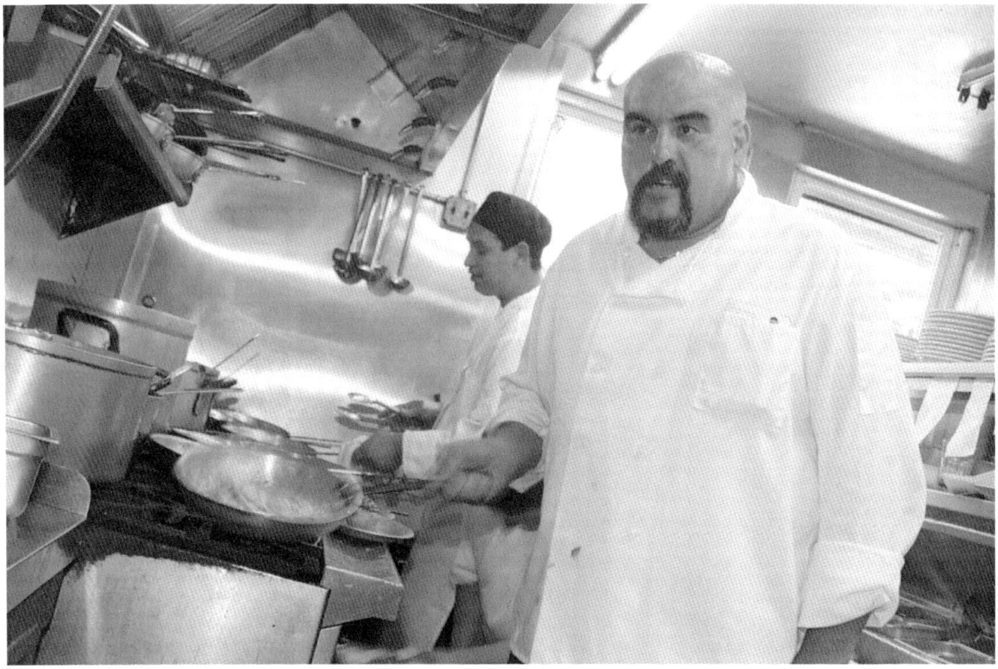

Rino's Place

Located on the first floor of a triple-decker house at 258 Saratoga Street, Rino's has been serving gourmet Italian cuisine since 1989. Originally opened by Rino and Anna DiCenso of Italy, it is now run by their son, Chef Anthony DiCenso. This unassuming spot, which always has long lines of customers waiting to get in, has won numerous awards and been featured on the Food Network, the *Phantom Gourmet*, and other television programs and websites. (Courtesy of John Lynds.)

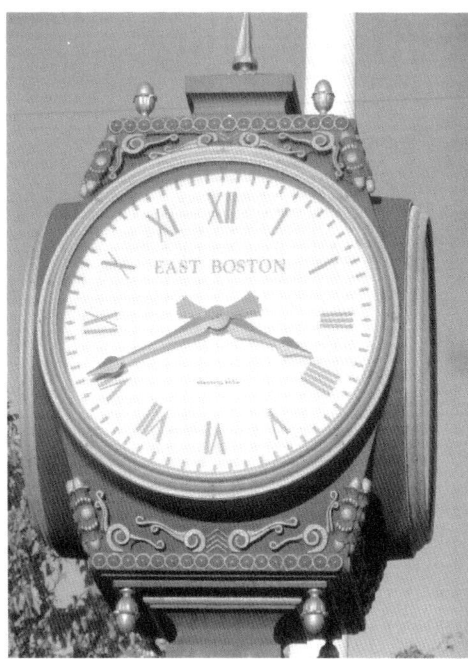

East Boston Times–Free Press

Established in 1935, the *East Boston Times* is East Boston's oldest existing newspaper. It was founded by lifelong East Bostonian Frank J. Tarbi (1916–2013), who developed an interest in news while working as a reporter for the *Stars and Stripes* during World War II. It is now owned by the Independent Newspaper Group, published weekly in print and online. (Author's collection.)

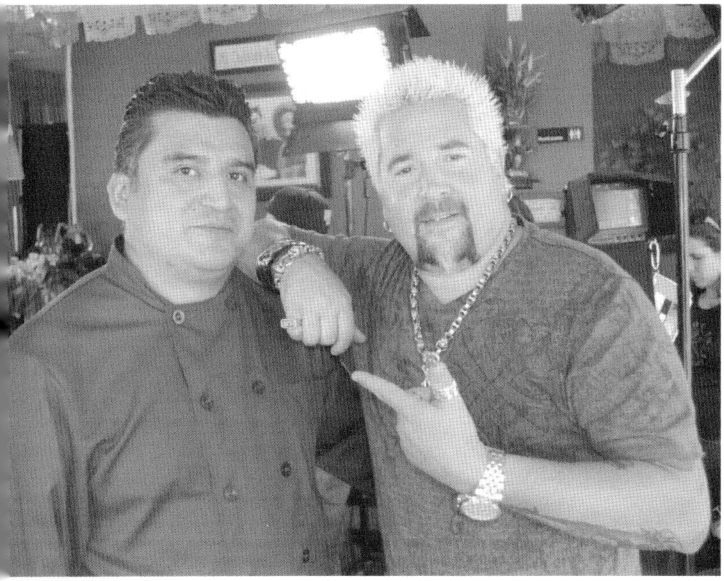

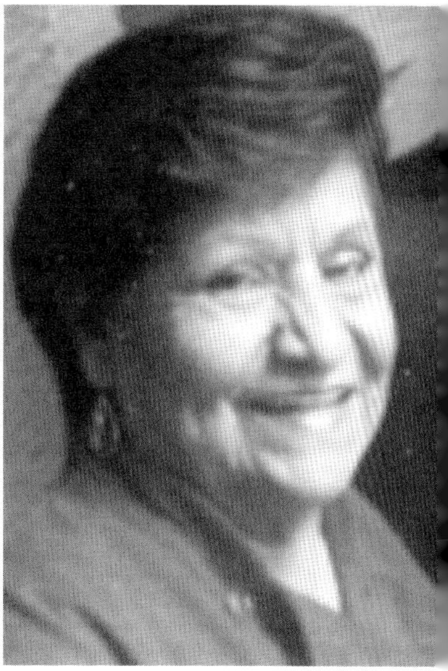

Angela's Café
Hailing from Puebla, Mexico, Angela Anteco Lopez (right) and her two sons, Luis (left) and Joel, opened Angela's Café in 2007, quickly becoming one of the most popular restaurants in East Boston. Angela's authentic Poblano cuisine has been featured on the Food Network's *Diners, Drive-ins and Dives* and has won awards and rave reviews from *Boston Magazine*, *The Improper Bostonian*, Zagat, and others. (Left, courtesy of John Lynds; right, courtesy of Angela's Café.)

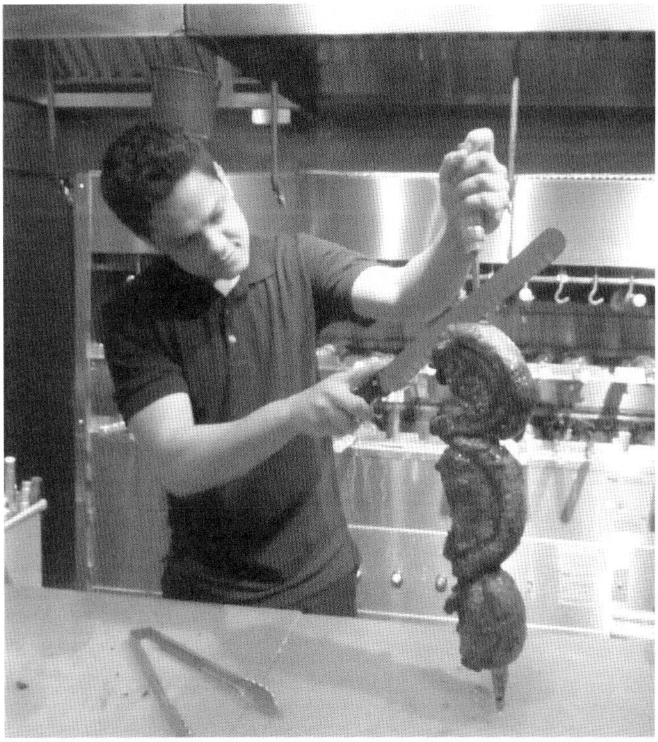

Oliveria's Steakhouse
Owned by Iziquel Di Souza and Clayton Goncalves, natives of Brazil, Oliveira's Steakhouse at 297 Chelsea Street has served traditional Brazilian *churrasco* (barbecue) since 2004. There are additional locations in East Boston's Central Square and in Somerville. (Author's collection.)

Saul Perlera

When he was just 16, Saul Perlera, owner of Perlera's Realty, left his hometown of Metapán in war-torn El Salvador to migrate alone to the United States. He arrived in East Boston on a sunny day in 1986. "I took one look and it was love at first sight!" He found work in the Covercraft factory on Condor Street, stitching car covers for Trans-Ams and Camaros. The other factory workers were older immigrants from Avellino, and Italian was spoken almost exclusively. They adopted Perlera, inviting him to their homes for Sunday dinners, and soon he became fluent in Italian. "We had so many similarities—being family-oriented, Catholic, having a strong work ethic, and similar languages. And, I loved the pasta and braciole!" He later got a job at the Sterlingwear factory on Orleans Street, sewing pea coats, and supplemented it with jobs cleaning a garage and a hair salon. Working seven days a week for five years, he sent money to El Salvador to pay for his sibling's schooling and to build his mother a new home, while finding time to study English at the Most Holy Redeemer Church. Looking to rent a new apartment, he met Tony Giacalone of Tony's Realty. Impressed that Perlera spoke four languages, Tony offered him a job as a rental agent. They worked together for 12 years, serving Italian, American, and Latino clients. Perlera got his GED and studied business administration, eventually getting his real-estate broker's license. In 2003, he opened Perlera's Realty on 142 Meridian Street. "Tony was a great mentor and we're still good friends," he notes. A fan of historic architecture, Perlera bought a run-down brick building at 137–141 Meridian Street and restored it, at great personal expense, recreating the original slate mansard roof and copper details. He still lives in East Boston and has been actively involved in the community's business and civic life for more than 25 years. (Author's collection.)

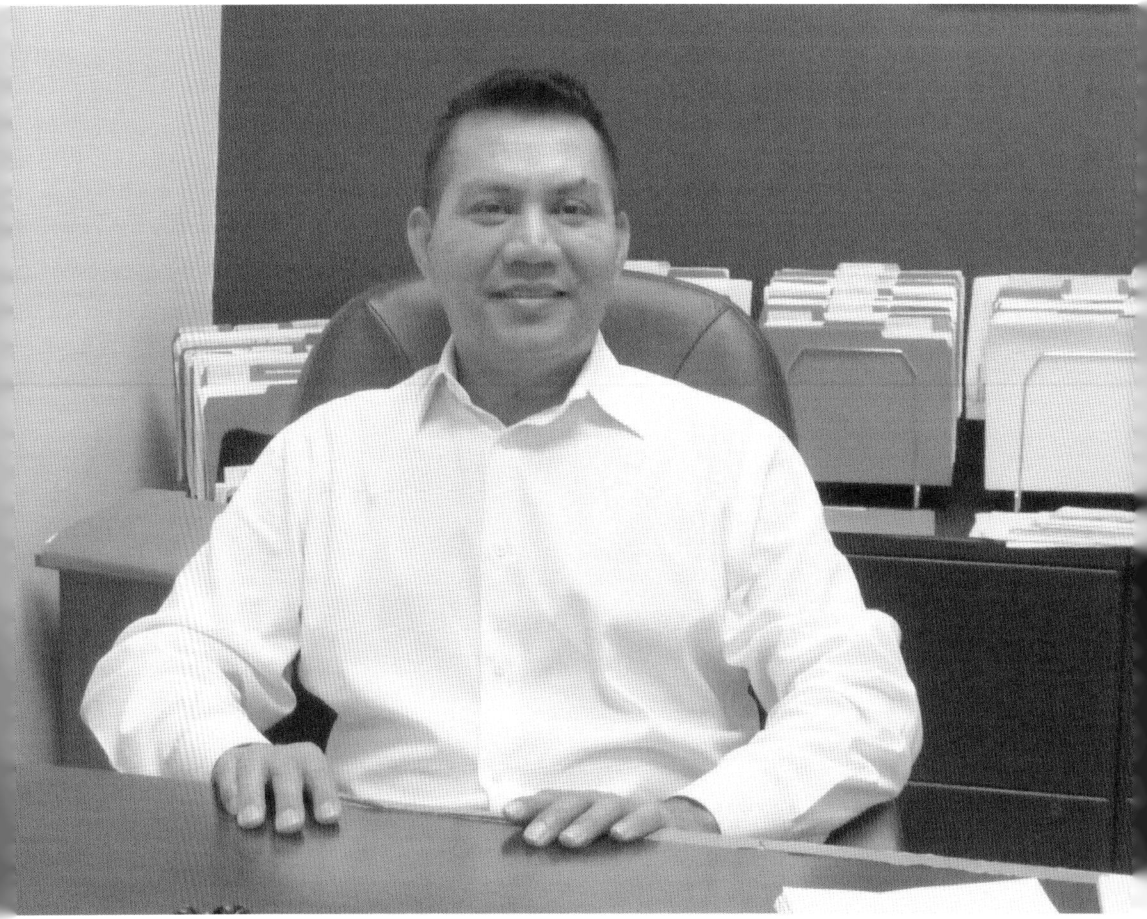

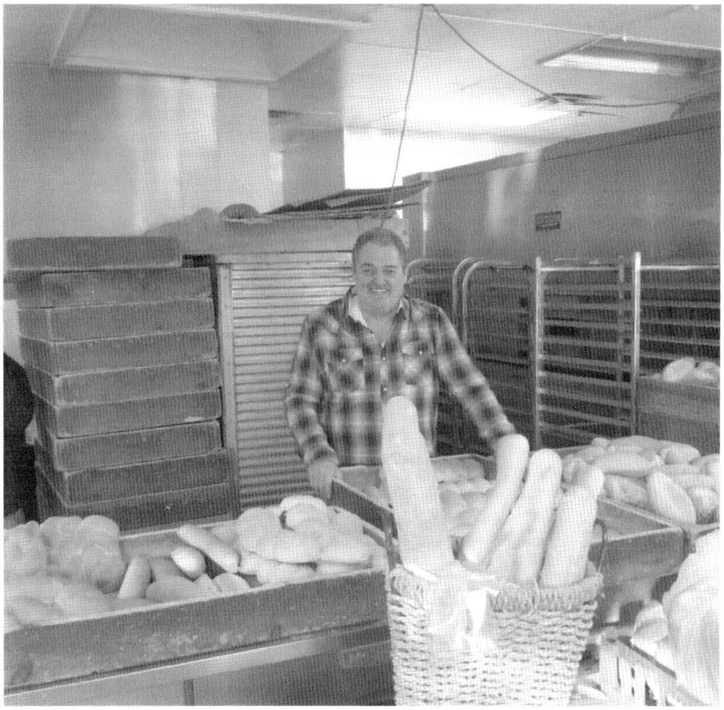

Cuchiello's Bakery

East Boston used to have fresh Italian bread shops on nearly every corner, but Cuchiello's is the oldest of the few remaining bread stores. With parents from Abruzzi, brothers Sonny, Agostino "Cookie," Frank, Richard, and Michael Cuchiello went into the bread business in 1969, opening Logan Bakery on Bennington Street and later changing the name to Cuchiello's when they relocated to Day Square in 1999. The shop is a family affair with wives and grandchildren helping out. (Courtesy of Debra Cave.)

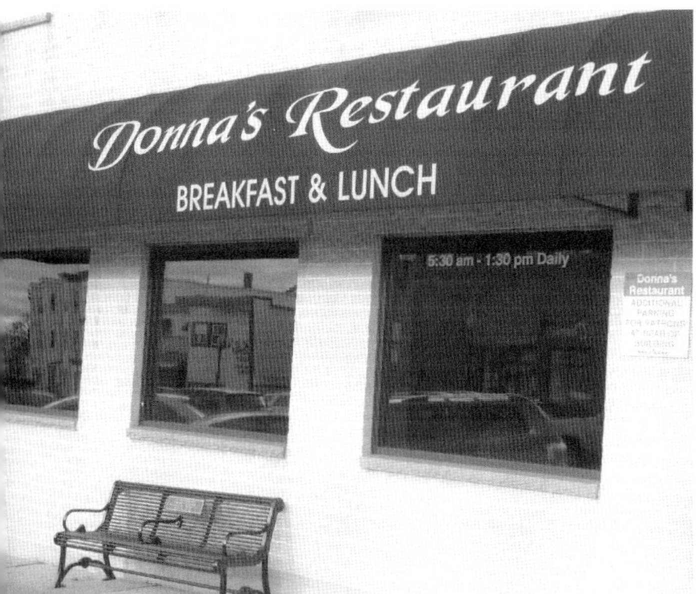

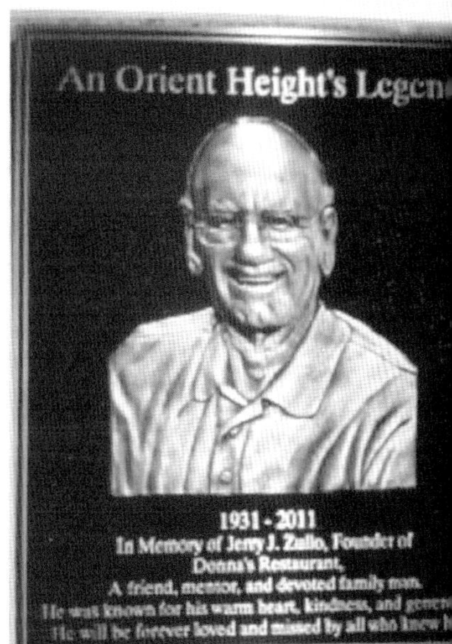

Donna's

In 1960, Jerry and Loretta Zullo of Orient Heights opened a family diner, naming it after their little girl, Donna. Specializing in classic all-American breakfasts and lunches, it is run today by Donna, who has worked at the diner since age 10. It is still a family affair, with her husband, children, cousins, uncles, and other family members working as cooks and servers, providing customers with an old-fashioned friendly diner experience. (Left, author's collection; right, courtesy of Donna Zullo Marquardo.)

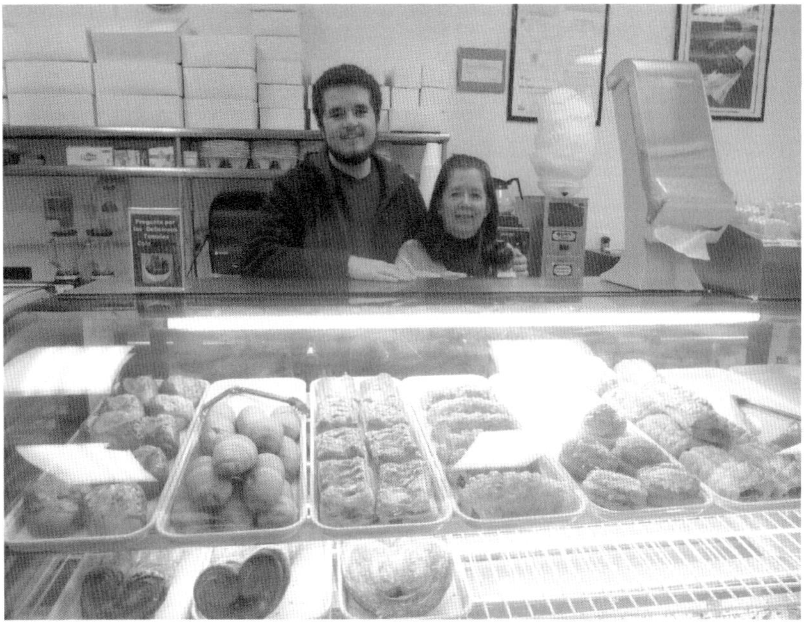

Amelia Sanchez and Family

In 1980, Amelia and Faustino Sanchez from Bogotá, Colombia, were some of the earliest Colombians to arrive in East Boston. They got jobs in a factory assembling audio components. To earn extra money, Amelia began selling homemade *empanadas* and *arepas* from a cart in Franklin Park during Sunday soccer games. By 1993, she had saved enough to open La Sultana Bakery in Maverick Square. Specializing in Colombian baked goods and other specialties, the bakery is a central meeting point for the Colombian community. When new immigrants fly into Logan Airport from Colombia, they come directly to La Sultana to be picked up by friends and family. Amelia is pictured above with her son Christian. (Both, author's collection.)

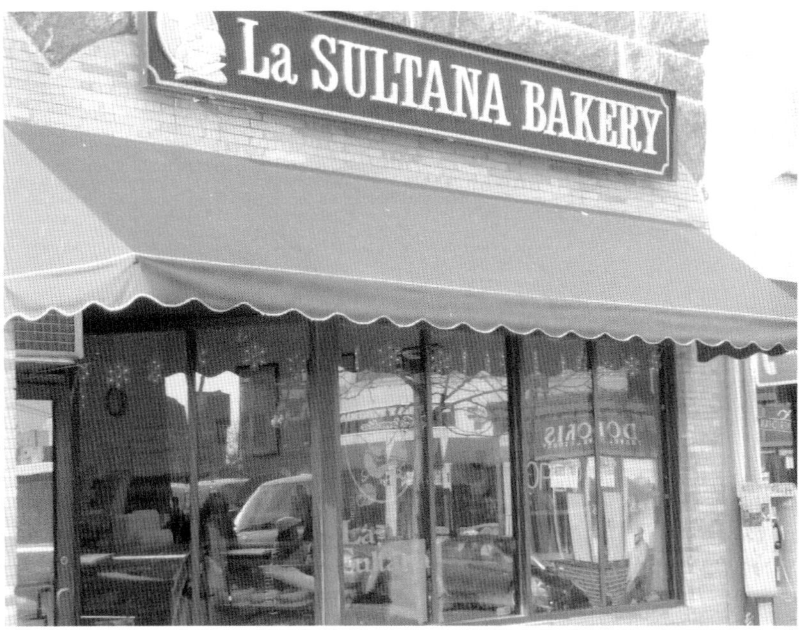

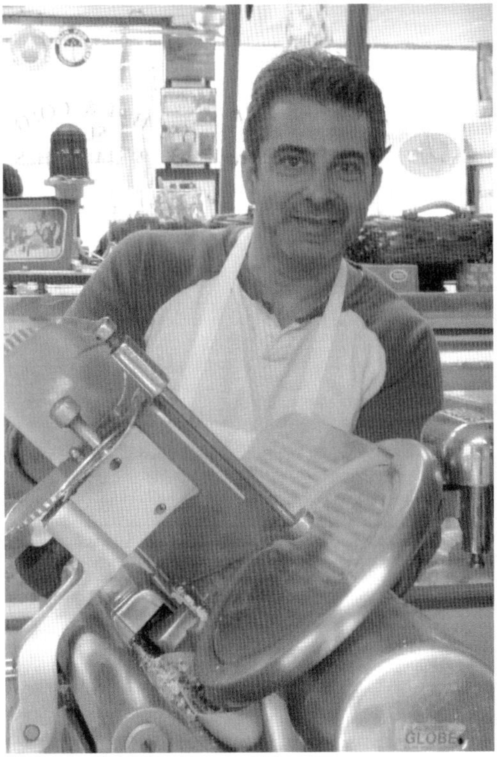

Carlo's Market and Cold Cuts

Four generations of the Scire family have worked at Carlo's delicatessen, named after Carmelo "Carlo" Scire, who came to East Boston from Sicily in the 1930s with his wife, Mary. They first ran a basement grocery shop in Drake Place, then inherited a corner store on Bennington and Putnam Streets from Mary's family. In the 1950s, their son Sammy and his wife, Carmela, moved the store to Orient Heights. Since 1984, their son Steve (left) has run the shop at 567 Bennington Street with his wife, Kathy (below). Their three children and nephew (below) have also worked at the store while going to college. Having grown up in the business, Scire says, "From the time I was six, I loved spending time at the store, playing and helping my parents. All my friends lived around here. This is my neighborhood and I'll be here until I die." (All, author's collection.)

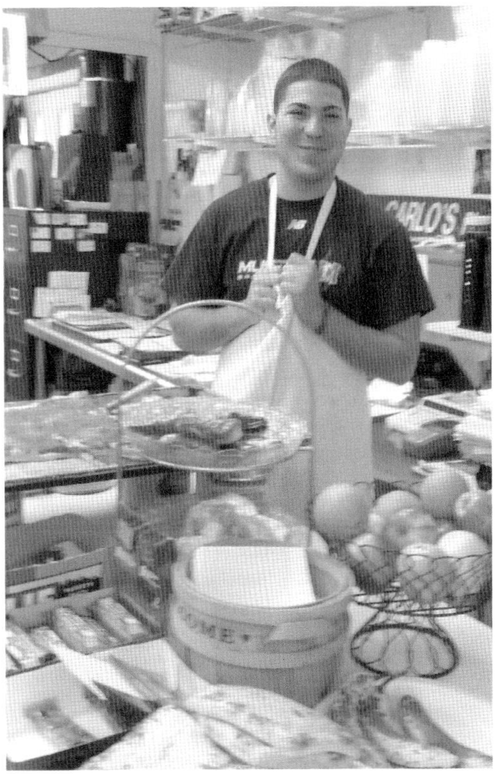

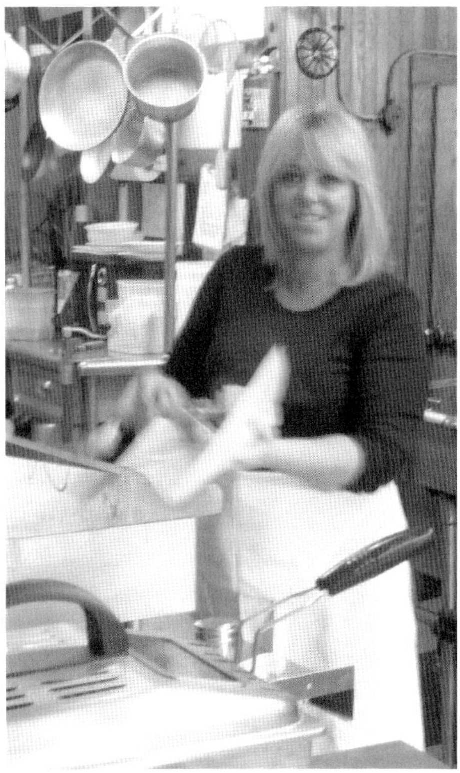

BIBLIOGRAPHY

Graves, E.F. and I. Steinbarger (eds.). *Biographical Sketches of Representative Citizens of the Commonwealth of Massachusetts.* Boston, MA: Graves & Steinbarger Publishers, 1901.

Buckingham, J.T. *A Sketch of the Recent Improvement at East Boston.* Boston, MA: self-published, 1836.

Condensed History and Manual of Maverick Congregational Church. Boston, MA: Maverick Congregational Church, 1894.

Drake, Samuel G. *The History and Antiquities of Boston: From Its Settlement in 1630 to the Year 1770.* Boston, MA: Luther Stevens Publishing, 1856.

East Boston. Boston 200 Neighborhood History Series. Boston, MA: Boston 200 Corporation, 1976.

East Boston: A Survey and a Comprehensive Plan. Boston, MA: City of Boston Printing Department, 1915.

Haynes, Guy. *Journal of East Boston: Buildings Erected, Families Removing on, Occurrences, etc.* Private journal of Guy C. Haynes. Available at R. Stanton Avery Special Collections, New England Historic Genealogical Society, Boston.

Knoblock, Glenn. *American Clipper Ships 1845–1920: A Comprehensive History, with a Listing of Builders and Their Ships.* Jefferson, NC: McFarland & Company Inc., 2014.

Maier, Thomas. *The Kennedys: America's Emerald Kings.* New York: Basic Books, 2003.

Moffett, Marian S. "The Physical Development of East Boston" (master's thesis). Massachusetts Institute of Technology Department of Architecture, 1973.

Nicholls, John, S.C. *The Rise and Growth of the East Boston Courts.* Cambridge, MA: University Press, 1933.

Pinckney, Warren, R. "Puerto Rican Jazz and the Incorporation of Folk Music," *Latin American Music Review,* v.10, n. 2, (1989), 239.

Sumner, William, H. *A History of East Boston with Biographical Sketches of Its Early Proprietors.* Boston, MA: J.E. Tilton and Company, 1858.

Winsor, Justin, ed. *The Memorial History of Boston: Including Suffolk County, Massachusetts 1630–1880,* v. 4. Boston, MA: James E. Osgood and Company, 1881.

Woods, Robert A. and Albert J. Kennedy. *The Zone of Emergence: Observations of the Lower Middle and Upper Working Class Communities of Boston, 1905–1914.* Cambridge, MA: MIT Press, 1969.

INDEX

LEGENDARY LOCALS

AN IMPRINT OF ARCADIA PUBLISHING

Find more books like this at
www.legendarylocals.com

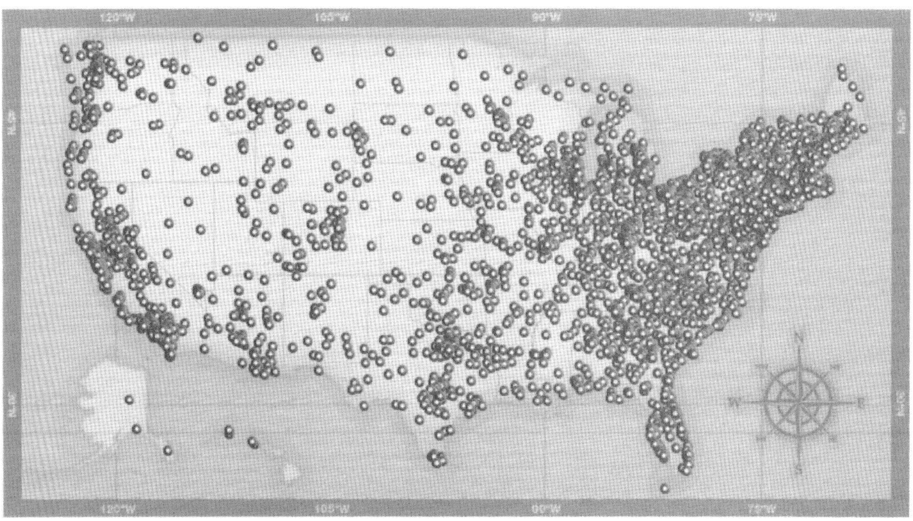

Discover more local and regional history books at
www.arcadiapublishing.com

Consistent with our mission to preserve history on a local level, this book was printed in South Carolina on American-made paper and manufactured entirely in the United States. Products carrying the accredited Forest Stewardship Council (FSC) label are printed on 100 percent FSC-certified paper.

MADE IN THE USA